Arabic
For Nerds

270 Questions on
Arabic Grammar

Fully Revised First Edition – With Index

BY
Gerald Drissner

IMPRESSUM / IMPRINT

1. Auflage, Oktober 2015 (fully revised 1st edition; 100417)

© 2015 Gerald Drißner (Drissner), 12045 Berlin, Germany

Umschlag, Illustration: Gerald Drißner

Internet: http://www.gerald-drissner.de

E-Mail: post@gerald-drissner.de

ISBN-13:   978-1517538385

ISBN-10:   1517538386

For my love
who hates grammar

ARABIC FOR NERDS - 270 QUESTIONS AND ANSWERS

ACKNOWLEDGEMENTS

This book consumed huge amount of work, research and dedication. I would like to express my gratitude to the many people who saw me through this book; to all those who taught me Arabic and allowed me to quote their remarks.

I would like to thank

Michael Guggenheimer

for his numerous comments which I am going to miss

Judith Zepter, in Hamburg,

for her profound and helpful remarks

Badrul Aini Sha'ari, in Kuala Lumpur,

for his valuable comments.

Above all, I want to thank

my wife

who supported and encouraged me

in spite of all the time it took me away from her.

1. INTRODUCTION

A: كَيْفَ الْحال؟

B: دائِمًا مَنْصُوب !

(A joke shared among Arabic grammar nerds.)

The cover picture was taken when I started to fall in love with Arabic. It happened in 2009 in Egypt after my first lesson with Dr. Mustafa (مصطفى حميدة), a highly esteemed professor at the University of Alexandria. When I showed it to my friends at home in Austria, they thought of mathematics or physics – as there are a lot of arrows and arithmetic signs.

This is what Arabic is all about: patterns and structures. If you want to feel the beauty and strength of the Arabic language, you have to understand its inner logic. I used to play chess at a young age and grandmasters told me that you have to study pawn structures and patterns – and not opening moves. I guess it is quite the same with Arabic.

I have been collecting interesting facts about grammar, vocabulary and expressions, hints and traps for almost ten years. Now, I have compiled them to a book: *Arabic for Nerds*.

This book should fill a gap. There are plenty of books about Arabic for beginners and some for intermediate students but it is difficult to find good material on the advanced level.

Which leads us to the question: What is advanced?

If your mother tongue is English, it is said that you need 700 hours (of instruction) to become fluent in French, German, Spanish, Danish or Swahili. You need 1400 hours for Greek, Hindi, Russian or Urdu. And you need 2800 hours if you want to reach the level *advanced high* in Japanese, Korean, Chinese – and Arabic.

This book is suitable for you if you have been studying Arabic intensively for at least two years. You have a sound knowledge of vocabulary (around 3000 words) and know about tenses, verb moods and plurals.

During my studies in the Middle East and North Africa I met students from Europe and the USA. They all shared a similar experience: They studied Arabic the same way they had learned German, English, French or Spanish – by using the grammar terms and syntax they knew from their native language. This only works in some cases. However, it will definitely make it difficult to achieve an advanced level in Arabic – because you won't get the feeling how this fascinating Semitic language works.

When I decided to study Arabic I wanted to study it the Arab way. I realised that Arabic grammar is actually much easier than German grammar – but only if you use the Arabic terms. If you read German books on Arabic grammar, you need a Latin dictionary and eventually get frustrated.

I was happy to find an old Arabic teacher who couldn't speak English. I avoided translating words. English has a word for nearly everything. In Arabic, a single word can mean dozens of things depending on the context. Arabic is a poetic language but have you ever felt its poetic core?

Let us have a look at the word دُنْيا: It is translated in books as *world*. The meaning is correct but if you have a closer look, you will understand that it is not a good idea to focus on translations too much (see chapter 146).

This book doesn't teach you vocabulary, nor are there exercises. This book explains how Arabic works and gives you hints in using and understanding the language better. Since most of the Arabic words are given in translation, you should be able to read this book without a dictionary. I used تَشْكِيل for the correct pronunciation wherever it is necessary – especially when dealing with cases and verbs. Since the vowel before a ة is always a فَتْحة, I didn't add the vowel marker on top of the preceding letter. I also mix English and Arabic. I hope you don't mind the strange combination sometimes.

Since there are already a lot of points in the Arabic alphabet I sometimes don't follow the correct English punctuation (e.g. full stops or commas) to make it easier for the reader.

This book isn't scientific, nor academic. This book is a working paper and will be updated after some time. I am sure there are inaccuracies as I have a mere practical view.

If you spot mistakes, have ideas or corrections, please kindly let me know by e-mail: post@gerald-drissner.de

Berlin, October 2015

2. WHAT IS THE SECRET OF ARABIC VOWELS?

Arabic is like a mathematical game. You take the root of a word, which normally consists of three letters, and you start playing. Your tools are pre- and suffixes, three vowels and a mark of silence or anti-vowel.

The vowels at the end of words are essential for understanding the inner meaning and logic of Arabic. If you think about the pronunciation and how this influences the rhythm, you will improve your understanding of a sentence. You will also get a better feeling how to vocalize texts: الْإِعْراب

Let us have a closer look at the main sounds in Arabic:

u	ضَمّة	This is the regular ending. Endings in "u" mark normal situations. They are used for primacy and for action. It represents complete meanings and essential things. In grammar, we use the word مَرْفُوع. It comes from the root رَفَعَ meaning: to raise; to place; to take off/to start; to pronounce the final consonant with "u". It occurs in nouns (إِسْم) and verbs (فِعْل). Closest meaning in English grammar: nominative (nouns) or indicative (verbs).
a	فَتْحة	The word فَتْحة comes from the root *to open*. The vowel "a" is an open vowel and it is used for situations of installing, setting up or appointing things (نَصْب). In grammar, we use the word مَنْصُوب.

		It literally means *set up, installed*. Generally said, the فَتْحة at the end of a word enriches a sentence with additional information, it unfolds the action. It is like a supplement of information (e.g. the object of a verb). It occurs in nouns and verbs. Closest meaning in English grammar: accusative.
i	كَسْرة	The vowel "i" requires the lips to be stretched way out to the sides. At the end of a noun it marks situations of reduction, dragging and causing (جَرّ) and sets up a dependency in meaning (e.g. after a preposition or the second part of a إِضافة-construction). In grammar, we use the word مَجْرُور. It literally means *dragged* or *pulled*. The كَسْرة specifies and coordinates information. It occurs in nouns only. Closest meaning in English: dative. Sometimes: genitive.
-	سُكُون	Quiescence: mark of silence or anti-vowel (سُكُون). At the end of a verb it evokes the action of cutting, clipping or decision (جَزْم). If there is a weak letter in the word (حَرْف الْعِلّة – namely و or ي), it will regularly get cut off. In grammar we use the word مَجْزُوم. It literally means *cut short; clipped*. It occurs in verbs only.

<u>Some remarks:</u>

I strictly recommend to stick solely to the Arabic grammar terms. In this book I occasionally use the Latin terms just to give readers (who aren't familiar with the Arabic terms yet) a hint. There is one big advantage: Most people have no clue what the Latin grammar terms actually mean. However, Arabic grammar terms are Arabic words with a meaning (see chapter 153). So always try to translate the grammar term literally. It will help you to remember the terms. You will also understand the idea of the grammar concept better. If you use the Arabic terms only, Arabic grammar will eventually become much easier.

For example: A verb or a noun can be مَنْصُوب in Arabic.

- Regarding a noun, it might be a direct object (Latin term: *accusative*). See example 1 in the table below.

- Regarding a verb, we might deal with a subordinate clause (Latin term: *subjunctive*). See example 2.

Forget these two complicated Latin terms! Practically speaking, the two ideas are the same. And so it is in Arabic grammar! Arabic uses the same term for both which perfectly makes sense: مَنْصُوب. Remember: A فَتْحة at the end of a word enriches a sentence with additional information, it unfolds the action.

I want a book. (*A book* is what <u>I want</u>.)	أُرِيدُ كِتابًا	1
I want to read a book. (*To read a book* is what <u>I want</u>.)	أُرِيدُ أَنْ أَقْرَأَ كِتابًا	2

6

3. HOW MANY ROOTS DOES THE ARABIC LANGUAGE HAVE?

There are a lot of Arabic dictionaries. You might know "Hans Wehr" named after the German scholar. It is called *Arabisches Wörterbuch für die Schriftsprache der Gegenwart* and was published in 1952. It is the most complete dictionary of standard Arabic ever published in the West, and its English version is probably the most common one in use by non-Arab scholars. It contains 2967 roots (جِذْر) with 3 letters and 362 with 4 letters.

As the Arabic alphabet consists of 28 letters there are 21,952 theoretical combinations. (We are talking about theoretical three-radical-roots only.)

The most common root letter is the ر with 722 times followed by the و which occurs 547 times. The ل is found 519 times and the م occurs 511 times. The ذ is the least common: only 98 times.

- The ن is the most common first radical: 235 times – followed by the ح which occurs 161 times.

- The ر is the most common second radical: 258 times – followed by the و with 244 times.

- The ر is also the most common third radical: 282 times – followed by the ل with 220 times.

By the way: The oldest Arabic text was written approximately 150 years before the religion of Islam was founded at the beginning of the 7th century. The text which was found in Najran near Yemen is the oldest form of Arabic writing known to date, the "missing link" between Nabatean and Arabic writing.

4. WHICH LETTERS CAN YOU ADD TO A ROOT?

Almost every Arabic word - except proper nouns and foreign words - has a root that consists of three or four letters, so called radicals. In Arabic, a radical is called حَرْف أَصْلِيّ. The word أَصْلِيّ means *original* or *authentic*.

It is pretty easy to identify a root (جِذْر) as there are <u>only ten letters</u> in Arabic which can be added to a root. They are called حُرُوف الزِّيادة.

You can remember them easily because they can be summed up in this word: سألتمونيها

Difficult to remember? Well, think of a possible pronunciation, and it will be easy: "sa'altumuuniiha".

5. LETTERS WITHOUT DOTS - DOES IT WORK?

It did, a long time ago. At first Arabic was written without vowel-signs above or under letters.

Furthermore, letters were written without dots which makes reading pretty difficult – as the letters ف and ق as well as the letters ب and ن and ي might look the same in certain situations.

Try to read the following sentence without the dots:

This sentence can mean a lot depending where and how you add the dots, e.g. the first word can mean:

killed	قَتَل		before	قَبْل		elephant	فِيل

This is how you could read the sentence:

It was said that the elephant killed an elephant in front of the river.	قيل إن فيل قتل فيل قبل النهر.
This is the sentence with all the vowels.	قِيلَ إِنَّ فِيلاً قَتَلَ فِيلاً قَبْلَ النَّهْرِ.

6.   WHO WAS THE FIRST ARABIC GRAMMAR EXPERT?

His name was أَبُو الْأَسْوَد الدُّؤَلِي - in transliteration: Abu al-Aswad al-Du'ali (603 - 688). He became Muslim during the time of the prophet Muhammad and later migrated to Basra (which is today in Iraq) where a mosque was named after him. When more and more people converted to Islam, a lot of them couldn't read the Qur'an without making mistakes which led to a misunderstanding of words.

Historians also say that it was أَبُو الْأَسْوَد الدُّؤَلِي who marked the letters with points approximately in the year 664 (42 ﻫ), at a time when the vowel signs (تَشْكِيل), which we use now, had not existed.

Remark: In the 8th century, a grammarian from modern day Oman invented a writing system which we basically use in standard Arabic till today.

- His name was أَبُو عَبْد الرَّحْمٰن الْخَلِيل ابن أَحْمَد الْفَراهِيدي commonly known as *al-Farahidi* or *al-Khalil*. It is said that he started using a small س for the الشَّدّة (*Shadda*).ᵗ

7. WHAT DOES THE WORD نَحْو MEAN?

It has a lot of meanings: *direction; side; way; manner, fashion; corresponding to; similar to; like* – <u>and</u> it means: <u>*grammar*</u>!

In its early original meaning the root ن - ح - و meant *direction*. In old grammar books the word نَحْو was used to express the meaning of *to show someone the direction*. Later, it also had the meaning of: *for example*. So what we call *grammar* now was in old times just a way to show people how Arabic works.

What is important to know: The word نَحْو is a اِسْم and can be used in several ways.

- It can be used as an adverbial accusative of place or time - نَحْوَ - which is often (not entirely correct) treated as a preposition. The word نَحْوَ always stays the same in this application. It always ends with a single فَتْحة.

- If you connect نَحْو with a true preposition - like in the expression بِنَحْوِ -, the word is treated as a اِسْم – which implies that the word نَحْو takes case endings.

10

Notice that the "preposition" نَحْـوَ is synonymous with the "preposition" صَوْبَ.

The girl is as nice as...	...الْبِنْتُ لَطِيفَةٌ نَحْوَ	١
Here, the word نَحْوَ is used as a preposition and not as a اِسْم. We could use a synonym: مِثْل		
He came to us.	أَتَى نَحْوَنا.	٢
Here, the word نَحْوَ is used as a preposition and not as a اِسْم. We could use a synonym: إِلَى		
around five o'clock...	...فِي نَحْوِ السَّاعَةِ الْخَامِسةِ	٣
Here, the word نَحْو is not a preposition – instead, it is a اِسْم and gets a case ending.		
in this way...	...عَلَى هٰذا النَّحْوِ	٤
Here too, the word نَحْو is not the preposition نَحْوَ – instead, it is a اِسْم and needs a case ending.		

Notice: نَحْو can also be used together with numbers meaning: *about, approximately*:

approximately eleven years...	...نَحْوَ أَحَدَ عَشَرَ عَامًا
about four thousand men...	...نَحْوَ أَرْبَعةِ آلافِ رَجُلٍ

8. ARE THERE LONG VOWELS?

In Arabic, precisely speaking, no. The term *long vowel* is used to make things easier to understand, also in this book.

So called long vowels are described in Arabic by the term حُرُوف الْمَدّ. The word مَدّ has the meaning of *additional* and causes a lengthening of the preceding sound – which is: a, i or u.

Arabic does not have real long vowels. It has only three short ones (a, i, u). The letters و and ي are treated as consonants. The letter ا (Alif) is a special case – see chapter 10.

Actually, for example, the long vowel "ii" is composed of a كَسْرة under the preceding letter plus the silent consonant يْ – which all together results in a lengthening or prolongation of the preceding sound. This is what we are talking about:

long a	aa	ـَا
long i	iy = "ii"	ـِيْ
long u	uw = "uu"	ـُوْ

9. CAN A WORD START WITH A VOWEL?

No. This brings us to a golden rule: <u>Every Arabic utterance or sentence has to start with a consonant followed by a vowel</u>. Standard Arabic forbids initial consonant clusters and more than two consecutive consonants in other positions.

If you see

- the definite article الـ like in the word الْكِتابُ
- an imperative, for example: أُكْتُبْ!
- the word for *son* اِبن or the word for *name* اِسْم

at the beginning of an utterance or in isolation, then the first sound coming out of your mouth has to be a هَمْزة or so called glottal stop.

The sound of a هَمْزة exists in English or German in speech but is not written. It is phonetically a catch in the throat by holding one's breath and suddenly releasing it.

Little is an example in colloquial English – if you don't pronounce the "tt", which means you pronounce the word like "li'le". *Spiegel-Ei* is an example for a German word with a glottal stop; the glottal stop is pronounced where the dash is.

10.   WHY IS THE LETTER ا (ALIF) SO SPECIAL?

There are three letters in Arabic that cause difficulties: ا - و - ي

Especially the Alif (أَلِف) is a tricky letter. We will have a look at three rules which will help us to deal with it:

RULE I: An Alif can never be part of the root.

The three (weak) letters ا - ي - و are called حُرُوف الْعِلّة. But only two of them - و and ي - can be part of the root. If you spot an Alif ا in a word, it will never be a root letter. The Alif is in fact originally a و or a ي which has changed its form to ا

Watch out: Notice the difference between the ا (long vowel) and the أ (هَمْزة) – for example the verb *to point at*: أَدَّى إِلَى

Here, the Alif is a real هَمْزة - written in the shape of an Alif with a هَمْزة on top - because the following vowel has an "a"-sound. The root of the word is: ء - د - و

RULE II: The letter آ is called ألِف مَدّ – in grammar: الْمَدّة.

Don't confuse it with the Alif functioning as a مَدّ حَرْف known as *long vowel a*.

The ألِف مَدّ is a combination of two letters. In the first example below it marks the phonetic process that produces the مَدّ while in the second example it moves from singular to plural:

meaning		example	construction	
to believe		أَأْمَنَ -> آمَنَ	أْ + أَ	1
	آ =	Notice: This is verb pattern IV أَفْعَلَ from the I-verb أَمُنَ (*to be be faithful; reliable*). Watch out: The I-verb أَمِنَ with a كَسْرة means *to be safe*.		
rewards; compensation		مُكافَأة -> مُكافآت	آ + أ	2

Notice that - in both cases - you have to pronounce it (all togeth-er) as a <u>glottal stop plus a long "a"</u>. It is <u>not a long glottal</u> stop as this would be a هَمْزة with شَدّة.

And pronunciation matters! Notice the difference in the following two examples:

translation	root	example
tragedies	ء - س - و	مآس
diamond	proper noun	ماس

RULE III: <u>An Alif can't start an utterance.</u>

This might sound strange but as we have seen above, no sentence in Arabic can start with a vowel. The Alif at the beginning of a word is never pronounced – unless it marks the beginning of a sentence (= glottal stop).

The letter I at the beginning might get mixed up with a regular هَمْزة - so called هَمْزة الْقَطْع – which is written as أ and is pro-nounced as a glottal stop. It is therefore important to understand the function of the Alif when it starts a word.

There are two different kinds of an Alif that don't function as a long vowel:

هَمْزة الْوَصْل	هَمْزة الْقَطْع
Written as أ - آ - إ but it is in fact a form of هَمْزة	Always written with a small هَمْزة on top = أ
Only treated as a consonant (هَمْزة) when it marks the beginning of an utterance.	Always treated as a consonant (هَمْزة).
Literal meaning: *connecting* هَمْزة	*disconnecting* or *cutting* هَمْزة
This هَمْزة is only pronounced as a glottal stop if it marks the beginning of a sentence. Apart from that, it is not pronounced at all. You need a helping vowel in the preceding word to connect the word with the هَمْزة الْوَصْل	This هَمْزة is always pronounced as a glottal stop.

Examples

هَمْزة الْوَصْل		هَمْزة الْقَطْع	
The إ is found in some verb patterns.	اِفْتَعَلَ, اِسْتَفْعَلَ	The أ here marks the first person singular *I* or the comparative form.	أَفْعَل
Definite article	ال	Personal pronoun *you*	أَنْتَ
		إفْعال of a IV-verb مَصْدَر	إفْعال

16

The هَمْزة الْوَصْل could be translated into English as *joining* or *elidable* Alif.

The following verb patterns in the imperative, past tense as well as their مَصْدَر all have a هَمْزة الْوَصْل at the beginning which is (depending on the position of the word) pronounced as a glottal stop, as a vowel – or it is even unpronounced.

verb form	مَصْدَر	past tense
VII	اِنْفِعال	اِنْفَعَلَ
VIII	اِفْتِعال	اِفْتَعَلَ
IX	اِفْعِلال	اِفْعَلَّ
X	اِسْتِفْعال	اِسْتَفْعَلَ

If it is connected to a وَ or فَ for example, the ا is not pronounced at all. For example the verb *to get away* - اِنْصَرَفَ - turns, if preceded by a و or ف, into "wansarafa", "fansarafa".

11. WHAT IS A WEAK LETTER?

If there is a و or a ي in the root, we call it a root with a weak letter. These letters complicate Arabic grammar as the و or ي sometimes has to be elided or even changes into a different letter. The Arabic term for a weak letter is حَرْف الْعِلّة which literally means *weak, deficient* letter. A verb that contains a weak letter is called فِعْل مُعْتَلّ (*sick, defective* verb).

17

There are several types of weak verbs:

1	Quasi-sound verb: This verb has a و or a ي as a first root-letter. It is usually translated as *assimilated verb*.	فِعْل مِثال
	But watch out: Verbs with initial ي are not really assimilated. In I-form-verbs, the ي usually stays. For example the (past tense) verb يَئِسَ هُوَ (*to give up all hope*). The present tense is: يَيْأَسُ Whereas in the I-verb وَأَدَ (*to bury alive*), the و drops in the present tense: هُوَ يَئِدُ	
	to arrive – وَصَلَ	

2	Hollow verb: This verb has a و or a ي in the middle of the root.	فِعْل أَجْوَف
	to say – قالَ	

3	Defective verb: This verb has a و or a ي as the last letter of the root.	فِعْل ناقِص
	to call – دَعا	

4	Double weak verb: Has two weak letters in its root.	فِعْل لَفيف
	to grill – شَوَى	
	to carry out – وَقَى	

12. WHEN DOES A ‏ا‎ OR A ‏ى‎ AT THE END CAUSE TROUBLE?

You should always be careful if you spot a weak letter or a هَمْزة in a word – but especially if a word ends in:

- a) a ‏ا‎ (Alif)
- b) a ‏ى‎ – no matter if pronounced ‏ي‎ or ‏ا‎ ("i" or "a"-sound)
- c) ‏اء‎

Here is an overview of all three different possibilities and how they are called in Arabic:

الْاِسْم الْمَمْدُود	الْاِسْم الْمَنْقُوص	الْاِسْم الْمَقْصُور
‏اء‎ at the end	‏ي‎ at the end	‏ا‎ or ‏ى‎ at the end
Lit.: *the extended*	Lit.: *the reduced*	Lit.: *the shortened*
Noun with extended ending; *prolonged noun*	Noun with curtailed ending; *defective, deficient noun*	Noun with shortened ending; *abbreviated, indeclinable noun*
desert صَحْراء	the judge الْقاضِي	stick عَصًا
red حَمْراء	the club النَّادِي	young man فَتًى

So what does this mean practically?

It is important to identify the correct type of word

- a) if you want to إعْراب the word
- b) if you need to form a <u>dual</u> or <u>plural</u>

We will get back to all this in the following chapters. Notice: In all three groups we are talking about a اِسْم. The grammar we are dealing with has nothing to do with verbs (e.g. قَضَى) or prepositions (إِلَى).

13. زُمَلائه OR زُمَلاؤُه, زُمَلاءَه - WHAT IS CORRECT?

The expression means *his colleagues*. And to give you the answer to our question: All of them are correct!

It depends on the function and position in the sentence, to say it short: on the case. Grammatically speaking, the word زُمَلاء is a so called اِسْم مَمْدُود which is important to keep in mind.

Let us have a look at all three forms:

1 *his colleagues*		زُمَلاؤُه
Used as a subject	مَرْفُوع	زُمَلاؤُه
His colleagues came.		. جاءَ زُمَلاؤُه

2 *his colleagues*		زُمَلاءَه
Used as an object	مَنْصُوب	زُمَلاءَه
I met his colleagues.		.قابَلْتُ زُمَلاءَه

20

3	*his colleagues*	زُمَلائِهِ
	Used after a preposition (1st example) or as a second part of a إضافة	مَجْرُور	زُمَلائِهِ
	I took the books from his colleagues.	أَخَذْتُ الْكُتُبَ مِن زُمَلائِهِ.
	his colleagues' house	بَيْتُ زُمَلائِهِ

14.   الْمَقْصُور - WHY DO ENDINGS GET SHORTENED?

We are only talking about a اِسْم مَقْصُور if there is an Alif at the end of the word and if this <u>Alif belongs to the root</u>. This Alif is called أَلِف لازِمة

Don't forget: The ا (Alif) can never be part of the root. It was originally a و or ي which has changed into a ا (Alif).

So watch out:

1. Sometimes the <u>Alif is just a case marker and is not part of the root</u>. Let us take for example the word أَب which means *father*. For example: قابَلْتُ أَبا بَكْرٍ (*I met Abu Bakr.*) The Alif here is not part of the root. It marks the مَنْصُوب-case.

2. The ا is a *fixed, invariable letter* and stays the same in all cases, so called مَبْنِيّ. For more information about that see chapter 58.

Let us have a closer look:

أَلِف at the third position?	explanation	feminine plural	dual	e.g.	root
yes	و is part of the root – أَلِف changes into و	عَصَوات	عَصْوانِ	عَصًا	ع - ص - و
yes	ي is part of the root	فَتَيات	فَتَيانِ	فَتًى	ف - ت - ي
no	–	كُبْرَيات	كُبْرَيانِ	كُبْرَى	ك - ب - ر

Let us now check the masculine plural of أَعْلَى, the Arabic word for *higher*:

explanation	masculine plural	root	
You have to delete the أَلِف and add a سُكُون on top of the و. Notice the correct pronunciation of أَعْلَوْن. It is not: "'a3luun" – it is "'a3lawn"	أَعْلَوْن	ع - ل - و	أَعْلَى
	أَعْلَيْن or if it is مَجْرُور or مَنْصُوب		

And what about the تَنْوِين (*nunation*)?

Nothing changes in any case! Notice in the following examples that the تَنْوِين at the end of the word الْفَتَى - which is not written - is a *hidden marker* or *presumptive vowel* (مُقَدَّرة).

<u>So it is ى in all cases!</u> You always pronounce the word "al-Fata". This is because the last letter is actually a أَلِف and not a ي!

فاعِل مَرْفُوع بِضَمّة مُقَدَّرة	The young boy came.	١ جاءَ الْفَتى.
مَفْعُول بِهِ مَنْصُوب بِفَتْحة مُقَدَّرة	I met the young boy.	٢ قابَلْتُ الْفَتى.
مَجْرُور بِكَسْرة مُقَدَّرة	I greeted the young boy.	٣ سَلَّمْتُ عَلَى الْفَتى.

15. رَأَي AND الْقاضِي - SAME ENDING, SAME PROBLEM?

No – we have to deal with different grammatical problems.

Generally speaking, if you see the letter ي at the end of a word, you have to watch out. There are several reasons and all of them have an impact on the تَنْوِين, the dual and the plural.

In this chapter we will have a look at the اِسْم مَنْقُوص. The word مَنْقُوص means: *reduced; deficient; insufficient.*

Let us have a look at some words.

All of them end in a ي – but not all of them are a اِسْم مَنْقُوص. The numbers on the left side correspond to the conditions listed below.

	grammar term	اِسْم مَنْقُوص	example, meaning	
4	It is a regular اِسْم	NO	opinion	رَأْيٌ
	The word رَأْيٌ has a سُكُون on the letter before the ي. But to be considered a مَنْقُوص it needs a كَسْرة			

3; 2	This is a so called اِسْم مَنْسُوب	NO	Egyptian	مَصْرِيٌّ
	Any noun in Arabic can easily be turned into an adjective (صِفة) by adding the so called ي *of relation* (also called: النِّسْبة). Notice the شَدّة on the ي			
	Note here the كَسْرة before the ي which is typical for a اِسْم مَنقُوص	YES	the lawyer	الْقاضِي

3	This is the اِسْم الْمَفْعُول of the root بَنَى	NO	built	مَبْنِيٌّ
	Although we have a منقوص-root (e.g. active participle بانٍ) it isn't a اِسْم مَنْقُوص – as the ي has a شَدّة (see condition no. 3). Watch out: The اِسْم الْمَفْعُول of a مَنْقُوص-root (فاعٍ) follows إِسْم الْفاعِل) has the pattern: مَفعيّ			

So let us sum up the conditions for a اِسْم مَنْقُوص:

1. The word can take تَنْوِين – also called اِسْم مُعْرَب. Therefore, words like الَّذِي can't be a اِسْم مَنْقُوص

2. The ي must be part of the root – ياء لازمة

3. There is no شَدّة above the ي

4. The vowel before the ي has to be a كَسْرة – not a سُكُون

<u>This brings us to an important question:</u>

What is actually the problem with the الْإِسْـم الْمَنْقُـوص؟ Answer: It is not always necessary to write the ي!

Let us check all possible situations:

1. Keep the ي – in the dual and the feminine plural

a messenger; delivery boy	ساعٍ	indefinite
the messenger; the delivery boy	السَّاعِي	definite
the two delivery boys	السَّاعِيانِ السَّاعِيينِ	dual
the delivery boys	السَّاعِيات	feminine plural

2. Delete the ي – if it is a sound masculine plural

a lawyer	مُحامٍ	indefinite
the lawyer	الْمُحامِي	definite
the lawyers	الْمُحامُونَ الْمُحامِينَ	masculine plural

25

Notice the difference between the pronunciation of the last letter in the dual and the masculine plural: السَّاعِيانِ ("e"-sound; dual) and الْمُحامُونَ ("a"-sound; plural).

So what about the correct case endings?

Let us check this too:

1. If the word functions as a subject (فاعِل)

explanation	case marker	example	
The judge came.	مَرْفُوع	جاءَ الْقاضِي.	١
The judge of the city came.	بِضَمّة مُقَدَّرة	جاءَ قاضِي الْمَدِينةِ.	
The ending is not pronounced "u" – it is "e/i". *The judge* is مَرْفُوع – but the marker is hidden.			
A judge came.	مَرْفُوع بِضَمّة مُقَدَّرة	جاءَ قاضٍ.	٢
Here, *a judge* is مَرْفُوع – but the case "un" is hidden and pronounced "in". That's why you see two كَسْرة under the ض			

2. If the word functions as a direct object (مَفْعُول بِهِ)

explanation	case marker	example	
I met the judge.	مَنْصُوب	قابَلْتُ الْقاضِيَ.	١
I met the judge of the city.	بِفَتْحة ظاهِرة	قابَلْتُ قاضِيَّ الْمَدِينَةِ.	

The "a" at the end of *the judge* is pronounced "a" ("ya").			
I met a judge.	مَنْصُوب بِفَتْحة ظاهِرة	قابَلْتُ قاضِيًا.	2
The ending is pronounced "an".			

3. If the word comes after a preposition (حَرْف جَرّ)

translation/explanation	case marker	example	
I greeted the judge.	مَجْرُور بِكَسْرة مُقَدَّرة	سَلَّمْتُ عَلَى الْقاضِي.	1
I greeted the judge of the city.		سَلَّمْتُ عَلَى قاضِي الْمَدِينةِ.	
The ending of *the judge* is pronounced "e/i" as there is a ي Watch out: The ي has no case marker! (no كَسْرة under the ي)			
I greeted a judge.	مَجْرُور بِكَسْرة مُقَدَّرة	سَلَّمْتُ عَلَى قاضٍ.	2
The ending of *judge* is pronounced "in" – but the (actual) case marker is hidden! Don't be confused: Yes, there are two كَسْرة. But don't forget that the ي was elided! So the ending is actually <u>not under the last letter.</u>			

To sum it up:

You only pronounce the actual case marker...

... if the الْإِسْم الْمَنْقُوص is مَنْصُوب !

27

indefinite, مَنْصُوب	"qaadiyan"	قَاضِيًا
definite, مَنْصُوب	"qaadiya"	الْقَاضِيَ

16.   ARE THERE WORDS THAT LOOK THE SAME IN ALL CASES?

Well will see. Let us take a root with a weak letter (و or ي) as the last radical, e.g. ع - ن - ى which means: *to concern; to regard; to mean*. From this root, we can form the word for *meaning*: مَعْنًى

Words like this are called a اِسْم مَقْصُور. There is something special about them: These words are <u>indeclinable</u> in all 3 cases. This is also the reason why you call the الْاِسْم الْمَقْصُور the *indeclinable noun*. See also chapters 12 and 14.

Let us have a look at an example – the word for *meaning*:

case	indefinite	definite
مَرْفُوع	مَعْنًى	الْمَعْنَى
مَجْرُور	مَعْنًى	الْمَعْنَى
مَنْصُوب	مَعْنًى	الْمَعْنَى

Here are some other examples:

level; standard	مُسْتَوًى	س - و - ي
villages	قُرًى	ق - ر - ى
given	مُعْطًى	ع - ط - ي

17. سَماء - HOW DID THE هَمْزة GET INTO THIS WORD?

The word سَماء means *sky*.

If we want to answer our question, we need to have a look at the root for this word, which is: و - م - س

The root means: *to be high, elevated; to be above*. Actually, the word for *sky* should normally be: سَماو. But this would be difficult to pronounce. So the و turned into a ء.

Notice that in the النِّسْبة-form (adjective; صِفة) - which is سَماوِيّ and means *heavenly* -, the و is still there. This is also important for the correct form of the plural which will be dealt in chapter 18. By the way: The word سَماء can theoretically be used as masculine or feminine but is more frequently considered to be feminine.

By the way, the same is applied to the word *building* - بِناء

Here, the root is: ي - ن - ب. So the word should actually be بِناي - but this would be difficult to pronounce.

Watch out: Of course it isn't always like that. There are plenty of Arabic words that do end in the usual way, although the pronunciation is a bit difficult, e.g.: مُتَساوِ (*equal, similar*).

18. سَماء - WHAT IS THE PLURAL OF "SKY"?

The ending اء of the Arabic word for *sky* brings us again to the topic of the الاِسْم الْمَمْدُود.

مَمْدُود literally means *lengthened* or *extended*. Grammatically speaking, all words that end with ١ء belong to this group.

So what is the answer? What is the plural of سَماء? In the case of *sky* you can choose between سَماوَات or سَماءَات. In the Qur'an you find سَماوَات more often. But both forms are correct.

Let us now examine the الْاِسْم الْمَمْدُود in detail. We have to look at three cases:

Case 1: The ء is part of the root – هَمْزة أَصْلِيّة
In this case the ء remains

meaning	masculine plural*	feminine plural	dual*	root	word
construction		إِنْشاءات	إِنْشاءانِ إِنْشاءَيْنِ	ن - ش - ء	إِنْشاء
sb. who reads a lot	قَرّاءُون قَرّائِين		قَرّاءانِ قَرّاءَيْنِ	ق - ر - ء	قَرّاء

* مَرْفُوع and مَنْصُوب / مَجْرُور

Case 2: The ء is additional – هَمْزة زائِدة
• There is <u>no masculine</u> plural
• All words of this pattern are feminine
• The ء turns into a و

30

meaning	feminine plural	dual*	root	word
desert	صَحْراوَات	صَحْراوَانِ صَحْراوَيْنِ	ص - ح - ر	صَحْراء

* مَجْرُور/ مَنْصُوب and مَرْفُوع

> **Case 3: The ء was originally a و or ي**
> - The ء remains or, alternatively, it turns into a و. The latter is used in the Qur'an more often.

meaning	masculine plural*	feminine plural	dual*	root	word
building		إِناءَات	إِناءَانِ إِناءَيْنِ	ب - ن - ي	إِناء
		إِناوَات	إِناوَانِ إِناوَيْنِ		

runner	عَدّاؤُونَ عَدّائِينَ		عَدّاءَانِ عَدّاءَيْنِ	ع - د - و	عَدّاء
	عَدّاوُونَ عَدّاوِينَ				

* مَجْرُور/ مَنْصُوب and مَرْفُوع

Notice the spelling of the ء in the <u>dual form</u> of the مَجْرُور- and
مَنْصُوب-case of عَدّاءَيْنِ. Since there is a سُكُون on the letter ي

31

of the dual ending you should write a <u>lone</u> ء and not a ئ (which is, by the way, also called *"ya chair"*).

Here are some more examples:

The tallest building was built in front of the club.	أُقِيمَ الْبِناءُ الْأَعْلى أَمامَ النَّادِي ١
The (two) tallest buildings were built in front of the (two) clubs.	أُقِيمَ الْبِناءانِ= الْبِناوَانِ الْأَعْلَيانِ أَمامَ النَّادِيَيْنِ

Promote virtue and prevent vice.	كُنْ داعِيًا إِلَى الْمَعْرُوفِ, ناهِيًا عَنْ الْمُنْكَرِ ٢
dual form	كُونا دَاعِيَيْنِ إِلَى الْمَعْرُوفِ, ناهِيَيْنِ عَنْ الْمُنْكَرِ
masculine plural	كُونوا داعِينَ إِلَى الْمَعْرُوفِ, ناهِيَيْنِ عَنْ الْمُنْكَرِ

Notice that in the second sentence, we use the verb كانَ – so the predicate (خَبَر) has to be مَنْصُوب.

19.   حَرْفُ عَطْفٍ - WHAT IS SO SPECIAL ABOUT IT?

The word عَطْف means *sympathy* in Arabic. In grammar it is used to describe words which don't change the case of the following word. A حَرْف عَطْف stands in the middle of two words which have the same case.

Here are the most important ones:

but	لٰكِنْ		and	و
but rather; in fact	بَلْ		even; even though	حَتَّى

Watch out for the difference!

With a شَدّة on top of the ن at the end, this word means *but* as well. You have to use this form when a full sentence comes after it. This sentence has to follow the rules of إِنَّ : • the subject (اِسْم إِنَّ) is مَنْصُوب • the predicate (خَبَر إِنَّ) is مَرْفُوع	لٰكِنَّ

Let us have a look at an example:

My two sisters are dark skinned, but Mustafa's two sisters are fair skinned.	أُخْتايَ سَمْراوانِ وَلٰكِنَّ أُخْتَيْ مُصْطَفَى شَقْراوانِ

• Note 1: "ukht**aaya**"

The first word is the dual-form of *sister* أُخْت with the possessive pronoun *my* – this is the reason for the Alif: أُخْتايَ

• Note 2: the pronunciation after لٰكِنَّ

It is "ukht**ai**": A dual in the 1st part of a إِضافة merely loses the final ن. Nothing else happens. If the 2nd part of a إِضافة is a word beginning with الـ, then you need a helping vowel on the ي. But the helping vowel is always a كَسْرة, not a فَتْحة. For example: أُخْتَي الطَّالِبِ

33

20. شُؤُون OR شُئُون - WHAT IS CORRECT?

Both are correct. Both words are the plural of شَأْن which means: *affair* or *matter*.

In Egypt, the form شُئُون is more common whereas in most other parts of the Arab world, the form شُؤُون - with the ء over the و - is more used.

21. WHY DOES THE DEFINITE ARTICLE SOMETIMES HAVE A RIBBON?

The definite article consists of two parts: ا and the letter ل

The ا in the definite article is a so called هَمْزة وَصْل. It is never pronounced unless it marks the beginning of a sentence or utterance – in that case it must be pronounced as a glottal stop. But as soon as the definite article is preceded by a word, the ل in the definite article is elided and gets a special form:

This Alif is treated as if it wasn't there. That is why you mark it with a وَصْلة or صِلة which looks like a ribbon above the ا – like a ضَمّة with a tail. It is rarely used in books or newspapers.	ٱ

Let us have a look at some examples to make it clearer:

explanation; translation	example	
'al-kitaabu - *the book*	أَلْكِتابُ	١

34

The هَمْزة وَصْل is written like this - أ - if it marks the beginning of a sentence. So you start with a glottal stop! The ل is pronounced like the following letter if that following letter is a so-called sun letter. The phonetic characteristic of sun letters is that in all of them, the tongue is raised towards the front part of the upper palate.		
Haadhal-kitaabu – *this book*	هٰذا ٱلْكِتابُ	2
Here, you don't pronounce a glottal stop! You take the preceding vowel "a" of the word هٰذا and connect it with the ل		

A remark: The purist grammarians never write the definite article as أَلْ with a هَمْزة قَطْع. Instead, they prefer the writing of a simple Alif with a vowel on the top or at the bottom of the letter – even at the beginning of a sentence or in isolation when it has to be pronounced as a هَمْزة.

An excursus: sun letters and moon letters

In Arabic, we have two different kinds of consonants: sun letters (ٱلْحُرُوف الشَّمْسِيّة) and moon letters (ٱلْحُرُوف الْقَمَرِيّة).

The rule is that all letters of the first group (sun letters) assimilate the letter ل in a definite article – this eventually results in doubling the sun letter (شَدّة).

The names are no coincidence: The word for *the sun* - الشَّمْس - is pronounced "ash-shams" and assimilates the ل whereas the word for *the moon* - الْقَمَر - doesn't. It is pronounced "al-Qamar".

35

The sun letters are:

ت	ث	د	ذ	ر	ز	س	ش	ص	ض	ط	ظ	ل	ن
t	th	d	dh	r	z	s	sh	ṣ	ḍ	ṭ	ẓ	l	n

The moon letters are:

ء	ب	ج	ح	خ	ع	غ	ف	ق	ك	م	و	ي	ه
'	b	j	ḥ	kh	'	gh	f	q	k	m	w	y	h

22. THE WORD „BUT" - HOW DO YOU WRITE IT?

The Arabic word for *but* is لكن

It is pronounced with a long „aa"-sound after the ل – although it is usually not written. This has to do with a speciality: the writing of the Aleph. It should be: لٰكِنْ

It is called *dagger Aleph* (أَلِف خَنْجَرِيّة as خَنْجَر means *dagger*) and has to do with the history of the script. The original Semitic alphabet had no vowel signs. Eventually some vowels came to be marked with letters, but in the Qur'an you still have many words in which the vowels are not marked.

Usually people don't notice this because the Qur'an is fully vocalized, but for example if you read the first sura (الْفاتِحة) you will see that the word الْعالَمِين in the second verse has no Aleph. Nor does the word مالِك in the fourth verse. Today they have daggers instead.

translation	example in the Qur'an, sura الْفَاتِحة	verse (Ayah)
(All) praise is (due) to Allah, Lord of the worlds	الْحَمْدُ لِلهِ رَبِّ الْعَٰلَمِينَ	2
The Entirely Merciful, the Especially Merciful	ٱلرَّحْمَٰنِ ٱلرَّحِيمِ	3
Sovereign of the Day of Recompense	مَٰلِكِ يَوْمِ ٱلدِّينِ	4

Eventually the script became more orderly and today we have absolute rules.

However, some words, including grammar words like هٰذا and religious words like ٱلرَّحْمَٰنِ, are still spelled the old way and vocalized with daggers.

By the way: The same happens in Hebrew. Old Biblical names like כהן ("Cohen" which means priest in Hebrew) or שלמה ("Shlomo"; meaning: Solomon, son of David; سُلَيْمان in Arabic) are spelled in the old way, instead of כוהן and שלומו.

23. "THIS" AND "THAT" - WHY ARE THEY SPECIAL IN ARABIC?

If we want to understand the words for *this* or *that* - so called - إِسْم إشارة, we have to take a closer look at their origin.

In Arabic, هٰذا (ha:ða:) means *this* and ذٰلِكَ (ða:lika) means *that*. Both have a long a-vowel after the first letter (which is usually written with a vertical dash – see chapter 22 for details about the so called "dagger Alif" or أَلِف خَنْجَرِيّة). Why is that?

Let us first have a look at the source for these words:

feminine, singular (several options)	ذِى, ذِةْ تا, تَةْ	masculine singular	ذا
feminine, dual	تان	masculine, dual	ذان
feminine, plural	أولاءِ <->	masculine, plural	أولاءِ
		for places	هُنا

If you want to talk about <u>something that is close</u> to you, you'll have to combine these words with a ه – so called: هاء التّنْبيه.

تَنْبيه means *warning* or *alarm*. The so called هاء التّنْبيه literally has the meaning of *look!* or *there!* Usually the ه has an additional Alif – ها

Here are some examples:

Look, there he is!	ها هُوَ !
Hey, you!	ها أَنْتُم !
Here I am! (Notice that the final Alif of أنا is omitted.)	ها أَنَذا !

Let's continue with the expression *this*.

In Arabic, these words are called أَسْماء الإشارة إلَى الْقَريب.

A hint: Since it is <u>near</u> to you, you put the additional letter ه at the <u>beginning</u>!

fem., singular	هٰذِهِ	mas. singular	هٰذا
* feminine, dual; *these two*	هَاتَانِ	masculine, dual; *these two*	هٰذانِ
feminine, plural; *these*	هٰؤُلَاءِ <->	masculine plural; *these*	هٰؤُلَاءِ
		* for (near) places	هَهُنا or هَٰهُنا

* A remark: Take a close look at the spelling of the Alif. If the consonant after the هاء التَّنْبِيه is a ت or a ه, you don't write the "dagger Alif" (see chapter 22). This is just a convention. The pronunciation is the same.

Now, let's see how it works for <u>something that is further away</u>; the expression *that*.

In Arabic, these words are called أَسْماء الإِشارة إِلَى الْبَعِيد.

A hint: Since it is <u>far</u> from you, you put the additional letter(s) – a ك or a combination of ك + ل - at the <u>end</u>!

feminine, singular	تِلْكَ	masculine singular; *those*	ذاكَ or ذٰلِكَ
feminine, dual	تانِكَ or تَيْنِكَ <->	masculine dual; *those two; both of those*	ذانِكَ or ذَيْنِكَ
feminine, plural	أُولَٰئِكَ <->	masculine plural; *these*	أُولَٰئِكَ

39

for places	هُنَاكَ or هُنَالَكَ

Some important remarks:

- The ل is a long-distance indicator and usually signals that something is *further away;* it is called لام البُعْد.

- When you address another person, you add a ك. What precedes the ك relates to the person or thing <u>indicated</u>. The letter ك is the so called كاف الخِطاب (particle of allocution). This ك agrees in case number and gender with the addressee! (see chapter 178)

  كَ or كِ – singular

  كُما – dual

  كُمْ – masculine plural

  كُنَّ – feminine plural

- If there is a لَكَ or a لِكَ after the ذ, the long Alif is written as a vertical dash. After the letter ت, the long Alif is omitted (you just pronounce a short vowel a).

- You can never have ه and ل combined together as the ه denotes nearness and the ل remoteness.

Let us have a closer look at some combinations.

construction		explanation
ذا + ما = ماذا ١	*what*	ذا is the اِسْم الْإِشارة. It is combined with the word ما. See chapter 24.
ها + ذا = هٰذا ٢	*this*	The ها is only used for giving attention. The ها is used to give notice, to a person addressed, to something about to be said to him. Only the ذا is the اِسْم الْإِشارة
ذا + ل + ك ٣ = ذٰلِكَ	*that*	For things that are further away.
هُوَ ذا, هِيَ ذي ٤		Combined with a personal pronoun, it means: *that one; look at that one!*

Some notes on the grammatical terms concerning *this* and *that*:

هٰذِهِ مُدَرِّسةُ اللُّغةِ الْعَرَبِيّةِ.	This is a teacher of the Arabic language.
اِسْم الْإِشارة مَبْنيٌّ عَلَى الْكَسْر في مَحَل رَفْع مُبْتَدَأ	هٰذِهِ ١
خَبَر الْمُبْتَدَأ مَرْفُوع بِالضَّمة	مُدَرِّسةُ ٢
مُضاف إِلَيْهِ مَجْرُور بِالْكَسْرة	اللُّغةِ ٣
نَعْت لِلْمُضاف إِلَيْهِ مَجْرُور بِالْكَسْرة	الْعَرَبِيّةِ ٤

Watch out if you have a <u>definite noun after the demonstrative pronoun</u>:

This student is diligent.	هٰذا الطَّالِبُ مُجْتَهِدٌ.

إِسْم الْإِشارة مَبْنِيٌّ عَلَى الْكَسْر فِي مَحَل رَفْع مُبْتَدَأ	هٰذا	1
بَدَل لِاسْم الإِشارة مَرْفُوع بالضَّمّة	الطَّالِبُ	2
خَبَر الْمُبْتَدَأ مَرْفُوع بالضَّمّة	مُجْتَهِدٌ	3

Have a look at number 2: The word student is grammatically speaking an apposition, a so called بَدَل. See chapter 210 for more details.

To sum it up:

Words like هٰذا or هٰؤُلاءِ are actually a construction of two or three words.

24. ذا - Does it only mean "this"?

No, it doesn't.

Let's check why and start with the characteristics of ذا

- ذا is a *demonstrative pronoun* – a so called اِسْم إِشارة

- ذا basically means *this one; this;* in combinations also *that.*

- The feminine form of ذا is ذي (also written as: ذِهِ).

- The plural is: أُولاءِ

42

Sometimes, however, the word ذا is mistaken with another word: ذُو – which means *master of; a possessor; an owner of.*

The reason for this is that ذُو in the مَنْصُوب-case turns into ذا and in the مَجْرُور-case, it turns into ذِي

Here are some examples:

مَرْفُوع – nominative		١
The man with a hat	الرَّجُلُ ذو قُبْعةٍ	
مَجْرُور – genitive		٢
Next to the man with the hat	إِلَى جِوارِ الرَّجُلِ ذِي الْقُبْعةِ	
مَنْصُوب – accusative		٣
I saw a man with a hat.	رَأَيْتُ رَجُلاً ذا قُبْعةٍ	

Watch out: In Egyptian Arabic, instead of هٰذا and هٰذِهِ, you say: دَه ("da") and دِي ("di") – so don't get confused.

25. ماذا AND ما ذا (WITH SPACE) – WHAT IS THE DIFFERENCE?

There is a tricky difference. Let's check it step by step:

1. You can combine the word ذا with two other words: ما or مَنْ. Grammatically speaking, this form of a ذا is a so called إِسْم مَوْصول (relative pronoun).

    It has the meaning of الَّذِي

2. The words مَنْ and ما are both a اِسْم اِسْتِفْهام, an interrogative particle; مَنْ is for human beings only. (Note: About the different applications of ما, have a look at chapter 133.)

3. However, ذا is only a relative pronoun if it is <u>not connected</u> with the preceding word ما. If it is (merged), the single word is used as an interrogative particle: ماذا

Let us now have a closer look:

grammar	meaning of	example	
ذا here is a demonstrative pronoun; اِسْم إِشارة Both words - ما and ذا - are written separately.			I
ما: مُبْتَدَأ	= ما هٰذا الكتاب؟	ما ذا الكتاب؟	
ذا: خَبَر	What is this book?		

ذا here is a relative pronoun; اِسْم مَوْصُول Both words - ما and ذا - are written separately (notice the space). It is translated as *that which*, or simply *that* or *what* or *which*.			2
ما: مُبْتَدَأ	= ما الَّذي أَتى بِكَ؟	ما ذا أَتى بِكَ هُنا؟	
ذا: خَبَر			
What brings you here? (Lit.: What is it that brings you here?)			

		3
إذا merges with ما to one word. In Arabic we say: مُرَكَّبة مع ما		

- There is NO space between the first two words
- ماذا has the meaning of أَيُّ شَيْءٍ
- ماذا can function as a direct object (مَفْعُول بِهِ) or a prepositional phrase
- The grammatical function of ماذا depends on the position of the sentence

ماذا: مَفْعُول بِهِ		
ماذا: مَفْعُول بِهِ direct object	What did you write?	ماذا كَتَبْتَ؟
جارّ وَمَجْرُور prepositional phrase	Meaning: Why did you come?	لِماذا جِئْتَ؟

Watch out for the difference:

What does he exactly want?	ماذا يُرِيدُ بِالضَّبْطِ؟	1
What is it that he wants?	ما ذا يُرِيدُ بِالضَّبْطِ؟	
	= ما الَّذِي يُرِيدُ بِالضَّبْطِ؟	
Who is it that is in the office?	مَنْ ذا فِي الْمَكْتَبِ؟	2
Who is this who is in the office?	مَنْ ذا الَّذِي فِي الْمَكْتَبِ؟	

Some last remarks:

1. ماذا (interrogative particle)

- ماذا is normally used in verbal sentences (جُمْلة فِعْلِيّة)

45

- ماذا can serve as a subject (فاعِل) or object (مَفْعُول بِهِ) of a verb

| subject | <u>What</u> happened after that? | ماذا حَدَثَ بَعْدَ ذلِكَ؟ |
| object | <u>What</u> do you want? | ماذا تُرِيدُ؟ |

2. ما ذا (with space; ذا used as a relative pronoun)

After a relative pronoun a lot of things can follow:

جُمْلة فِعْلِيّة – verbal sentence		1
I read the book that you bought.	قَرَأْتُ الْكِتابَ الّذِي اِشْتَرَيْتَهُ.	
جُمْلة اِسْمِيّة – nominal sentence		2
The ones who came they are my friends.	حَضَرَ الّذِينَ هُمْ أَصْدِقائِي.	
(جارّ وَمَجْرُور ;3.1) prepositional or شِبْه جُمْلة – (ظَرْف مَكان ;3.2) adverbial phrase		3
Give me the pen that is in the office.	أَعْطِنِي الْقَلَمَ الّذِي فِي الْمَكْتَبِ.	3.1
Give me the pen that is in front of you.	أَعْطِنِي الْقَلَمَ الّذِي أَمامَكَ.	3.2

26. ARE THERE BILITERAL ROOTS?

Some people say yes, there are biliteral roots; some say no, and others even believe that biliteral roots are the origin of Semitic languages. In the end, it all depends on definitions.

Georges Bohas (University of Paris) has written a lot about this subject. He basically says that Arabic roots are derived from what he calls *etymons* – a combination of two letters to which a third letter is added. The added letter can precede the *etymons*, follow them, or it can be put in between.

It is worth thinking about the meaning of roots which look similar.

Let us take the roots: ح - م - د and م - د - ح and م - د - ج

They all share two root letters - م and د - although in different positions. And somehow they mean similar things.

1. حَمِدَ basically means *to praise* in the meaning of *to thank*. It is mainly used with the word *God*.

2. مَدَحَ also means *to praise* – but more in the meaning of *to commend, to say good things about something or someone*.

3. مَجُدَ too has meanings that are related to *being glorious, exalted, praised*.

However, many other verbs have the same letters in different positions – with totally different meanings.

For example: نَقَشَ (*to paint*) versus شَنَقَ (*to hang; to execute*).

A remark: In colloquial Arabic, root letters are sometimes twisted. For example the word for husband: جُوز (Egyptian Arabic) versus زَوْج (standard Arabic).

<u>So let us go back to our question: Are there biliteral roots?</u>

Andrzej Zaborski, a professor from Poland, writes in his article *Biradicalism* (2006) that there are 37 nominal roots in Arabic consisting of only two consonants. They belong to the basic vocabulary going back to Proto-Semitic and even Proto-Hamito-Semitic/Afro-Asiatic and describe mainly basic things human beings needed to survive.

Some grammarians say that most of the words listed below have only two radicals:

water	ماء	father in law	حَم	hand	يَد
father	أَب	blood	دَم	mouth	فَم
				vulva	جِر

Also the following words (as most grammarians argue) have only two root letters:

son	اِبْن	tongue	لِسان	name	اِسْم
root	بن	(with lexicalized suffix)		root	سم

However, in dictionaries you will find them occasionally under a triliteral root which is sometimes based on their plurals:

root	plural	word
ف - و - ه	أقْواه	فَم
ب - ن - و	أبْناء	اِبْن
ل - س - ن	أَلْسُن	لِسان
ح - م - و	أحْماءُ	حَم

root	plural	word
د - م - و	دِماء	دَم
م - و - ه	مِياه	ماء
س - م - ي	أسْماء	اِسْم
ء - ب - و	آباء	أب
ح - ر - ح	أحْراح	جِر

Notice: The word جِر is an exception from the rule.

27. ARE ROOTS SOMETIMES RELATED TO EACH OTHER?

Yes. As seen in chapter 26, some scholars believe that Arabic words had only two root letters at an early stage. It is worth checking similar roots to get a better feeling for Arabic. Of course, you have to watch out: The root doesn't always help you find the correct meaning of a word.

Let us have a look at the following examples. Notice that all verbs start with the same two letters: قط

to cut	قَطَعَ
to cut off	قَطَلَ
to cut off; to break off	قَطَمَ
to knit; to stitch; to concentrate	قَطَبَ

to skim off; to harvest (to cut off a fruit)	قَطَفَ
to trim; to sharpen	قَطَّ
to trickle; to drip	قَطَرَ

28.   DOES THE WORD ORDER MATTER IN ARABIC?

In most cases, in Arabic, the word order <u>doesn't</u> change the meaning of a sentence.

But sometimes it does.

Let us have a look at some examples:

Umm Kulthum is the (<u>one and only</u>) singer.	إِنَّما أُمُّ كُلْثُم مُطْرِبةٌ.
Umm Kulthum was <u>only</u> a singer.	إِنَّما الْمُطْرِبةُ أُمُّ كُلْثُم.
The beginning of civilization started in Egypt.	أَصْلُ الْحَضارةِ في مِصْرَ.
<u>In Egypt</u> started the beginning of civilization.	في مِصْرَ أَصْلُ الْحَضارةِ.
We are studying in the centre.	نَتَعَلَّمُ في الْمَرْكَزِ.
<u>Only</u> in the centre we are studying.	في الْمَرْكَزِ نَتَعَلَّمُ.

29. WHAT IS SO SPECIAL ABOUT THE ARABIC WORD FOR "SON"?

The word for *son* is: اِبْن

It belongs to a group of special words in Arabic. Some of them have only two root letters – and all of them start with an Alif.

two, masculine	اِثْنانِ	son	اِبْن
two, feminine	اِثْنَتانِ	daughter	اِبْنة
name	اِسْم	man	اِمْرُؤٌ
I swear by God	آيْمُ اللّٰهِ		

The letter ا in these words is a هَمْزة وَصْل

Classical Arabic does not know the occurrence of two consonants at the beginning of a word – which means that no Arabic word can begin with a سُكُون on top, like the original word for *son*: بْن

We solve this problem with a هَمْزة وَصْل. That's why in the table above all words start with ا

But what happens if the word اِبْن marks the start of your utterance or sentence?

Then the Alif is pronounced as a هَمْزة – as no Arabic sentence/utterance can start with a vowel, thus with a consonant followed by a vowel. In the word اِبْن you pronounce a هَمْزة and a كَسْرة resulting in: 'ibn

51

This brings us to some other specialities regarding the correct pronunciation. If the letter Alif in words like اِبن or اِسْم isn't the first letter of your utterance, watch out for the bindings:

- واسْمُهُ – *and his name* becomes: "wasmuhu"

- يا اْبني – *oh my son!* becomes "yabni"

- ما اسْمُكَ – *what is your name?* becomes "masmuka?"

Some remarks:

This is a special case! In the sentence *in the name of God*, the Alif is omitted.	بِسْمِ اللّهِ
If you start a question with the particle أ (similar to هَلْ), then the Alif is omitted too.	أبْنُكَ مَوْجُودٌ؟

30. OSAMA BIN LADEN OR OSAMA IBN LADEN - WHAT IS CORRECT?

In English and other foreign languages, you will hear and read the name *Osama bin Laden*, the name of the former head of the terrorist organisation *al-Qaida*. His name is the transliterated form of: أسامةُ بنُ لادِن. (Have a look at chapter 56 if you are wondering about the ة although it is a name for a man.)

Let us start with an important remark: *Bin,* which is common in English or German writing, is wrong – speaking purely in terms of Arabic grammar. In classical Arabic, when the word is not at the beginning of an utterance (that is, when it is بن), then it is always pronounced "bn" + whatever the proper case for it: *bnu, bna, bni.*

Of course, it is also always preceded by a vowel (either a case ending, a mood ending or a helping vowel), so the entire sequence is: *"u/a/I bn u/a/i"*. This is true even if there is nunation! The pronunciation depends on the preceding word – whether it is مَرْفُوع ("ubn") or مَنْصُوب ("abn").

For example:

The son of Karim came.	.جاءَ ابْنُ كَرِيم
pronunciation: "jaa'-**abn**ukarim"	

This shows: If you only state the name *Osama bin Laden* without a verb or preposition, it is impossible to get "ibn" – as this could only be the case if the preceding word was مَجْرُور.

In standard Arabic, the word for son is: اِبْن

That is also why Arabic newspaper sometimes write the name *Bin Laden* like this: "بن لادن" – with inverted commas (quotation marks).

But there is an exception: The word بْن - written without the Alif - is used in combination with the father (*son of...*) but never with the mother. Also, you can never write بْن if this word starts a sentence - it has to be اِبْن

So let us have a look at this example (the parents of the prophet Muhammad):

بْن	مُحَمَّد بِنْ عَبْد اللّٰهِ	Muhammad, son of Abdallah (= his <u>father</u>) Notice: The actual pronunciation is "muhammadun(i) bnu 'abd…" There an unwritten helping vowel (كَسْرة) after the nunation, and the word for "*son of*" is vocalized بْنُ
	مُحَمَّد اِبْن آمِنة	Muhammad, son of Aminah (= his <u>mother</u>)
اِبْن	مُحَمَّد اِبْن عَبْد الْمُطَّلِب	Muhammad, son of Abd al-Muttalib (= his <u>grandfather</u>). Don't get confused: Some-times, the Arabic word for *son* is used to de-scribe the relationship between the name of a person and the name of the grandfather.

Now let us check the grammar: The important point here is the letter ا – the so called هَمْزة الْوَصْل

The word behaves exactly in the same way as اسم, except that in the latter you don't drop the Alif in the spelling: ما اسْمُكَ؟ (ex-cept in the expression بِسْمِ اللّٰهِ).

The only thing that is unique about ابن is the Alif that is dropped. There are in fact a number of words and forms in Ar-abic that begin with a consonant cluster and that therefore have an added vowel before, preceded by a هَمْزة when at the begin-ning of an utterance.

All form VII, VIII, XI and X verbs are like this, as are the nouns اِسم, اِمْرَأة. Phonetically, all these forms behave identically.

If the word اِبْن is written between two names, the هَمْزة الْوَصْل (which is only there for grammatical reasons as no Arabic word can start with two consonants in a row) is not pronounced – and written as اّبْنُ

This also happens to the word اِسْم in similar situations as well as to some other words that we already dealt with in chapter 29.

The whole construction of the name *Osama bin Laden* is grammatically speaking a إِضافة. The entire 2nd part of the name - *son of Laden* - is an apposition to the son's name which is: *Osama*.

A remark: If you want to read it correctly, you should pronounce the ا as a هَمْزة – as in names you normally don't bind words and rather stop after the word *Osama*.

To sum it up: It is written *Osama bin Laden* – but the correct pronunciation, as you make a small pause after *Osama,* would be: *Osama 'ibn Laden*

Watch out: Sometimes you have to be careful as there are two possibilities for writing names. Both mean approximately the same – but they have a different grammatical background!

Here is an example: Khalid (whose father is Muhammad).

| 1 | Literally: *Khalid is the son of Muhammad.* Here, the part *son of Muhammad* is the خَبَر (predicate) of the مُبْتَدأ (subject). Note: The Alif (هَمْزة الْوَصْل) is written! You can't write بِنْ | خَالِدُ اّبْنُ مُحَمَّدٍ |

2	Literally: *Khalid, son of Muhammad* Here, the part *son of Muhammad* (a إِضافة) is an apposition (بَدَل) to Khalid. In this case, the Alif is not written.	خالِدُ بْنُ مُحَمَّدٍ

One last example: مُحَمَّد بْنِ عبدِ اللهِ ابْنُ/ابْنِ عبدِالْمُطَّلِب

The word ابْن is either pronounced with a ضَمَّة at the end or - if you consider it as part of a إِضافة - with a كَسْرة

31.   HOW ARE FAMILY NAMES CONSTRUCTED IN ARABIC?

In Europe or the USA we have a first name (given name), maybe a middle name, and a surname (family name). How is it in the Arab world? Let us check for example this name:

Muhammad al-Farouq Abu Karim ibn Khalid al-Baghdady

In Arabic: مُحَمَّد الْفارُوق أَبُو كَرِيم اِبْن خالِد الْبَغْدادِيّ

In general, Arabic names consist of five parts which don't have to follow a particular order:

	مُحَمَّد اِسْم	1
(First) name. This could be a traditional Arab name that is found in the Qur'an, a (nice) attribute, a foreign name or a compound with the most famous prefix: عَبْد – which means *servant of* and is followed by one of the 99 names (attributes) of Allah.		

2	لَقَب	الفارُوق

The لَقَب is defined most simply as an epithet, usually a religious or honorific or descriptive one, often also a title. The لَقَب can precede the اِسْم and sometimes comes to replace it.

There are mainly three possibilities:

- physical qualities: الطَّويل - *the tall*
- virtues: الْفارُوق means *he who distinguishes truth from falsehood* or الرَّاشِد meaning *the rightly guided*.
- compounds with الدّين (*religion*) like نُور الدّين

3	كُنْية	أَبُو كَريم

Name under which people call somebody on the street; mostly named after a child: *father of* or *mother of* or *son of*.

The كُنْية is a honorific name. It is not part of a person's formal name and is usually not printed in documents. It indicates that the man or woman is the father or mother of a child. The كُنْية is very important in Arabic culture – so even a person who has no child might have a كُنْية which makes him (or her) symbolically the parent of a special quality, such as *father of good deeds*.

4	نَسَب	اِبْن خالِد

The نَسَب is the patronymic. It is more or less a list of ancestors, each introduced with *son of* (اِبْن) or - if we are talking about a woman - *daughter of* (بِنْت).

It is often given for two or more generations. That's why Arabic names can be very long, for example:... اِبْن خالِد اِبْن فَيْصَل اِبْن In this case, Khalid is the father and Faisal the grandfather. See chapter 29 for the special case بن

5	نِسْبة	الْبَغْدادِيّ

The نِسْبة is similar to what people in the West call the surname.

It is rarely used in Egypt and in Lebanon where the لَقَب incorporates its meaning.

It is usually an adjective (نِسْبة) derived from the place of birth, origin or residence like الْبَغْدادِيّ (*the people of Baghdad*); the name of a religious sect or tribe or family like الْقَذَّافِيّ (*al-Qadhafi*); and occasionally it is derived from a profession like الْعَطَّار (*the perfume vendor*). A person may have several نِسْبة which in Arabic are usually preceded by the definite article الْ

Watch out:

In the Arab world - unlike in a lot of Western countries – women don't take their husband's surname when they get married. They keep their names they were given at birth.

Children, however, do take their father's name – which is expressed in the نَسَب by *daughter of* (name of the father).

32. الْبَرادِعيّ - WHAT IS THE MEANING OF THIS NAME?

You might have heard of the Egyptian Nobel peace prize winner and one-time presidential-hopeful Muhammad Mustafa el-Baradei. His name in Arabic is: مُحَمَّد مُصْطَفى الْبَرادِعيّ

The origin of his name - الْبَرادِعيّ - goes back to بَرْدَعة whose plural is: بَرادِع

Sometimes the word is written with a ذ instead of the د. It is an old word which means: *the saddle of a donkey or horse.* Muhammad el-Baradei's name describes a person who makes these saddles; *the saddle-maker*: الْبَرادِعيّ

In Arabic, family names often go back to professions. You can use a نِسْبة or a صيغة الْمُبالَغة

weaver	نَسَّاج	tiler	بَلَّاط	perfume vendor	عَطَّار
bone setter	مُجَبِّر	butcher	قَصَّاب		

33. ARE THERE PET NAMES IN ARABIC?

Yes, they are very common. The word for *pet name* is اِسْم الدَّلْع. The root ع - ل - د means *to loll; to let the tongue hang out.*

There are a lot of pet names in Arabic and you will hear them quite often. Some of them are tricky as the person is masculine - but the nickname looks feminine.

Here are some examples:

pet name	meaning of the name in Arabic	proper name	
هيما	Ibrahim is a name of a prophet	Ibrahim	إِبْراهِيم
حَمادة	Ahmad: *more praiseworthy*; Ahmad has also the meaning of Muhammad which means: *praised*	Ahmad, Muhammad	أَحْمَد مُحَمَّد
دَرْش	*Chosen; selected; the chosen one* Mustafa has also the meaning of Muhammad. دَرْش originally means *black leather*.	Mustafa	مُصْطَفى
زَنُوبة	*an aromatic tree*	Zainab	زَيْنَب

Here are less formal pet names that are used in various countries:

pet name	name
أَبو تُوت	تَوْفيق
سُوسُو	إِسْماعِيل
كَوْكَب الشَّرْق	أُمّ كُلْثُوم

34. WHAT ARE THE MAIN PLURAL FORMS?

In Arabic, we have to deal with regular and irregular („broken") plurals. Let us have a look at the main forms:

جَمْع مُذَكَّر سالِم – Regular masculine plural			

It is easily formed by adding ونَ in the مَرْفُوع-case or ينَ in the
مَجْرُور/ مَنْصُوب-case.

Notice that the letter ن at the end always takes a فَتْحة

translation	plural مَجْرُور/ مَنْصُوب	plural مَرْفُوع	singular
engineer/s (m)	مُهَنْدِسينَ	مُهَنْدِسونَ	مُهندِسٌ

جَمْع مُؤَنَّث سالِم – Regular feminine plural			

It is easily formed by adding ات in the مَرْفُوع-case or ات in the
مَجْرُور/ مَنْصُوب-case. Note: There is <u>never</u> a فَتْحة on the letter ت at
the end!

Watch out: The singular can be in the masculine form, but the plural
looks like a regular human feminine plural (e.g. *hospital*).

شاهَدْتُ مُسْتَشْفَياتٍ كَبيرةً - I saw big hospitals.

translation	plural مَجْرُور/ مَنْصُوب	plural مَرْفُوع	singular
engineer/s (f.)	مُهْنْدِساتٍ	مُهْنْدِساتٌ	مُهْنْدِسٌ

جَمْع تَكْسِير – Irregular plural			
There are a lot of patterns and some of them are مَمْنُوع مِنْ الصَّرْف			
translation	plural مَجْرُور/ مَنْصُوب	plural مَرْفُوع	singular
man/men	رِجالاً	رِجالٌ	رَجُلٌ
book/books	كُتُبٍ - كُتُبًا	كُتُبٌ	كِتابٌ

35. WHAT IS A PREPOSITION IN ARABIC?

Prepositions in English are words like: *in, at, on, above, with*. In Arabic, however, some prepositions we know from English are adverbs. In Arabic, we call only the following words prepositions. Notice that also a one letter word can be a preposition:

مُذ, مِنْ, عَنْ, فِي, إِلَى, حَتَّى

مُنْذُ, بِ, ك, ت, و, لِ, عَلَى

All other words like بَعْدَ (*after*) or تَحْتَ (*under*) which we call prepositions in English or German were originally nouns in the adverbial accusative of place or time – which explains why they all have a فَتْحة at the end, the indicator for مَنْصُوب

Arabic has only few pure adverbs, e.g. فَقَط (*only*) or هُنا (*here*). An adverb is a word that qualifies the meaning of a verb. An adverb indicates manner, time, place, cause or degree and gives answers to questions such as *when, where, how* or *how much*.

If we think about the function which the most common adverbs have in a sentence, we call them مَفْعُول فِيهِ (*adverbs of time or place*). Notice: Especially adverbs of place or time can theoretically appear anywhere in the sentence.

adverb of time	ظَرْف الزَّمان	1
You travelled on day off.	سافَرْتَ يومَ الْعُطْلةِ.	
adverb of place	ظَرْف الْمَكان	2
The bee sat on the tree.	جَلَسَتْ النَّحْلةُ فَوْقَ الشَّجَرةِ.	
Notice the فَتْحة at the end of يَوْمَ and فَوْقَ		

Here is a list of some important adverbs of place. Don't be confused – in English, most of them are called prepositions!

above	فَوْقَ	towards	ناحِيةَ
under	تَحْتَ	during; through	خِلالَ
behind	خَلْفَ	beside	جانِبَ
near	قُرْبَ	right	يَمِينَ
around	حَوْلَ	left	يَسارَ
towards	تُجاةَ	north	شَمالَ
in front of	أَمامَ	south	جَنُوبَ
between; among	بَيْنَ	east	شَرْقَ
middle; amongst	وَسْطَ	west	غَرْبَ

36. IS THE WORD مَعَ A NOUN OR A PREPOSITION?

This is a question that does not have a clear answer: اِسْم or حَرْف? There is a debate going on but most grammarians think that مَعَ - which means *with* - is a اِسْم

But why is the word *with* rather a noun than a preposition?

Because the word مَعَ can sometimes have تَنْوِين ! For example:

They came together.	جاؤوا مَعًا.

What is important here:

A حَرْف is by definition مَبْنِيّ, which means that it always (no matter what position or case) stays the same, e.g. the word فِي

مَعَ treated as a اِسْم is a اِسْم لِمَكان الِاصْطِحاب أَو وَقْتَهُ

This basically means that it functions as an adverb of place or time. It takes تَنْوِين and has one فَتْحة above the last letter (as it has an adverbial meaning).

The word which comes after it is the second part of a إِضافة - so called مُضاف إِلَيْهِ - and therefore has to be مَجْرُور

Let us have a look at two examples:

Karim sat with Muhammad.	جَلَسَ كَرِيمٌ مَعَ مُحَمَّدٍ.

ظَرْف مَكان مَنْصُوب بِالْفَتْحة	مَعَ	1
مُضاف إِلَيْهِ مَجْرُور بِالْكَسْرة	مُحَمَّدٍ	2

Karim came with Muhammad.	جاءَ كَرِيمٌ مَعَ مُحَمَّدٍ.

ظَرْف زَمان مَنْصُوب بِالْفَتْحة	مَعَ	١
مُضاف إِلَيْهِ مَجْرُور بِالْكَسْرة	مُحَمَّدٍ	٢

37. WHY IS IT IMPORTANT TO COUNT SYLLABLES?

It is useful to find out how a word is stressed. Arabic has two
kinds of syllables (C = consonant; V = vowel):

1. Open syllables: CV and CVV

2. Closed syllables: CVC

Every syllable begins with a consonant and never with a vowel!
The سُكُون is the marker for a consonant without a vowel. Literally, the word means *tranquillity* or *quietude*. It is the absence
of sound and cuts the word into syllables.

light syllable	C V	open
heavy syllable	C V V	
	C V C	closed

Notice: The verb ظَنَّ for example actually consists of the letters
ظَنْنَ. The first ن takes a سُكُون.

Therefore, grammatically speaking, it has two syllables C V C V
– although they are not pronounced.

<u>So how can we find the right stress?</u>

In Arabic, there are no fixed rules that tell you where you should put the stress. There are regional differences especially in dialects. As a general rule, the <u>penultimate</u> (second-to-last) <u>syllable</u> should be stressed.

Here are some hints:

- The ultimate (last) syllable is never stressed.

- The stress falls on the first long syllable counting from the end of the word. If there is no long syllable or if only the last syllable is long, the first syllable receives the stress, e.g. شَرِبَ - <u>sh</u>ariba

- If the penultimate (second-to-last) syllable is a heavy syllable (C V V or C V C), it receives the stress. Otherwise, the stress is put on the ante-penultimate syllable (the one before the penultimate).

- The stress can't be put on the definite article الـ, nor on a preposition or conjunction.

In Egyptian Arabic too, the stress is put on the penultimate syllable (even on the light penultimate syllable) – which is different to Eastern Arabic dialects. In the following examples the apostrophe ' tells you where to put the stress:

Eastern dialect	Egyptian Arabic		example
'madrasa	mad'rasa	C V - C V - C V	مَدْرَسة
mu'darrisa	mudar'risa	C V - C V C - C V - C V	مُدَرِّسة

38. WHY DO YOU NEED HELPING VOWELS?

You need a helping vowel for the correct pronunciation.

For example: If the second word in a sentence starts with a definite article, you'll have to add a helping vowel under/above the last letter of the preceding word – to combine the two words.

Here is an example: أَنْتَ الْمُدَرِّسُ (*You are the teacher*)

explanation	pronunciation
This is, precisely speaking, wrong. Beginners who are still reading sentences word by word are likely to pronounce it like that – and make a pause after the word أَنْتَ	'anta al-Mudarris
This is how a native speaker would pronounce the sentence. The sentence is pronounced as it would only be one word, without a pause.	'antalmudarris

So what is the difference?

The هَمْزة الْوَصْل in the definite article ال was omitted and it basically disappeared. The word أَنْتَ ends with a فَتْحة which is pronounced as "a". This final فَتْحة replaces the Alif in the definite article! So without the هَمْزة the sentence above is pronounced as it would be one word.

This is typical for Arabic, especially, as most words end with a vowel (case ending, verb mood, hidden/implied pronoun, etc.)

But what happens if the preceding word ends with a سُكُون?

For example the words: هَلْ ,مِنْ or مَنْ. So what happens if we change the sentence above to a question?

Is the teacher present?	هَلْ الْمُدَرِّسُ مَوْجُودٌ؟

In almost all cases we use a كَسْرة as a helping vowel, so the words are connected with an "i"/"e"-sound. This is how it is pronounced correctly:

The particle هَلْ which ends with a سُكُون is now connected to the next word with the vowel "i"/"e"	halilmudarrisu mawjuudun?

But there are exceptions:

- The preposition مِنْ normally takes فَتْحة as a helping vowel. But strictly speaking, the helping vowel of the preposition مِن is a فَتْحة only when the word is followed by the definite article: مِنَ ال. Otherwise, it is كَسْرة, for example: مِنِ امْتِحان

- If the last vowel (not the case-marker!) of a word is a ضَمّة (u), the helping vowel will be a ضَمّة.

  But watch out: The helping vowel is ضَمّة only at the end of pronouns or pronominal endings that end in ضَمّة, e.g.: هُم, كُم, تُم

  Otherwise, the helping vowel is كَسْرة even when the word ends in ضَمّة, e.g.: لَمْ يَعُدِ الرَّجُل

39. فَاسْمَعُوا - HOW DO YOU PRONOUNCE THAT?

The sentence فَاسْمَعُوا means: *and listen*.

If you read it, you should a) not stop and b) you should forget about the Alif with the كَسْرة after the letter ف – which means you should pronounce it like: "fasmaʒu!"

And not: "fa-ismaʒu!" – as you don't pronounce the ا

Without فَ it would be pronounced 'ismaʒu! – with glottal stop and "i"

40. CAN YOU STUDY ARABIC GRAMMAR IN VERSES?

Yes! If you want to study Arabic in the most cultivated way, there is a book for you. It contains most of the Arabic grammar – in verses. It was written by: اِبْن مالِك

The book is from the 13ᵗʰ century and is called: أَلْفِية ابن مالِك (*"Alfia"*) which means *1000 verses*. It contains the essential things about نَحْو (*grammar*) and صَرْف (*morphology*). But I'll have to warn you: It is only for very proficient readers.

Ibn Mālik died in Damascus in 1274 (672 هـ).

41. WHAT IS ESSENTIAL TO KNOW ABOUT VERB FORMS?

Many Arabs don't know what a I-verb or X-verb is. They only know patterns, so called أَوْزان.

This word is the plural form of وَزْن which means *weight; form* (grammar) or *noun or verb pattern*.

The word *weight* is a good description for what we are actually doing. Imagine a pair of scales and image weights in form of vowels and extra letters. In order to keep the balance with the pattern, we have to add weights (vowels and/or extra letters) to the root.

The Roman numerals which are widely used in the West to describe the different verb forms were invented by Western scholars. If you want to increase your understanding of Arabic, it is important to switch from numbers to patterns as this will automatically give you a better feeling for the language.

Theoretically, each triliteral Arabic root could be transformed into one of 15 possible verb forms. Forms 11 through 15 (as well as number 9) are very rare. It is usually sufficient to focus on the first 10 forms only.

There are basically two groups of verbs:

unaugmented The verb consists only of the three or four root letters	مُجَرَّد	1
augmented This means we are talking about verbs from II to X	مَزِيد	2

We distinguish between roots that consists of 3 radicals - ثُلَاثِيّ - and roots with 4 radicals (root letters) which are called رُبَاعِيّ

If the term ثُلَاثِيّ is mentioned in the book, it means we are talking about the I-verb. Otherwise, we would call it مَزِيد

Let us now have a look at the most common verb patterns. The capital letters next to the examples refer to the capital letters in the list:

					2.1 مَزِيد يِحَرْف
Only one Arabic letter is added to the root. A) تَضْعِيف (doubling of a letter) B) أَلِف C) هَمْزة D) ت					
root has 3 radicals	to teach	عَلَّمَ	II	فَعَّلَ	A
	to meet	قابَلَ	III	فاعَلَ	B
	to take out	أَخْرَجَ	IV	أَفْعَلَ	C
root has 4 radicals	to quake	تَزَلْزَلَ	IV	تَفَعْلَلَ	D

					2.2 مَزِيد يِحَرْفَيْن
Two Arabic letters are added to the root. A) تَضْعِيف plus ت B) أَلِف plus ت C) هَمْزة plus ن D) هَمْزة plus ت E) هَمْزة plus تَضْعِيف					
root has 3 radicals	to study	تَعَلَّمَ	V	تَفَعَّلَ	A
	to cooperate	تَعاوَنَ	VI	تَفاعَلَ	B

	to be broken	اِنْكَسَرَ	VII	اِنْفَعَلَ	C
	to take part in	اِشْتَرَكَ	VIII	اِفْتَعَلَ	D
	to become green	اِخْضَرَّ	IX	اِفْعَلَّ	E
root has 4 radicals	to be reassured	اِطْمَأَنَّ	IV	اِفْعَلَّ	E

Three Arabic letters are added to the root. This is a combination of: • هَمْزة • س • ت			مَزِيد بِثَلاثة أَحْرُف	2.3
root has 3 radicals	to import	اِسْتَوْرَدَ	X	اِسْتَفْعَلَ

42. DOES EVERY VERB FORM HAVE A DIFFERENT MEANING?

Yes and no.

Some verb forms have a similar meaning. It is good to know the general meaning of the verb forms from II to X.

Let us have a look at them. The capital letters next to the examples refer to the capital letters in the list.

				قَفَّلَ	II

A) Strengthens the meaning of a I-verb (often an intensive version of the I-verb)

B) Makes a I-verb transitive

C) Makes a I-verb causative

to teach	دَرَّسَ	A	to study	دَرَسَ
to clean sth.	طَهَّرَ	B	to be clean	طَهَرَ
to remind sb.	ذَكَّر	C	to remember	ذَكَرَ

				فاعَلَ	III

A) Shows the attempt to do something – *try to...*

B) *To do to* (someone); *to involve someone.*

Describes someone doing the action in question to or with someone else. Notice: I-verbs need a preposition to connect the action with the other part – III-verbs don't.

to try to kill (to fight)	قاتَلَ	A	to kill	قَتَلَ
to do business with	عامَلَ	B	to work	عَمِلَ
to correspond	كاتَبَ	B	to write	كَتَبَ

		أَفْعَلَ	IV

A) Makes a I-verb transitive

B) Makes a I-verb causative (main usage) – *to make or cause*

			someone or something to do or be	
			C) Can also strengthen a I-verb	
to make happy	أَسْعَدَ	A	to be happy	سَعِدَ
to inform sb.	أَعْلَمَ	B	to to know	عَلِمَ
to lock	أَغْلَقَ	C	to close	غَلَقَ

				تَفَعَّلَ	V

A) Reflexive or passive meaning of a II-verb. But watch out: This form is (grammatically speaking) not the passive tense. The action happens to the subject without an (implied) agent.

B) Sometimes it is an intensive version of a I-verb

to be separated	تَفَرَّقَ	A	to separate	فَرَّقَ
to congregate, to flock together	تَجَمَّع	B	to gather, collect	جَمَعَ

				تفاعَلَ	VI

A) Reflexive form of a III-verb (*to do something together; to do something between or among each other*).

to share with one another	تَشارَكَ	A	to share	شارَكَ

			اِنْفَعَلَ	VII

A) Reflexive or passive meaning of a I-verb. But watch out: This form is not the passive tense (similar to a V-verb). The action happens to the subject without an (implied) agent.

to be broken	اِنْكَسَرَ	A	to break sth.	كَسَرَ

			اِفْتَعَلَ	VIII

A) Reflexive or passive meaning of a I-verb. Similar to VII.

to burn	اِحْتَرَقَ	A	to burn sth.	حَرَقَ

			اِفْعَلَّ	IX

A) Reflexive meaning of a II-verb (referring to colours or physical deficiencies).

to blush; become red	اِحْمَرَّ	A	to be red	حَمَّرَ

			اِسْتَفْعَلَ	X

A) *To regard/find/consider something as...*

B) Derived meaning from a noun (اِسْم)

C) Expresses a wish or a desire (*to let sb. do sth. for you; to demand sth. for yourself*). *To seek, ask for, require an action.*

D) Reflexive of أَفْعَلَ (form IV)

to find ugly	اِسْتَقْبَحَ	A	to be ugly	قَبُحَ
to ask for permission	اِسْتَأْذَنَ	C	to allow	أَذِنَ
to invest	اِسْتَثْمَرَ	B	fruit	ثَمَر
to inquire	اِسْتَعْلَمَ	C	to know	عَلِمَ
to prepare oneself	اِسْتَعَدَّ	D	to prepare	أَعَدَّ

43. HOW DO YOU SAY "BOTH" IN ARABIC?

In Arabic, you need a dual noun (مُثَنَّى) to express the English
word *both*. There are two words for it:

both; masculine singular	كِلَا	1
both; feminine singular	كِلْتَا	2

The only difference between كِلَا and كِلْتَا is the gender: The first
is masculine and the second is feminine. Typically, they serve as a
مُضاف in an إضافة structure (1ˢᵗ part), but they can also be used
as an apposition (بَدَل) – the meaning is the same.

Both words must agree in gender with the noun or pronoun
they refer to. So we match كِلْتَا and كِلَا either with

- the gender of the مُضاف إلَيْهِ (which is the gender of the
  2ⁿᵈ part) or with

- the gender of the 1ˢᵗ part of the apposition

إضافة 2nd part must be a def. dual noun	both men	كِلَا الرَّجُلَيْنِ	١
	both times	كِلْتَا الْمَرَّتَيْنِ	
بَدَل (apposition) connected to a dual pronoun suffix	both men	الرَّجُلَيْنِ كِلَاهُما	٢
	both times	الْمَرَّتانِ كِلْتاهُما	

What is important here:

1. The expressions that are connected with كِلَا or كِلْتَا are grammatically treated as singular – although they are both dual nouns. So a following verb, adjective or noun that is connected to the expression is either masculine or feminine <u>singular</u>.

2. When governing a اِسْم, they are <u>not inflected</u> for case!

3. However, when they are <u>combined with a pronoun suffix</u>, they <u>must be inflected for case</u> in مَنْصُوب and مَجْرُور. This goes for the ending ا which turns into a ي

   This is similar to the dual of nouns or verbs which also have a ا in the nominative case (مَرْفُوع) and a ي in the مَجْرُور- and مَنْصُوب-case.

   So we eventually get for example: كِلْتَيْهِما or كِلَيْهِما

   (pronounced as "kilaihima" and "kiltaihima")

Let us have a look at some more examples.

Notice: The numbers in the table refer to the rules above.

It belongs to both of you (plural). Notice: The expression كِلْتَيْكُم is used as an apposition. It has to agree in case and gender with the word it is referring to which means: Since there is the preposition لِ in لَكُمْ the word كِلْتَيْكُم has to be مَجْرُور too!	هُوَ لَكُمْ كِلَيْكُمْ. هِيَ لَكُمْ كِلْتَيْكُم.	3
Both of them are teachers.	كِلَاهُما مُدَرِّسٌ.	1
Everything that happened to both of us...	كُلُّ ما حَدَثَ لِكِلَيْنا.	3
In both times... Note: Although كِلْتا comes after a preposition, it is not inflected for case as a اِسْم follows!	فِي كِلْتا الْمَرَتَيْنِ	2
with both of us Note: Since it is not connected to a اِسْم but to a personal pronoun, we have to use the مَجْرُور-case! (The Alif turns into a ي)	بِكِلَيْنا	3
Both were nice. Note: The Alif stays – it is مَرْفُوع	كانَ كِلاهُما لَطِيفًا.	1
Both men saw her. Note: The verb is used in singular (3rd person masculine) and not dual although we are referring to a dual.	كِلا الرَّجُلَيْنِ رَآها.	1

44. How do you say: "My two colleagues"?

Sounds easy. But it is actually pretty tricky to express *my two colleagues*. There are three problems you have to deal with:

1. The dual
2. The possessive marker for the first person (*my*): ي
3. The possessive form: The possessive pronoun is part of a إِضَافة-construction.

<u>Here is a step-by-step-guide:</u>

1. First form the dual
2. Delete the ن of the dual
3. Add the possessive pronoun: ي
4. Add a فَتْحة on top of the last letter: يَ

case	how to pronounce it	*my two colleagues*	*two colleagues*	*colleague*
مَرْفُوع	"zamiil**aa**-ya"	زَمِيلايَ	زَمِيلانِ	زَمِيلٌ
مَجْرُور or مَنْصُوب	"zamiilai**yy**a"	زَمِيلَيَّ	زَمِيلَيْنِ	

79

45. وَالِدَيَّ - WHAT DOES THIS WORD MEAN?

First of all let us have a look at the pronunciation. It is pronounced: "waalidayya".

وَالِدَيَّ means *my (two) parents* - if the word is مَنْصُوب or مَجْرُور
Let us now check it in more detail:

translation	remarks	word	
father		وَالِد	١
(two) parents	مَرْفُوع; subject	وَالِدانِ	
(two) parents	مَجْرُور or مَنْصُوب	وَالِدَيْنِ	
my (two) parents	مَرْفُوع; subject; NO شَدّة at the end !	وَالِدايَ	
my (two) parents	شَدّة Notice the ;مَجْرُور or مَنْصُوب	وَالِدَيَّ	
brother		أَخ	٢
my two brothers	مَرْفُوع; subject; NO شَدّة at the end!	أَخَوايَ	
my two brothers	شَدّة Notice the ;مَجْرُور or مَنْصُوب	أَخَوَيَّ	

Watch out:

- The ن of a dual form is omitted in a إِضافة-construction or if a possessive pronoun is added (which is in fact a إِضافة)

- In a مَنْصُوب or مَجْرُور-case we would theoretically have two ي falling together.

  This is expressed by a شَدّة over the ي

46. HOW DO YOU SAY: "THIS CAR IS MINE"?

In Arabic, there are no words like *mine; yours; his* or *hers* which we call possessive pronouns in English.

In order to express the same meaning in Arabic, you could for example repeat the thing being possessed and add the appropriate pronoun suffix.

Here are some examples:

This car is mine.	هٰذِهِ السَّيَّارَةُ سَيَّارَتِي.
The book is hers.	الْكِتابُ كِتابُها.

47. شِبْه الْجُمْلة - WHAT IS THAT?

First of all the word شِبْه means *like; quasi or semi*. The word جُمْلة means *sentence*. So literally, this is a *quasi/semi sentence*.

In Arabic, we know two different types of sentences:

1. جُمْلة مُفِيدة: It consists of two or more words. It provides a full meaning. To this group belong:

   * the nominal sentence (جُمْلة اِسْمِيّة) and

   * the verbal sentence (جُمْلة فِعْلِيّة) which starts with a verb

2. شِبْه الْجُمْلة: This is not a full sentence.

   There are two possibilities:

adverb (time or place) + noun (إِضافة)	ظَرْف + مُضاف إلَيْهِ	١
above the tree	فَوْقَ الشَّجَرةِ	
afternoon	بَعْدَ الظُّهْرِ	
preposition + noun (genitive)	حَرْف الْجَرّ plus مَجْرُور	٢
in the house	فِي الْبَيْتِ	
on the desk	عَلَى الْمَكْتَبِ	

48. HOW MANY TYPES OF WORDS ARE THERE IN ARABIC?

In Arabic, the definitions we use in German or English - adverb, adjective, preposition, etc. - don't really work as they are sometimes different from our languages.

In Arabic, there are only three main kinds of words:

إِسْم - فِعْل - حَرْف

We can roughly translate them with: noun, verb and particle.

A حَرْف (*particle*) is a word that makes no sense unless there is a word that comes after it. Some examples: فِي, هَلْ, لَمْ, أَن

A فِعْل (*verb*) is a word that is stuck in time. It indicates an action or occurrence. In Arabic, we basically only know two tenses: an action is completed (الْماضِي) – or not (الْمُضارِع).

A إِسْم (*noun*) refers to a place, time, person, thing, condition, idea, adverb, adjective, etc. It is not affected by time.

In German, for example, students learn that there are ten types of words: nouns, articles, verbs, adjectives, pronouns, numerals (which are all irregular) and adverbs, prepositions, conjunctions and interjections (which are all regular).

So how can there are only be three kinds of words in Arabic?

Well, Arabic works differently. Understanding the fundamental meaning of the root and what can be derived from it is essential.

What we call in English or German an adjective (*nomen adjectivum*) like the word *beautiful* - جَمِيل - is in fact a اِسْم in Arabic. According to its function in a sentence we could translate it as an *adjective*. This can be confusing. The meaning, form and the way it is being derived can be very different to English or German.

Here is a list of some common types of a حَرْف:

translation	grammatical term	example
preposition; particle of subordination	حَرْف جَرّ	فِي
letter of negation; negative particle	حَرْف نَفْي	لا, لَمْ
particle of digression; retraction particle	حَرْف إِضْراب	بَلْ
conjunction; copulative particle	حَرْف عَطْف	و
interrogative particle	حَرْف اِسْتِفْهام	هَلْ
conditional particle	حَرْف شَرْط	لَوْ

83

49. HOW DO YOU RECOGNIZE A اِسْم IN A TEXT?

A noun (اِسْم) can easily be identified in a sentence. Every اِسْم must have one of the following three characteristics which no other type of word can have.

Let us take the word كِتاب (*book*):

	grammar term	grammatical explanation	example
I	تَنْوين	Only a اِسْم can have تَنْوين, which means only a اِسْم has a case-ending	هٰذا كِتابٌ.
2	تَعْريف بِأل	Only a اِسْم can take the definite article!	أَعْطَى الكِتابَ.
3	إضافة	Only a اِسْم can be part of a إضافة	أَعْطَى كِتابَ النَّحوِ.

Don't forget that there are only three types of words in Arabic - see chapter 48. This is important as e.g. an active participle is a اِسْم in Arabic.

50. WHAT IS AN ADJECTIVE IN ARABIC?

This is something complicated and confusing for native speakers of English, German or French.

In linguistics, an adjective is a describing word, the main syntactic role of which is to qualify a noun or noun phrase. The Latin word *ad-icere* (*adiectum*) means to *throw down; to add*.

The grammatical terms in Arabic are صِفة or نَعْت – which means *description, characterization*. This definition is pretty logical as it describes the preceding اِسْم.

The following grammatical forms can serve as a نَعْت and are all used for what we call in English an adjective or attribute or attributive adjunct:

شِبْه الْجُمْلة	صِيغة الْمُبالَغة	الصِّفة الْمُشَبَّهة	اِسْم الْمَفْعُول	اِسْم الْفاعِل

But if you take a closer look at these forms, you will find out that they are very different in their core meaning.

<u>Let us check them in detail:</u>

1. The <u>active participle</u> (اِسْم الْفاعِل) is a description of an action. In Arabic, we would call this: صِفة بِالْحَدَث. This is the same in English or German, for example the active participle for *to go* is *going* (*gehend* in German).

2. The <u>passive participle</u> (اِسْم الْمَفْعُول) refers to something having undergone the action of the verb. For example: *to break – broken* (*gebrochen* in German).

3. The <u>verbal adjective</u>; or: assimilate epithet (الصِّفة الْمُشَبَّهة) describes something that has nothing to do with a (verbal) action. This also explains why the root of a صِفة مُشَبَّهة can't build a اِسْم فاعِل

The الصِّفة الْمُشَبَّهة functions like a representative or substitute for the non-existent اِسْم الْفاعِل.

The word مُشَبَّه literally means *to make similar*. Grammatically speaking, it is a اِسْم مُشْتَقّ, a derived noun from the root. This is the reason why it is usually better to use the مَصْدَر for analysing and forming derived words – and not the past tense.

4. The so called <u>form of exaggeration</u> (صِيغة الْمُبالَغة) is built from a verb which <u>can</u> build a اِسْم الْفاعِل. So can every verb build an active participle?

As shown in chapter 142, the answer is no!

The صِيغة الْمُبالَغة is basically just the description that somebody is doing the "active participle" (an action, a movement, etc.) often/a lot of times/intensively.

In Arabic we would say it like that: يَحْدُث كَثِيرًا لَهُ اِسْم الْفاعِل

5. The شِبْه الْجُمْلة which functions as a نَعْت is basically an <u>adverb of time or place or a preposition + information</u>. For example: *under the table; before midnight; in the house.*

51. WHAT IS A "REAL ADJECTIVE"?

Normally, an adjective has to agree with a noun. But what does agreement - so called الْمُطابَقة - actually mean?

If we talk about agreement, we mean four grammatical things words have to share:

1) negated/not negated

2) case

3) singular/dual/plural

4) gender

Let us have a look at an example:

The honourable man came.	جاءَ الرَّجُلُ الْفاضِلُ

In the sentence above, we call the description a نَعْت حَقيقيّ (literally: *true description*). This is because it takes the same agreement as the preceding اِسْم

This brings us to the three main different forms of the النَّعْت الْحَقيقيّ. What is important to know here: <u>The adjective is put after the noun which it describes.</u>

I	noun	إسْم ظاهِر
	Damascus is a great city.	دِمَشْق مَدينةٌ عَظيمةٌ.
	نَعْت	عَظيمةٌ

2	adverb or preposition = ظَرْف or حَرْف جَرّ	شِبْه الْجُمْلة = ظَرْف or حَرْف جَرّ
	I listened to a professor on the platform.	اِسْتَمَعْتُ إِلَى أُسْتاذٍ فَوْقَ الْمِنْبَرِ.
	ظَرْف نَعْت أُستاذ	فَوقَ
3.1	nominal sentence	جُمْلة اِسْمِيّة
	It was very cold at night.	مَضَى يَوْمٌ بَرْدُهُ قارِصٌ.
	نَعْت لِيَوْم	بَرْدُهُ قارِص
3.2	verbal sentence	جُمْلة فِعْلِيّة
	This is a work which is useful. (meaning: This is a useful work). Instead of the verb you could also use مُفِيدٌ	هذا عَمَلٌ يُفِيدُ
	نَعْت لِعَمَل	يُفِيدُ
	Notice that for 3.1 and 3.2 the الْمَنْعُوت has to be indefinite.	

Watch out: There is also a so called *causative description* (نَعْت سَبَبِيّ) – see chapter 143.

52. Do all English tenses exist in Arabic?

No, they don't.

In Arabic, as we only distinguish between an ongoing action and an action which was completed, we need helping constructions to express tenses which we know from other languages.

Tenses are one of the easy parts in Arabic grammar. In French, for example, there are five past tense forms: *l'imparfait, le passé simple, le passé composé, le plus-que-parfait, le passé antérieur.*

Here is a list of the most important English tenses and how they can be expressed in Arabic. Watch out for the endings!

1. Present tense

he does	يَفْعَلُ
he doesn't	لا يَفْعَلُ
he does indeed	لَيَفْعَلَنَّ
he doesn't (augmented); rarely used	ما يَفْعَلُ

2. Past tense

he did it/he has done it	فَعَلَ
he did not do it/he has not done it	لَمْ يَفْعَلْ
he has already done it	قَدْ فَعَلَ
he has not done it yet	لَمْ يَفْعَلْ بَعْدُ
he (indeed) did it	لَقَدْ فَعَلَ
he has not done it (augmented)	ما فَعَلَ

89

3. Past tense progressive

1	he was doing	كانَ يَفْعَلُ
	he was doing	ظَلَّ يَفْعَلُ
2	he was not doing* (negation of فَعَلَ)	كانَ لا يَفْعَلُ
	he was not doing (negation of كانَ)	لَمْ يَكُنْ يَفْعَلُ
	* The negation of فَعَلَ is more common than the negation of كانَ	

4. Past perfect (pluperfect) tense:

1	he had done it	كانَ قَدْ فَعَلَ
2	he had not done it* (negation of كانَ)	ما كانَ قَدْ فَعَلَ
		لَمْ يَكُنْ قَدْ فَعَلَ
	he had not done it (negation of فَعَلَ)	كانَ ما فَعَلَ
		كانَ لَمْ يَفْعَلْ
	* The negation of كانَ is more common than the negation of فَعَلَ	

5. Future tense (I)

he will do (in near future)	سَيَفْعَلُ
he will do (distant future)	سَوْفَ يَفْعَلُ
he will not do (near future)	لَنْ يَفْعَلَ
he will not do (distant future)	سَوْفَ لا يَفْعَلُ

6. Future tense progressive

he will be doing	سَيَظَلُّ يَفْعَلُ

7. Future perfect (II)

Notice that we use the particle قَدْ plus past tense to distinguish the future perfect *(will have done it)* from the subjunctive (<u>*would*</u> have done it).

1	he will have done it	كَانَ سَوْفَ يَفْعَلُ
	he will have done it	سَيَكُونُ (قَدْ) فَعَلَ
2	he will not have done it* (negation of كَانَ)	سَوْفَ لا يَكُونُ (قَدْ) فَعَلَ
		لَنْ يَكُونُ (قَدْ) فَعَلَ
	he will not have done it (negation of فَعَلَ)	كَانَ سَوْفَ لا يَفْعَلُ
		كَانَ لَنْ يَفْعَلَ
	* The negation of كَانَ is more common than the negation of فَعَلَ	

7. Subjunctive (German: Konjunktiv II)

If you want to express the subjunctive mood (something impossible), you usually use a conditional clause with لَوْ and لَ – see chapters 125 and 255.

He would have done it	كَانَ سَيَفْعَلُ
He would not have done it	لَمْ يَكُنْ سَيَفْعَلُ

8. Imperative

do!	إِفْعَلْ - إِفْعَلِي - إِفْعَلُوا - إِفْعَلْنَ
don't do!	لَا تَفْعَلْ - لَا تَفْعَلِي - لَا تَفْعَلُوا - لَا تَفْعَلْنَ

53. "Prayer is better than sleep" - Is it really "better"?

Yes, at least regarding the grammar of the sentence.

You might know that in Sunni Islam there is a special line that the muezzin says if he calls people to come to pray during dawn. This is only said for the الْفَجْر-prayer.

It goes like this: الصَّلَاةُ خَيْرٌ مِن النَّوْمِ

The sentence means *prayer is better than sleep.*

This is an interesting grammatical construction. We do not use the regular اِسْم التَّفْضِيل here, following the pattern: أَفْعَل

So why do we have a comparative in these examples? The word خَيْرٌ is usually translated as *good*, which is correct. But it also has another meaning – the meaning of a اِسْم تَفْضِيل.

The word خَيْرٌ has the same meaning as أَحْسَن – *better*. Let us have a closer look at some examples:

Prayer is better than sleep.	الصَّلَاةُ خَيْرٌ مِن النَّوْمِ.
Work is better than laziness.	الْعَمَلُ خَيْرٌ مِن الْكَسَلِ.
He is better than...	هُوَ خَيْرٌ مِنْ...

I am not better than the student.	لَسْتُ خَيْرًا مِن الطَّالِبِ

The word for *better* was originally أَخْيَر – but it was changed into خَيْر. This happened a long time ago as in the Qur'an, خَيْر is already used in the meaning of *better*.

The word comes from the root خ - ي - ر. The corresponding I-verb is خَازَ. Watch out for the correct plural:

meaning	plural	singular	
good; excellent/better; best	خِيار or أَخْيار	خَيْر	١
good; blessing; good thing	خُيُور	خَيْر	٢

There are other words which follow the same logic as خَيْرٌ, for example the word شَرٌّ (*bad* or *evil*), but it is less common.

She is worse than... (Notice that there is no feminine form of شَرٌّ.)	هِيَ شَرٌّ مِنْ...

Be careful: If you use خَيْرٌ or شَرٌّ in a إِضافة-construction, they have the meaning of the superlative.

(the) best student	خَيْرُ طَالِبٍ
* In Arabic you don't use the definite article although it has a definite meaning in English.	
* As it is a إِضافة-construction, the word خَيْر doesn't get nunation	

54. WHAT DOES THE NAME "HUSSEIN" MEAN?

You might know the name Hussein. In Arabic, it is written like this: حُسَيْن. It literally means *small beauty*.

Forms like this are called diminutive, so called: تَصْغِير. These forms are pretty common in Arabic.

Let us have a look at some common patterns:

Derived from a اِسْم that consists in total of three letters (here, as always, we don't mean 3 root letters)			فُعَيْلٌ	1
door	بابٌ	small door	بُوَيْبٌ	
child	وَلَدٌ	small child	وُلَيْدٌ	
river	نَهْرٌ	small river	نُهَيْرٌ	

Notice: Also adverbs of place/time (prepositions) use this pattern: قَبْلَ - قُبَيْلَ (*shortly before*) or بَعْدَ - بُعَيْدَ (*shortly after*)

When the original nouns consists in total of four letters (again, we don't mean 4 root letters!)			فُعَيْلِلٌ	2
friend	صاحِبٌ	small friend	صُوَيْحِبٌ	

Feminine nouns. They have a ة and follow the rules of number 2. If the original noun is feminine but does not have a ة, the diminutive will take a ة (e.g. *market*)	3

tree	شَجَرةٌ	bush	شُجَيْرةٌ
drop	نُقْطةٌ	droplet	نُقَيْطةٌ
market	سُوقٌ	small market	سُوَيْقةٌ

		فُعَيِّلٌ 4
This pattern is used when the original إسْم is of this form: The second letter of the إسْم is followed by a long vowel.		
book	كِتابٌ	small book	كُتَيِّبٌ
small	صَغيرٌ	tiny	صُغَيِّرٌ

55. IS حَرْب ("WAR") MASCULINE OR FEMININE?

Strangely, the word for *war* - حَرْب - is feminine in Arabic. The same is true for French (*la guerre*). The problem in Arabic is that you cannot see it as the definite article is the same for masculine and feminine words. Let us first have a look at the regular feminine endings. In Arabic, there are 3 different indicators or signals to define a word as feminine>

تاء تَأْنيث		أَلِف تَأْنيث	
		مَمْدُودة	مَقْصُورة
1 ة	2 اء	3 يا or ى
طالِبة	صَحْراء	كُبْرى, عُلْيا

Notice:

- The ending اء is also the pattern for colours and physical deficiencies (صِفة) in the singular feminine form.

- The letter ى is the pattern for the feminine form of a comparative (اِسْم تَفْضيل). For example: *older, smaller*.

Here are some examples:

desert	صَحْراء
colour red	حَمْراء

smaller	صُغْرَى
memory	ذِكْرَى

So what about حَزْب؟

It doesn't look feminine – but it is! Like in other languages there are words that look masculine by shape but are exceptions.

Here is a list of common exceptions:

war	حَزْب
land	أَرْض
soul	نَفْس
market	سُوق

fire	نار
house	دار
cup	كَأْس
paradise	الْفِرْدَوْس

sun	شَمْس
wind	رِيح
well	بِئْر
Ghoul; ghost	غُول

Watch out! If you want to add an adjective (صِفة), you will need the feminine form:

central market	سُوق مَرْكَزِيّة

96

Be careful with body parts:

1. When you have <u>two parts</u> of one (mostly pairs) like:
   leg (رِجْل), *eye* (عَيْن), *ear* (أُذُن), *tooth* (سِنّ) or *hand* (يَد),
   then these words are also <u>feminine</u>.

2. In contrast, the words for *nose* (أَنْف), *mouth* (فَم), etc.
   are masculine as you only have one!

3. Some parts of the body can be either masculine or feminine, e.g.: *head* (رَأْس), liver (كَبِد), *upper arm* (عَضُد)

Also feminine are:

- names of newspapers and magazines, for example: *al-
  Ahram* (الْأَهْرام)

- names of countries, cities and towns, except:

  Morocco (الْمَغْرِب), *Jordan* (الْأُرْدُن), *Lebanon* (لُبْنان), *Iraq*
  (الْعِراق) and *Sudan* (السُّدان)

Watch out: Some nouns can be treated as either masculine or
feminine:

country	بَلَد	sky	سَماء	wine	خَمْر
way	سَبِيل	road	طَرِيق	alley	زُقاق
power	سُلْطان	situation	حال	salt	مِلْح
gold	ذَهَب	hell(fire)	جَحِيم	soul	رُوح

97

56. ARE THERE WORDS WITH A ة THAT ARE MASCULINE?

Yes, there are – but only a few. Normally, they refer to masculine human beings, to people. For native-speakers the ة doesn't sound wrong. There are no rules, you have to know it.

The most important are:

successor, caliph	خَليفة	tyrant	طاغِية
explorer	رَحّالة	distinguished man	نابِغة
very learned man	عَلّامة	Hamuda (man's name)	حَمُودة
eminent scholar	بَحّاثة	Osama (man's name)	أُسامة

So watch out for the agreement: The صِفة has to be <u>masculine</u>!

A great explorer	رَحّالةٌ عَظيمٌ
The great scholar	الْعَلّامةُ الْكَبيرُ

57. A MASCULINE ADJECTIVE FOR A FEMININE NOUN?

Yes, this is possible.

If you say that a woman is *pregnant*, you use the word حامِل which is, grammatically speaking, the اِسْم الْفاعِل of the root *to carry*. But why do we use the masculine form for a woman – and not the feminine?

If we are talking about something that can only happen to women or is applied to women - like being pregnant - then we don't
have to write a ة at the end. Let us have a look at an example:

a pregnant woman	اِمْرَأَةٌ حَامِلٌ

Here is a list of some other words that follow this rule.

A remark: Some of them are not really exclusively attributed to
women – but maybe were in the past.

pregnant	حَامِلٌ
divorced	طَالِقٌ
menstruating	حَائِضٌ
barren, sterile	عَاقِرٌ
unmarried and of middle age	عَانِسٌ

Notice the difference!

She is pregnant.	هِيَ حَامِلٌ.
She is carrying luggage.	هِيَ حَامِلَةٌ مَتَاعًا.

Sometimes, however, the صِفة can be used for men and women:

old woman	اِمْرَأَةٌ عَجُوزٌ
old man	رَجُلٌ عَجُوزٌ = شَيْخٌ

58. حَيْثُ - أَمْسِ - الآنَ - WHAT DO THEY HAVE IN COMMON?

These words mean *now*, *yesterday* and *where*. So what do they have in common?

Grammatically speaking, they are called مَبْنِيّ. This means that they never change their vowels at the end. Whatever their case or position in the sentence is – they are fixed.

Here are some examples:

meaning	fixed vowel at the end	example
this	a - ا	هٰذا
yesterday	i - كَسْرة	أمسِ
where	u - ضَمّة	حَيْثُ
now	a - فَتْحة	الآنَ

59. WHY IS THERE A و IN THE PROPER NAME عَمْرو (AMR)?

It is an old way of writing the proper name *Amr*. By adding the letter و, people can distinguish (graphically) between *Amr* and the proper name *Omar* – which is written in the same way: عُمَر

Notice that *Amr* takes تَنْوِين – but *Omar* not. *Omar* is a so called diptote. It doesn't take تَنْوِين (*nunation*).

It is مَمْنُوع مِن الصَّرْف like all proper names that follow the pattern فُعَل, e.g.: عُمَر, زُحَل, هُبَل, جُحا

Let us check both names again:

I saw Amr.	تَنْوِين; sometimes it is also seen with و Also in a إضافة the و is usually written.	رَأَيْتُ عَمْرًا.
I saw Omar.	No Alif – as it is مَمْنُوع مِن الصَّرْف	رَأَيْتُ عُمَرَ.

60.   قال - HOW DO YOU BUILD THE IMPERATIVE IN THE DUAL?

This is a rather unusual form as in most Arabic dialects, the dual (الْمُثَنَّى) is very rare. You hardly hear these forms as in colloquial Arabic you use the plural of the imperative (أَمْر) for the dual.

First of all, let us have a look at the imperative forms in singular and plural. Let us take the verb to say: قال. Notice that we have a weak letter (حَرْف الْعِلَّة) in the middle.

For building the imperative, the present tense (الْمُضارِع) is important: يَقُولُ

	قُلْ ! you, masculine	
say!	قُولِي ! you, feminine	
	قُولُوا ! you, masculine plural	
	قُلْنَ ! you, feminine plural	

What we learn from these examples: The vowel above the last root letter ل is crucial.

سُكُون	the weak letter disappears	قُلْ ؛ قُلْنَ
ضَمّة or كَسْرة	the weak letter is written	قُولِي ؛ قُولُوا

This has to do with a rule in Arabic:

It is impossible to have two سُكُون in a row. For example: قُوْلْ
or قُوْلْنَ – so the weak letter is omitted!

Let us examine the dual now:

meaning	dual	verb
(you both) say!	قُولا	قالَ, يَقُولُ
(you both) be!	كُونا	كانَ, يَكُونُ

Let us check some examples now for the dual form of the imperative for all verb forms (with or without a weak letter):

meaning	imperative dual	imperative; singular masc. and fem.	verb	form
write!	أُكْتُبا	أُكْتُبْ, أُكْتُبِي	كَتَبَ	I
stop!	قِفا	قِفْ, قِفِي	وَقَفَ	
want!	وَدّا	وَدَّ, وَدِّي	وَدَّ	
follow!	لِيَا	لِ, لِي	وَلِيَ	II
agree!	وافِقا	وافِقْ, وافِقِي	وافَقَ	III
arrest!	أَوْقِفا	أَوْقِفْ, أَوْقِفِي	أَوْقَفَ	IV

stop!	تَوَقَّفا	تَوَقَّفْ, تَوَقَّفِي	تَوَقَّفَ	V
be modest!	تَوَاضَعا	تَوَاضَعْ, تَوَاضَعِي	تَوَاضَعَ	VI
leave!	اِنْطَلِقا	اِنْطَلِقْ, اِنْطَلِقِي	اِنْطَلَقَ	VII
connect!	اِتَّصِلا	اِتَّصِلْ, اِتَّصِلِي	اِتَّصَلَ	VIII
blush!	اِحْمَرّا	اِحْمَرَّ, اِحْمَرِّي	اِحْمَرَّ	IX
stop (sb.)!	اِسْتَوْقِفا	اِسْتَوْقِفْ, اِسْتَوْقِفِي	اِسْتَوْقَفَ	X

61. اِزْدَحَمَ – WHAT IS THE ROOT OF THIS WORD?

The verb means: *to be crowded*. The root is: ز - ح - م

اِزْدَحَمَ is a VIII-verb of the pattern: اِفْتَعَلَ

This shows that the letter د takes the place of the letter ت in the pattern. The letter ت in this verb form always turns into a د if the first root letter is ز (زاي). Therefore, the pattern اِفْتَعَلَ will change into اِفْدَعَلَ. The reason for this is that it makes the pronunciation easier. Some examples:

meaning	root	verb
to be crowded	ز - ح - م	اِزْدَحَمَ
to swallow; to gulp	ز - ق - م	اِزْدَقَمَ
to increase	ز - ي - د	اِزْدَادَ

62. ARE THERE ABBREVIATIONS IN ARABIC?

Yes, there are. But they are less common than in English.

Here are some examples:

translation and meaning	full meaning	
May peace be upon him.	عَلَيْهِ السَّلَامُ	عم
Used for the prophet Muhammad whenever a Muslim says his name. Lit.: *May Allah honour him and grant him peace.* (eulogy)	صَلَّى اللهُ عَلَيْهِ وَسَلَّمَ	صلعم / صَلَّى اللهُ عليهِ وستلم
Whenever a Muslim says a name of a companion of the prophet Muhammad (*Sahabi*). Lit.: *May Allah be pleased with him.* (eulogy)	رَضِيَ اللهُ (تعالى) عَنْهُ	رضه
Said by Muslims if somebody died (eulogy for deceased). Lit.: *May Allah have mercy on him.*	رَحِمَهُ اللهُ	رحه
Meaning: *etc.* Lit.: *till its end*	إلَى آخِرِهِ	الخ

63. THE LETTER ء - HOW DO YOU SPELL IT CORRECTLY?

The letter هَمْزة is often misspelled, even in Arabic newspapers or books. The correct spelling is actually not difficult. It is important to know that the three Arabic vowels have different strengths.

The stronger vowel (usually) decides which related letter becomes the bearer of the هَمْزة. There is a general rule: The vowel
"i" is stronger than the "u". And the vowel "u" is stronger than
the vowel "a".

In short: i → u → a

Let us have a closer look:

	explanation	spelling of the ء	vowel before
1	The كَسْرة is the strongest vowel. If there is a كَسْرة before or after the ء it becomes ئ	ئ	⟋ِ
	The يْ with the سُكُون is considered to be as strong as the كَسْرة	ئ	يْ
2	The second strongest vowel is the ضَمّة. If there is no كَسْرة before or after the ء but a ضَمّة, it becomes ؤ	ؤ	ُ
3	The weakest vowel is the فَتْحة. If there is no other vowel involved the ء becomes: أ	أ	َ
4	As a first letter, the هَمْزة is written in the shape of an Alif – no matter what the vowel is.	إ - أ - أ	
5	At the end: after long vowel or سُكُون it is just ء	ء	
6	The سُكُون is not a vowel and has no related let-ter. It is considered as the weakest of all, except when it is written with يْ (see no. 1)		ْ

105

Let us have a look at some examples:

explanation	example	spelling of the ء
Beginning of the word	أُخْت	أ
No كَسْرة, no ضَمّة	رَأْس	أ
The ضَمّة is stronger than the فَتْحة	رُؤَساء	ؤ
The كَسْرة is stronger than the فَتْحة	رِئَاسة	ئ
At the end after a سُكُون it is ء	شَيْء	ء
At the end after a long vowel it is ء	سَماء	ء

Notice: In the middle of a word, after a سُكُون or a long vowel, the هَمْزة (in classical Arabic) used to be written as a ء

For example: مَسْءَلة

Nowadays, you can also find these forms: مَسْأَلة or even مَسْئَلة

64. WHAT IS SYNTAX, WHAT IS FORM?

In order to understand the proper meaning of a word in a sentence, you have to keep in mind that we have to look at it from two perspectives:

1. We have to deal with its form: صَرْف

2. We have to check its function in the sentence: بِناء الْجُمْلة

Let us have a look at the word *reader* - الْقَارِئ - in the following three sentences:

The reader sat in the library.	جَلَسَ الْقَارِئ فِي الْمَكْتَبِة.
I saw the reader.	شاهَدْتُ الْقَارِئَ.
I greeted the reader.	سَلَّمْتُ عَلَى الْقَارِئِ.

What does the word الْقَارِئ have in common in all three sentences? The word الْقَارِئ has the same form in each of the three sentences. It is an active participle (إسْم الْفَاعِل) which basically means that somebody is carrying out the action of a verb (*to read - the reader*).

If we want to analyse the form/type of word, we have to isolate it and look at its pure form: صَرْف or صِيغة. In order to identify the function of the word *reader* in all three sentences, we have to identify its position in a sentence.

The function of the إسْم الْفَاعِل in the examples is different.

In the <u>first sentence</u>, the word *reader* is the subject of the sentence, so called: فَاعِل. Notice that the grammatical term فَاعِل is in fact a إسْم فَاعِل, the active participle of the verb *to do*, as the grammatical term subject describes *the do-er*.

In the <u>second sentence</u>, the word *reader* is the direct object, so called مَفْعُول بِه. Notice that the term مَفْعُول بِه is the passive participle of the verb *to do*, so the direct object can never describe the person or thing which is doing the action – but the one to whom or which the action is being done.

In the <u>third sentence</u>, the word *reader* is مَجْرُور. The term مَجْرُور literally means *drawn* or *dragged*; *towed*. Grammatically speaking, it describes a word which is governed by a preposition (*dative*) or, as in other cases, a word in the genitive form (mostly used as the second part of a إِضافة-construction (مُضاف إِلَيْهِ).

An excursus: What does a إِضافة *consist of?*

<u>First</u> part of the إِضافة	"*the possessed thing*". Always indefinite. Can have all cases.	الْمُضاف
	A mnemonic: The grammatical term consists of <u>one</u> word (one = first).	
<u>Second</u> part of the إِضافة	"*the possessor*". Definite or indefinite. Always مَجْرُور	الْمُضاف إِلَيْهِ
	A mnemonic: The grammatical term consists of <u>two</u> words (two = second).	

Watch out:

In the third example the word *reader* would be the direct object in English (*I saw him*) and in German (*Ich sah ihn*). But in Arabic - as the verb *to greet* demands a preposition - it can't be the direct object (مَفْعُول بِهِ) as the direct object always follows the verb without a preposition.

Notice: There are some verbs in Arabic that can have two or three direct objects! See chapters 109 and 110.

65. الدَّرْسُ مَفْهُومٌ AND فُهِمَ الدَّرْسُ - ANY DIFFERENCE?

Basically, both sentences mean the same: *The lesson is understood*. But there is a tiny difference as we will see.

Let us look deeper into the structure of both sentences:

I	جُمْلة فِعْلِيّة	verbal sentence	فُهِمَ الدَّرْسُ.
	There is a verb. Every verb contains three things:		
	1) an indicator for time		
	2) a هَدَف (goal; what are you actually doing = the action)		
	3) the actor		
	If there is a verb, we will know about the time of the action; when it happened – now or in the past.		
2	جُمْلة اِسْمِيّة	nominal sentence	الدَّرْسُ مَفْهُومٌ.
	There is no verb!		
	This means there is <u>no indicator for time</u>. We don't know, when the action happened: now, in the past or in the future.		

So every time we see a verb we know something for sure:

Does the action happen now or was it in the past.

66. A VERBAL SENTENCE AS A PREDICATE - IS THAT POSSIBLE?

Yes. It is possible that the predicate (خَبَر) of a جُمْلة اِسْمِيّة is a verbal sentence, a جُمْلة فِعْلِيّة

Let us look at these two sentences which both mean exactly the same:

The child sat down.	جَلَسَ الْوَلَدُ.	جُمْلة فِعْلِيّة	١
The child sat down.	الْوَلَدُ جَلَسَ.	جُمْلة اِسْمِيّة	٢

- The first sentence is a جُمْلة فِعْلِيّة – since the sentence starts with a verb.

  A جُمْلة فِعْلِيّة consists of a فِعْل (verb) and a فَاعِل (subject). It may carry a (or some) مَفْعُول بِهِ (object).

- The second sentence is a جُمْلة اِسْمِيّة

  A جُمْلة اِسْمِيّة consists of a مُبْتَدَأ (subject) and a خَبَر (predicate).

  In our sentence, الْوَلَد is the مُبْتَدَأ and جَلَسَ is the خَبَر

But watch out:

If you look at the predicate - جَلَسَ - you will notice that جَلَسَ itself is a جُمْلة فِعْلِيّة

The verb جَلَسَ has a hidden/implied pronoun (he). If we only look at the verb, it means: he sat.

So the خَبَر is actually a جُمْلة فِعْلِيّة

67. أَوْ OR أَمْ - WHAT IS THE CORRECT WORD FOR "OR"?

In English, there is only one word to express doubt or equalisation (in your preference) – the word: *or*. In Arabic, we have two words: أَمْ and أَوْ. So when do you use which one?

The word: أَوْ

1	Used if there is doubt	الشَّكُّ
	Muhammad may come in the evening or at night.	قَدْ يَصِلُ مُحَمَّدٌ مَساءً أَوْ لَيْلاً.
2	Letting choose	التَّخْيِير
	I advise you to join the literature faculty or law faculty.	أَنْصَحُكَ بِأَنْ تَلْتَحِقَ بِكُلِّيَّةِ الْآدَابِ أَوْ كُلِّيَّةِ الْحُقُوقِ.

The word: أَمْ

1	Used to separate a single pair of choices – you have to choose one	طَلَب تَعْيِين أَحَدِ الشَّيئَين
	Normally, أَمْ is used after the non-translated question word: أ, which is similar to the French *est-ce que*	
	Do you want coffee or tea?	أَقَهْوَةً تُرِيدُ أَمْ شَايًا؟

	Pay attention to two things:
	    1. Word order!
	        The words for *coffee* and *tea* are the direct object.	

	2. You have to use a أ (هَمْزة) before you introduce the two possibilities!	
2	Equalization	التَّسْوِية
	It doesn't make any difference to me if you travel or stay here.	سَواءٌ عَلَيَّ أَ سافَرْتَ أَمْ بَقِيْتَ هُنا.
	You could also use أَوْ in the example above but if you do so, you will have to delete the أ before the word سافَرْتَ	= سَواءٌ عَلَيَّ سافَرْتَ أَوْ بَقِيْتَ هُنا.

Notice that أَمْ and أَوْ are a so called حَرْف الْعَطْف.

The word which comes after "or" always takes the same case as the word before.

68. WHY IS نَهْر A مَصْدَر BUT دِراسَة NOT?

The word دِراسة means *lesson*. The word نَهْر *river*.

A مَصْدَر is a so called اِسْم مَعْنى; something, that is abstract, that has no colour, no size – but that is connected to an action, like writing, swimming. It does not give us information about the actor, nor the time (like a verb) – but only about the action.

All the other nouns are called اِسْم ذات and can be recognized with your senses – you can see, smell, taste, hear them. That is why the words نَهْر (*river*), جَبَل (*mountain*) or كُرْسِيّ (*chair*) cannot be a مَصْدَر. A مَصْدَر doesn't have a body, nor a concrete shape or form. How can you describe the word *reading*? You can't say it is big, blue or loud. Every مَصْدَر - like every verb - needs a goal (هَدَف) and you can only grasp it with your mind.

69. الْمَصْدَر - How do you build it?

Except for all forms of a I-verb, this is easy. There are rules for building the مَصْدَر of a I-verb – but there are a lot of exceptions. You have to learn them by heart. Let's focus on the forms II to X:

مَصْدَر	verb pattern	form
تَفْعِيل	فَعَّلَ	II
تَفْعِلة		
فِعال	فاعَلَ	III
مُفاعَلة		
إِفْعال	أَفْعَلَ	IV
تَفَعُّل	تَفَعَّلَ	V
تَفاعُل	تَفاعَلَ	VI
اِنْفِعال	اِنْفَعَلَ	VII
اِفْتِعال	اِفْتَعَلَ	VIII
اِفْعِلال	اِفْعَلَّ	IX
اِسْتِفْعال	اِسْتَفْعَلَ	X

Notice: The مَصْدَر of a IV-verb always starts with a إ = ء. The Alif in all the other forms is only pronounced as a هَمْزة, if the مَصْدَر is the beginning of an utterance/sentence. See chapter 9.

70. HOW DO YOU EXPRESS "ALREADY"?

Already is a tricky word in English. In Arabic, similar to the word *still*, there is no single word for it. In spoken Arabic, especially people from the upper class use foreign words to express *already*.

In Algeria, the French *déja* is used; in Egypt, it is *already* (the English word itself) or خَلاص; in some other dialects, e.g. in Saudi-Arabia, you hear أَصْلاً (literal meaning: *originally*). In Palestine, it is صار (*to become*).

Let us have a look at some possibilities in standard Arabic:

already (*by now*; German: *schon jetzt*): مُنْذُ الآن
You can already see the house.	تَسْتَطِيعُ أَنْ تَرَى الْبَيْتَ مُنْذُ الآن.

already (*previously*): سَبَقَ لَهُ by or سابِقًا or مِن قَبْلُ
I have already been to Cairo. (Literally: *I visited Cairo before.*)	زُرْتُ الْقاهِرَةَ سابِقًا.
He had already done it before.	لَقَدْ سَبَقَ لَهُ أَنْ فَعَلَهُ.
Notice: After أَنْ we use the past tense here – in order to paraphrase the pluperfect! See chapter 107.

He had met him before.	سَبَقَ لَهُ أَنْ قابَلَهُ.
We have already said that...	...سَبَقَ لَنا الْقَوْلُ بِأَنَّ

already (*by that time*) – expressed by an emphasis, e.g.: قَدْ, إِنَّ	
She was already there when I arrived.	إِنَّها كانَتْ مَوْجُودةً عِنْدَما وَصَلْتُ.
Have you eaten your dinner already?	هَلْ قَدْ تَناوَلْتَ عَشاءَكَ؟

71. WHAT IS A HIDDEN (IMPLIED) PRONOUN?

In Arabic, you sometimes hear the expression *hidden (understood, implied) pronoun*, so called ضَمِير مُسْتَتِر. This is typical for a Semitic language. In a Semitic language, it is usually the verb that starts a sentence – and not a noun as in English or German.

In Arabic, we normally don't write the personal pronoun before the verb unless you want to emphasize it – as the verb can be marked by a hidden/implied pronoun.

But be careful what we understand by a hidden pronoun. Look at these two sentences:

The girl wrote the lesson.	كَتَبَتْ الْبِنْتُ الدَّرْسَ.	I
Here, the ت at the end of the verb is not a hidden pronoun. It is just a marker for femininity, 3ʳᵈ person, so called تاء التَّأْنِيث		

She wrote the lesson.	كَتَبَتِ الدَّرْسَ.	2
Here, the ت is a hidden pronoun, a so called ضَمِير مُسْتَتِر as the ت is actually substituting the pronoun هِيَ – meaning: كَتَبَتْ هِيَ الدَّرْسَ		

72. IS AN ACTIVE PARTICIPLE THE SAME AS A VERB?

No, it is not.

A verb (فِعْل) can carry more information and it can also form different tenses. The active participle is not a verb – it is a اِسْم as it says in its name: اِسْمُ الْفَاعِلِ

But despite all this: Both have the same meaning and function.

In general, the active participle (اِسْمُ الْفَاعِلِ) is treated like a verb regarding the grammatical implications. Some examples:

In this sentence we use the active par- ticiple instead of the verb.	كُنْتُ فَاهِمًا الدَّرْسَ.	1.1
	I understood the lesson.	
In this sentence we use the verb.	كُنْتُ أَفْهَمُ الدَّرْسَ.	1.2
	I understood the lesson.	
I turned on the lamp to light up the room.	أَنْوَرْتُ الْمِصْبَاحَ مُنِيرًا الْغُرْفَةَ.	2
Here, room is the direct object (مَفْعُول بِهِ) of the اِسْمُ الْفَاعِلِ		

73.   IS EVERY NOUN DERIVED FROM A ROOT?

No, it is not.

Let us check why: If we want to understand how the Arabic noun (اِسْم) works, we will need to have a closer look at its foundations.

A اِسْم can occur in two forms:

I. The first group is called اِسْم جامِد

The word جامِد literally means *frozen* or *in a solid state*. The grammatical term is translated into English as *primitive noun*.

This brings us to the answer of our question: No, these kinds of nouns are not derived from a root.

They describe either the core meaning of the root or describe things like: a mountain, a man, or a branch of a tree.

All forms of a مَصْدَر are part of this group.

The مَصْدَر is a word which

- describes the action without giving you information about the one who is doing the action

- nor does it give you information about the time

For example the English word *reading*: اَلْقِرَأة: This word is describing the action but we don't have information about the person who reads. In this group there are also all things that you can see, hear or smell; for example a mountain.

II. The second group is called الْمُشْتَقَّات

The word مُشْتَقّ means *derived* and that is why we call these nouns *derived nouns*. These nouns are <u>derived from the root</u>.

Look at the root ك - ت - ب, which means in its basic form: *to write*. If you want build the word for the place where the process of *writing* is done - *the desk* - you can use a special pattern and eventually get the word مَكْتَب (*desk* or *office*). It is the place where the action of *to write* is being done.

The derived nouns can be easily recognized by their patterns. (We will get back to each مُشْتَقّ in several chapters.)

The most common الْمُشْتَقَّات are:

meaning	example	formula	type	
liar	كاذِب	رَجُل + كَذَبَ person + verb	إِسْم الْفاعِل	I
Active participle. It can describe • a state of being (e.g. *understanding* - فاهِم) or • what a person is doing right now (e.g. *sleeping* - نائم) or • that someone/something is in a state of having done something (e.g. *having put something somewhere* - حاطِط)				

somebody who lies a lot	كَذَّاب	رَجُل + كَذَبَ كَثيرًا person + verb the person is doing the action a lot of times	صِيغة الْمُبالَغة	2

A form like this doesn't exist in English.

It describes the action of a person/thing – like the اِسْم الْفاعِل – but emphasizes the intensity of the action.

factory	مَصْنَع	مَكان + صِناعة مَصْدَر + place	اِسْم الْمَكان	3

A اِسْم الْمَكان describes the place where an action takes place. Since the person is not important for the place, the مَصْدَر is meant here and not the verb itself (as the verb always gives you information about the subject/the doer).

appointment	مَوْعِد	زَمان + وَعَدَ مَصْدَر + time	اِسْم الزَّمان	4

Time when an action takes place.

Since the person is not important for the time of the action, the مَصْدَر is used and not the verb.

known	مَعْرُوف	رَجُل + مَعْرِفة person + مَصْدَر	اِسْم الْمَفْعُول	٥

Passive participle. The action was done already but the word doesn't give us information who had done it. As the person isn't important in the passive, we use the مَصْدَر and not the verb.

stronger	أَقْوَى	رَجُل + قُوَّة أكْثَر + مَصْدَر + person comparison	اِسْم التَّفْضِيل	٦

Comparative or superlative of an adjective in English.

great	عَظِيم	رَجُل + عُظْمة person + مَصْدَر	الصِّفة الْمُشَبَّهة	٧

The مَصْدَر here has an abstract meaning which is sometimes not easy to translate into English. See chapter 50.

key	مِفْتاح	أَداة + فَتْح tool/thing + مَصْدَر	اِسْم الْآلة	٨

This kind of اِسْم has several patterns which are used to build words for all kinds of tools or instruments.

74. A مَصْدَر CAN NEVER BE INDEFINITE - IS THAT TRUE?

Yes, this is true – but <u>only</u> in the مَرْفُوع-case.

A مَصْدَر - if it is مَرْفُوع - has to be definite, either by the article ال or by a إِضافة-construction.

This can help you to identify a مَصْدَر in a sentence, especially if you don't understand the structure or the meaning of words.

75. WHY IS THERE A مَصْدَر مِيمِيّ IN ARABIC?

The مَصْدَر مِيمِيّ is a special form of a مَصْدَر. It is called مِيمِيّ as it always starts with the letter م.

So what is it good for? Well, the poets needed it. It has more rhythm and melody as the original مَصْدَر. Sometimes, however, it indicates a stronger meaning (regarding the action/event of happening) than the original مَصْدَر. See chapter 76 for more information about that.

Let's have a look at the patterns for the الْمَصْدَر الْمِيمِيّ:

<u>1. I-form verbs (الثُّلاثِيّ):</u>

- مَفْعَل

- or مَفْعِل (especially for verbs starting with a و, for example: مَوْعِد)

Watch out: The same patterns are also used for the اِسْم الْمَكان and the اِسْم الزَّمان

121

2. All other verb forms II - X (غَيْر الثُّلاثيّ):

- You use the pattern for the اِسْم الْمَفْعُول

Here are some examples:

translation	الْمَصْدَر الْمِيمِيّ / ج	الْمَصْدَر الْأَصْلِيّ	verb
question	مَسْأَلة, مَسائِل	سُؤال	سَأَلَ
existence, life	مَعِيشة, مَعايِش	عِيشة or عِيش	عاشَ
benefit, utility	مَنْفَعة, مَنْفَعات	نَفْع	نَفَعَ
demand, request	مَطْلَب, مَطالِب	طَلَب	طَلَبَ
killing, murder	مَقْتَل, مَقاتِل	قَتْل	قَتَلَ
food	مَأْكُل, مَآكِل	أَكْل	أَكَلَ
drink	مَشْرَب, مَشارِب	شُرْب	شَرِبَ

And finally, there is another reason for the الْمَصْدَر الْمِيمِيّ: The plural form is easier to build.

Let us see some examples to understand it better:

plural	الْمَصْدَر الْمِيمِيّ	plural	الْمَصْدَر الْأَصْلِيّ	translation	root
مَضارّ	مَضَرّة	أَضْرار	ضَرَر	damage	ض - ر- ر
مَنافِع	مَنْفَعة	نَوافِع	نَفْع	benefit	ن - ف - ع

Watch out if you have to identify the الْمَصْدَر الْمِيمِيّ. You will find the word مُسْتَخْرَج in every sentence in the following table – with a different meaning.

translation	example	type
The well is the place of extraction for petroleum.	الْبِئْرُ مُسْتَخْرَجُ النَّفْطِ.	إِسْم الْمَكَان
Petroleum is extracted from the well.	النَّفْطُ مُسْتَخْرَجٌ مِن الْبِئْرِ.	إِسْم الْمَفْعُول
The extraction of the oil is in the morning.	مُسْتَخْرَجُ النَّفْطِ صَبَاحًا.	إِسْم الزَّمان
I extracted petroleum quickly.	اِسْتَخْرَجْتُ النَّفْطَ مُسْتَخْرَجًا عَجِيلاً.	الْمَصْدَر الْمِيمِيّ

76. DO سُؤَال AND مَسْأَلة BOTH MEAN THE SAME?

Basically, there is no difference in meaning. Both mean *question*.

1. The word سُؤَال is the original مَصْدَر of the verb سَأَل. It is the so called الْمَصْدَر الأَصْلِيّ
2. The word مَسْأَلة is the so called الْمَصْدَر الْمِيمِيّ

The الْمَصْدَر الْمِيمِيّ is mainly used to make the pronunciation of a word easier. But it can also indicate a stronger meaning (regarding the action/event of happening) than the original مَصْدَر.

If you find a ة at the end of the الْمَصْدَر الْمِيمِيّ, it can indicate an exaggeration of the action or a special focus on the abundance/frequency of the action.

مَسْأَلة does not only mean *question*.

It also means *issue, problem; matter, affair*.

77. حُرِّيّة - WHAT KIND OF WORD IS THAT?

The word حُرِّيّة means *freedom*.

A word that ends in يّة is usually the feminine form of a اِسْم that is describing a person. It is a نِسْبة-form which is used to form adjectives (صِفة) from any اِسْم – mostly for nations or professions, e.g.: *American* - أَمْرِيكِيّ / أَمْرِيكِيّة

But the ending يّة can also indicate that the word is a مَصْدَر صِناعِيّ, which could be translated as: "*artificial* مَصْدَر".

Let us examine the following examples. You will notice that most of these words describe a political system.

	الْمَصْدَر الصِّناعِيّ		الْمَصْدَر الصِّناعِيّ
freedom	حُرِّيّة	socialism	اِشْتِراكِيّة
democracy	دِيمُوقراطِيّة	communism	شُيُوعِيّة
capitalism	رَأْسمالِيّة		

78. رَبَّى - WHAT IS THE مَصْدَر OF THIS VERB?

The verb رَبَّى means: *to raise; to grow*. It is a II-verb as it follows the pattern فَعَّلَ. But watch out: The last letter is not a ي – it is an Alif, spelled as a ى! The root of this verb is: ر - ب - و

The مَصْدَر of these verbs is built by using the pattern تَفْعِيل

But when the last letter of the root is a weak letter (حَرْف الْعِلَّة) the pattern changes to تَفْعِلة

The correct مَصْدَر of رَبَّى is therefore تَرْبِيَة

Notice: This pattern is often mispronounced. There is no شَدّة on top of the ي! So the stress is on the first letter ت

79. "TO HAVE" - HOW CAN YOU EXPRESS THAT?

Unfortunately, there is no Arabic equivalent for the English verb *to have*. So what to do? We can use an adverbial expression, a preposition or express it by another verb. Don't forget to choose the correct cases if you use a preposition or an adverb.

Let us have a look at some common expressions:

عِنْدَ and لَدَى literally mean *at* or *by*. لِ literally means *for* and is especially used to express ownership.	عِنْدَ * لِ * لَدَى + pronoun
Notice: The direct object in English becomes the subject (مُبْتَدَأ) in Arabic – and therefore is مَرْفُوع!	

125

Pay attention to the تَنْوِين ("un") in the following examples:

He has...	عِنْدَهُ شَيْءٌ	
	لَدَيْهِ شَيْءٌ	
	لَهُ شَيْءٌ	
He doesn't have...	عِنْدَهُ شَيْءٌ	لَيْسَ
He had...	عِنْدَهُ شَيْءٌ	كانَ
He didn't have...	عِنْدَهُ شَيْءٌ	ما كانَ لَمْ يَكُنْ

to have something with one	مَعَ
I didn't have money with me.	لَيْسَ مَعِي مالٌ.

meaning of: *to own*	مَلَكَ, يَمْلِكُ
He has a house.	يَمْلِكُ بَيْتًا.

to have to do	عَلَى plus pronoun
She has to go.	عَلَيْها الذَّهابُ.

English expressions with *to have* are expressed by stand-alone verbs	
to have fear	خافَ, يَخافُ
to have patience	صَبَرَ, يَصْبِرُ
I got it! (German: *Ich hab's!*)	وَجَدْتُهُ!

to have a cold	يُصابُ بِالْبَرْد
to have the chance	تَسْنَحُ لَهُ الْفُرْصة
to have a crush	يَنْجَذِبُ لِ
Have a good day!	نَهارُكَ سَعِيد
to have a good knowledge of	يَعْرِفُ جَيِّدًا
to have a good time	يُمَتِّعُ نَفْسه
Have a good weekend!	أَتَمَنَّى لَكَ نِهايةَ أُسْبُوعٍ سَعِيدة
to have a hangover	يُعانِي مِن تَأْثِيرِ الكُحُولِ
to have a hard time doing sth.	يُواجِهُ صُعُوبَةً في
to have a heart attack	يُصابُ بِأَزْمةٍ قَلْبِيّة
to have a look at	يَفْحَصُ
to have a piece of	يَتَشارَكُ في

80. أُرِيدُ الذَّهابَ AND أُرِيدُ أَنْ أَذْهَبَ - ANY DIFFERENCE?

No, there isn't. They both mean exactly the same: *I want to go.*
The word ذَهابُ is the مَصْدَر of ذَهَبَ.

The construction أَنْ plus فِعْل مُضارِع (present tense verb) has
the same meaning as the pure مَصْدَر. It is even called a مَصْدَر,
namely a مَصْدَر مُؤَوَّل or "interpreted" مَصْدَر as مُؤَوَّل means
interpreted.

مُؤَوَّل is the passive participle of أَوَّل (*to explain; interpret*).

The "candid" (usual, original) مَصْدَر is called الْمَصْدَر الصَّريح.

You can build the الْمَصْدَر الْمُؤَوَّل by using the particles أَنْ or ما. They are a so called حَرْف مَصْدَرِيّ. Let us have a look at it:

أَنْ يَذْهَبَ	=	ذَهابٌ
الْمَصْدَر الْمُؤَوَّل	=	الْمَصْدَر (الصَّريح)
going; go	=	going; go

Watch out: The verb in the sentence above has a فَتْحة at the end as it is preceded by أَنْ. Therefore, the verb has to be مَنْصُوب

Let us have a look at it in detail. Our examples also show how to change a مَصْدَر مُؤَوَّل into a مَصْدَر صَريح and vice versa:

Type of مَصْدَر	example	A
الْمَصْدَر الْمُؤَوَّل	أَنْ تَصُومُوا خَيْرٌ لَكُم.	١
الْمَصْدَر الصَّريح	صِيامُكُم خَيْرٌ لَكُم.	٢
Both sentences mean the same: (Your) fasting is good for you.		

grammatical explanation	مَصْدَر	A
مَصْدَر مُؤَوَّل فِي مَحَلّ رَفْع مُبْتَدَأ	أَنْ تَصُومُوا	١
مُبْتَدَأ مَرْفُوع (subject of a nominal sentence)	صِيامُكُم	٢

Type of مَصْدَر	example	B
الْمَصْدَر الْمُؤَوَّل	أَسْعَدَنِي ما عَمِلْتَ.	1
الْمَصْدَر الصَّرِيح	أَسْعَدَنِي عَمَلُكَ.	2
Both mean the same: Your work/What you did made me happy.			

grammatical explanation	مَصْدَر	B
مَصْدَر مُؤَوَّل فِي مَحَلّ رَفْع فاعِل	ما عَمِلْتَ	1
فاعِل مَرْفُوع (subject of a verbal sentence)	عَمَلُكَ	2

81. تَغْنِيَةٌ AND غِناءٌ - DO THEY MEAN THE SAME?

Yes, there is no difference in meaning. Both words mean *singing* or *song*. They are both the مَصْدَر of the verb: غَنَّى. But why do they look different?

You might know that the مَصْدَر of a II-verb (فَعَّلَ) follows a certain pattern: تَفْعِيل

For example: دَرَّسَ - تَدْرِيسٌ

This is correct for regular verbs. But the pattern looks different if the last letter of the root is a حَرْف الْعِلّة - one of these tricky letters namely و or ي. The pattern then changes to: تَفْعِلة

This is why the مَصْدَر of the verb غَنَّى is written like this: تَغْنِية

129

So what about the second word: غِناء؟ Why does it mean the same as تَغْنِية؟

Well, for native speakers the regular form of the مَصْدَر is a bit difficult to pronounce. So a simplified pronunciation became popular following the pattern of I-verb (فعل).

To sum it up:

- The original مَصْدَر is تَغْنِية and is called الْمَصْدَر الْأَصْلِيّ

- However, native speakers prefer to use the word غِناء instead. This is called the اِسْم الْمَصْدَر. Normally the اِسْم الْمَصْدَر is shorter than the original مَصْدَر

Forms like this occur quite often in Arabic and exist for almost all verb patterns.

But before dealing with them, let us have a closer look again at the correct pronunciation of the word: غناء

The word غَناء with a فَتْحة over the غ is the مَصْدَر of the verb: غَنِيَ This is a I-verb and means: *to be rich* The مَصْدَر can be translated as *wealth*	غَناء ١
Notice here the "i"-sound at the beginning of the word, the كَسْرة under the letter غ This is the alternative مَصْدَر of the II-verb غَنَّى as explained above. The word means *singing* or *song*	غِناء ٢
So watch out for the pronunciation as without vowels, the words for *song* and *wealth* look exactly the same!	

Here are some examples for the اِسْم الْمَصْدَر

meaning	verb	pattern	الْمَصْدَر الْأَصْلِيّ	اِسْم الْمَصْدَر
to sing	غَنَّى	فَعَّلَ	تَغْنِية	غِناء
to make a mistake	أَخْطَأَ	أَفْعَلَ	إِخْطاء	خَطَأ
to travel	سافَرَ	فاعَلَ	مُسافَرة	سَفَر
to buy things	اِشْتَرى	اِفْتَعَلَ	اِشْتِراء	شِراء
to marry	تَزَوَّجَ	تَفَعَّلَ	تَزَوُّج	زَواج
to speak	تَكَلَّمَ	تَفَعَّلَ	تَكَلُّم	كَلام
to talk	تَحَدَّثَ	تَفَعَّلَ	تَحَدُّث	حَدِيث
to pray	صَلَّى	فَعَّلَ	تَصْلِية	صَلاة

For a special application of the اِسْم الْمَصْدَر see chapter 205.

82. WHAT ARE THE SO CALLED "FIVE VERBS"?

Before we talk about the *five verbs* we will have a look at something else: How to put a verb into the مَجْزُوم-mood:

1	Add a سُكُون on the last letter	for example: لَم يَذْهَبْ
2	Delete the ن	for example: لَمْ يَذْهَبوا
3	Delete the weak letter	for example: لَمْ يَلْقَ and NOT: لَمْ يَلْقى

Now let's get right into our topic:

The five verbs, in Arabic: الْأَفْعال الْخَمْسة

Why did we start this chapter with the مَجْزُوم-mood? You will see now.

In the <u>present tense</u> (and future since this is expressed by the suffix سَ or سَوْفَ + verb in the present tense), we have only <u>three different suffixes which can be added to the verb</u> with regard to the doer (pronoun) of the verb.

These three suffixes are:

- the plural (و) for هُمْ ، أَنْتُمْ
- dual Alif (ا) for هُما ، أَنْتُما
- second person feminine (ي) for أَنْتِ

In the regular present tense, a ن is added to the suffixes above. The three suffixes finally make up <u>five</u> forms, the reason why we call them الْأَفْعال الْخَمْسة (Notice: don't mix it up with the "five nouns" – see chapter 219)

They (both) go	يَذْهَبانِ	هُما	١
You (both) go	تَذْهَبانِ	أَنْتُما	٢
They go	يَذْهَبُونَ	هُمْ	٣
You (plural) go	تَذْهَبُونَ	أَنْتُمْ	٤
You (feminine, singular) go	تَذْهَبينَ	أَنْتِ	٥

Now comes the crucial point: What happens if we put these verb forms into the مَجْزُوم-mood? Answer: The ن disappears!

Let us have a look:

They (two) did not go	لَمْ يَذْهَبا	هُما	١
You (two) did not go	لَمْ تَذْهَبا	أَنْتُما	٢
They did not go	لَمْ يَذْهَبوا	هُمْ	٣
You did not go	لَمْ تَذْهَبوا	أَنْتُمْ	٤
You (feminine, singular) did not go	لَمْ تَذْهَبي	أَنْتِ	٥

Some important remarks:

- After the negation لَمْ and the so called *prohibitive* لا - so called لا النَّاهِية - we have to use the مَجْزُوم-mood. The *prohibitive* لا is used to warn or admonish people and is usually translated as *don't...*

- What we have seen above is also applied to the مَنْصُوب-mood. Don't forget that we need a verb in the مَنْصُوب-mood after لَنْ * حَتَّى * أَنْ

- In both moods we elide the ن to mark it correctly

83. سَوْفَ يَذْهَبُ AND سَيَذْهَبُ - SAME MEANING?

They both mean: *I will go.*

But there is in fact a small difference:

suffix		grammatical term	example
سَ	near future	الْمُسْتَقْبَل الْقَريب	سَيَذْهَبُ غَدًا.
		I will go tomorrow.	
سَوْفَ	far future	الْمُسْتَقْبَل الْبَعيد	سَوْفَ يَذْهَبُ بَعْدَ شَهْرَيْنِ.
		I will go in two months.	

84.   IF SOMEONE HAS DIED, WHY DO YOU USE THE PASSIVE?

In Arabic, there are several possibilities to express that a person has died. The most common expression uses a verb: تَوَفَّى. It is a V-verb (تَفَعَّلَ) of the root: وَفَى

The root means *to be perfect, integral; to satisfy; to serve; to fulfil; to compensate fully.*

The V-verb has the meaning: *to exact fully; to take one's full share of; to receive in full.*

So what is so special about this verb and why is it used when somebody has died?

The active form of تَوَفَّى can only be used if God/Allah is the subject. For example: تَوَفَّاهُ اللهُ – *God has taken him unto Him.* This expression has the meaning of أَخَذَ رُوحَهُ (*he took his soul*) or أَماتَهُ (IV-verb: *to make sb. die; to cause the death of sb.*)

Another example: اللهُ يَتَـوَفَّى النَّاسَ (*God/Allah takes the people to Him.*)

In religious beliefs, only God knows and decides when death will happen. This is the reason why you should only use the active form of the verb with God/Allah as a subject (the doer).

In all other cases the verb is used in the passive form to express that somebody has died: تُوُفِّيَ. The <u>passive verb</u> is translated into English with: *to die; to pass away*.

Somebody died.	تُوُفِّيَ إِلَى رَحْمةِ اللهِ.

Watch out:

- The مَصْدَر in the meaning of *death* is: مُتَوَفَّاة
- The مَصْدَر in the meaning of *dead* is: وَفَّاة
- This should not be mistaken with وفاء which is a proper name (mostly for women) and means: *loyalty; fulfilment*

85.   كَذَّاب - WHAT KIND OF LIAR IS HE?

In Arabic, you can distinguish by a single word if somebody *has just lied to you once* (كاذِب) or is a *notorious liar* (كَذَّاب). The latter form is called صِيغة الْمُبالَغة (*form of exaggeration*).

It is frequently used, also to describe jobs. For example a *butcher* (جَزَّار) is literally *somebody who slaughters a lot*. In general, the صِيغة الْمُبالَغة expresses that something is *very...* or *notorious...* or *strong...* or just simply *often done*.

translation	word	example; root	pattern
notorious liar	كَذَّاب	ك - ذ - ب	فَعَّال
notorious liar	كَذُوب	ك - ذ - ب	فَعُول
merciful	رَحِيم	ر - ح - م	فَعِيل
audacious; courageous	مِقْدام	ق - د - م	مِفْعال
cautious, wary	حَذِر	ح - ذ - ر	فَعِل

The صِيغة الْمُبالَغة is built from a ثُلاثيّ-verb (I-verb; مُجَرَّد which means that no letter is added to the root) – with the exception of the pattern مِفْعال. As seen above, the صِيغة الْمُبالَغة of the II-verb قدَّمَ is مِقْدام. Let us have a look at another example: The verb أغارَ (*to invade*) has the exaggeration-form: مِغْوار (*being notorious aggressive*).

Some remarks:

- The forms فَعّال and فَعُول mean exactly the same

- For the feminine form, just add a ة

- Watch out for the exception فَعُول – as the masculine and the feminine form share the same pattern!

For example:

She is a (notorious) liar.	هِيَ كَذُوبٌ.
She is a (notorious) liar.	هِيَ كَذّابة.

136

86. HOW DO YOU SAY: "TO RESPECT EACH OTHER"?

Each other is indicating a so called reflexive meaning. There are several ways to express this in Arabic. Sometimes, you can use a III-verb of the pattern فاعَلَ and just add a ت which converts it to the تَفاعَلَ-form (VI-verb). The VI-verb usually has a reflexive meaning.

to fight with one another	تَقائَلَ	<--	to fight	قائَلَ
to share with one another	تَشارَكَ	<--	to share	شارَكَ
to argue with one another	تَجادَلَ	<--	to argue	جادَلَ

But what do you do if your verb doesn't have the pattern فاعَلَ?

Let us take the verb: *to respect* – اِحْتَرَمَ

It follows the pattern of a VIII-verb: اِفْتَعَلَ

In a case like this, you can't build a reflexive verb just by changing the pattern. You need an additional expression, like this one: بَعْضًا بَعْضًا

| We respect each other. | نَحْتَرِمُ بَعْضُنا بَعْضًا. |

87. HOW DO YOU EXPRESS PROBABILITY WITH A WORD?

In Arabic, there is a fine way of expressing probability:

قَدْ plus a verb in the present tense (الْمُضارِع)

It describes an action that might happen (but is not certain).

For example: قَدْ تَكْتُبُ can mean:

- *You might write.*

- *Sometimes you write.*

- *It could be that you write.*

- *It happens that you write.*

Notice that قَدْ plus past tense (الْماضِي) does the opposite!

It gives the meaning that something had happened or has definitely happened. Regarding time, it can also indicate that something had happened further in the past.

In case you read old texts:

In old classical Arabic (جاهِلِيّة) the particle قَدْ in combination with the present tense (not past!) had occasionally also the meaning of something that had happened, meaning *then* or *in those days*.

88. CAN, SHOULD, MUST, TO BE ALLOWED – IN ARABIC?

Should, can, must, etc. are modal verbs. They are used a lot in daily talk and strangely enough, these tiny words cause a lot of problems in Arabic, especially for beginners.

Here is a list of the most important ones. They are all connected with أَنْ plus verb (مَنْصُوب-mood):

	English; German	present tense	past tense
1	want; wollen	يُرِيدُ	أَرَادَ
2	can; können	يَسْتَطِيعُ	اِسْتَطَاعَ
3	must; müssen	يَجِبُ	وَجَبَ (عَلَيْهِ)
		This verb is always used in the 3rd person singular (*he*). If you want to express for example *I must,* you have to add a personal pronoun to the preposition عَلَى and will finally get: يَجِبُ عَلَيَّ	
4	should; sollen	يَنْبَغِي	اِنْبَغَى (عَلَيْهِ)
		يَلْزَمُ	لَزِمَ
		These two verbs are always used in the 3rd person singular (*he*). If you want to express e.g. *you should,* you have to add a personal pronoun to the preposition عَلَى and will finally get: يَنْبَغِي عَلَيْكَ	
	should; sollen	عَلَى الْمَرْءِ أَنْ = يَنْبَغِي عَلَى الْمَرْءِ أَنْ	
5	to be allowed, may; dürfen	يَجُوزُ	جَازَ لَهُ
		This verb is always used in the 3rd person singular (*he*). If you want to express e.g. *you were allowed,* you have to add a personal pronoun to the preposition لِ and will get: جَازَ لَكَ	

6	to like to; mögen	وَدَّ + مَصْدَر مَنْصُوب or أَنْ + فِعْل مَنْصُوب
		A remark: You can also use this expression for the subjunctive (Konjunktiv II). In fact, they are often used to express a wish that can't be fulfilled any more. Notice that you have to use the word لَوْ after وَدَّ
		She likes to go with him. — تَوُدُّ أَنْ تَذْهَبَ مَعَهُ.
		He <u>would like</u> to travel with you. — يَوُدُّ لَوْ يُسَافِرُ مَعَكَ.
		He <u>would have liked</u> to travel with you. — وَدَّ لَوْ سَافَرَ مَعَكَ.

89.   CAN YOU USE THE PRESENT TENSE TO DESCRIBE THE PAST?

Yes, this is possible. But it must be clear that you are talking about a situation in the past.

Usually you use a verb in the past tense at the beginning of the sentence and later switch to the present tense to describe what has happened (although the action is already over).

What is important here: The (second) action - expressed by the present tense - occurs at the same time as the (first) action which is expressed by the past tense.

Let us have a look at some examples:

I thought that the house <u>was</u> collapsing.	اِعْتَقَدْتُ أَنَّ الْبَيْتَ يَنْهارُ.
She instructed me what I <u>had</u> to do.	شَرَحَتْ لِي ما يَجِبُ أَنْ أَفْعَلَ.

90. PAST AND FUTURE TENSE TOGETHER – DOES IT WORK?

Yes, it does. There are some grammatical constructions in Arabic that look a bit strange – but are correct. They are used in conditional sentences in order to express *would* or *would have*.

Here is an example:

إذا + الْماضِي + الْمُسْتَقْبَل
إذا + كانَ + سَوْفَ + verb (present tense)
This construction expresses the future or conditional or subjunctive.

If he resigned... = If he would resign...	إذا كانَ سَوْفَ يَتَنَحَّى...

91. HOW DO YOU CALL PEOPLE IN ARABIC?

In Arabic - unlike in English or German - you have to use a small word if you want to address a person: يا

The whole concept is called *vocative* or in Arabic الْمُنادَى. The term مُنادَى refers <u>not to the particle but to the following noun</u>.

Let us have a look at the different particles that are used to address people: أَدَوات النِّداء or حُرُوف النِّداء

			أَ, أَيْ
I	Used in literature	to call a person who is <u>close/near</u>	
	Oh little son!		أَيْ بُنَيَّ!
	Oh Zainab!		أَ زَيْنَبُ!

			أَيا, هَيا
2	Used in literature	to call a person who is <u>far away</u>	
	Oh Karim!		أَيا كَرِيمُ!

			يا
3	Used in general speech and writing	to call a person who is <u>near or far</u>	
	Oh Muhammad!		يا مُحَمَّدُ!
	Oh Aisha!		يا عائِشَةُ!

Now let us focus on the most common one, the particle يا

You have to be very careful to add the correct ending on the addressee.

A. Uninflected - مَبْنِيّ عَلَى ما يُرْفَعُ بِهِ

	يا + عَلَم مُفْرَد
I	You are addressing a person with his or her name (proper noun). In this case, the proper noun (addressee) has to be مَرْفُوع – but with only one ضَمَّة
Oh Aisha!	يا عائِشَةُ!
Oh Khalid!	يا خالِدُ!

	يا + نَكِرة مَقْصُودة
2	Specifically intended vocative – a particular person is addressed but not with his or her name! The addressee is مَرْفُوع – but only with one ضَمَّة
Oh (female) student!	يا طالِبَةُ!
Oh man!	يا رَجُلُ!

B. The addressee has to be مَنْصُوب

	يا + مُضاف
I	This is a إِضافة. It is prefixed and it has to be مَنْصُوب. Pay attention: The first part of the إِضافة takes one فَتْحة
Oh employees of the company! Notice: The word was originally مُوَظَّفِينَ - the ن disappears!	يا مُوَظَّفِي الشَّرِكَةِ!

143

Oh students of the centre!	يا طُلابَ الْمَركَزِ!
Oh Abdallah (Notice that Abdallah is a إضافة literally meaning *servant of Allah*)	يا عَبْدَ اللّهِ!

2	يا + شِبْه بالْمُضاف

Quasi-prefixed. The addressee is not defined by a proper name or a إضافة, but is described by additional information which completes the meaning. The word after it has to be مَنْصُوب. The first part after the vocative takes two فَتْحة

The meaning can be completed by:

الْفاعِلِ, الْمَفْعُول بِهِ, الْجارّ والْمَجْرُور, الظَّرْف

Oh you, who reads the book!	يا قارِئًا الْكِتابَ!
Oh you (people), who love reading books!	يا مُحِبِّينَ الْقِراءَةَ!
Oh you, who are living in this house!	يا مقيمًا في البيتِ!
Oh you, who are sitting in the car!	يا جالِسًا فِي السَّيّارَةِ!
Oh you, who drinks the water of the Nile!	يا شارِبًا مِنْ ماءِ النّيلِ!

3	يا + نَكِرة غَيْر مَقْصُودة

If you don't address a particular person but want to address a group or people in general (e.g. in a speech), you use an abstract, indefinite word after the vocative particle. It is مَنْصُوب and takes regular تَنْوِين

144

Oh Arab!	يا عَرَبِيًّا!
Oh intellectual!	يا مُثَقَّفًا!

How is the situation if we want to address a person not by his or her proper name? Or if we use a single word to call the addressee which means that we have to use the definite article?

Then, we need something in between. This can be a اِسْم إِشارة or the expression أَيُّها (masculine) and أَيَّتُها (feminine).

For example:

Oh respected viewers!	يا أَيُّها الْمُشاهِدُونَ الأَعِزّاءُ!

Let us have a closer look at the construction:

Oh (this) girl!	يا هٰذِهِ الْقَناةُ!	١
حَرْف النِّداء	يا	
مُنادَى مَبْنِيٌّ	هٰذِهِ	
Oh citizens!	يأَيُّها الْمُواطِنُونَ!	٢
حَرْف النِّداء	يا	
مُنادَى مَبْنِيٌّ عَلَى الضَّمِّ	أَيُّها	

Some more remarks on أَيُّها and أَيَّتُها (أَيٌّ and أَيَّةٌ):

- Both always take the same case marker: a single ضَمّة

145

- The ها is just there to underline the attention. The اِسْم which comes after it takes a ضَمَّة and is in the مَرْفُوع-case.

- They can merge with يا to يَاَّيُها but don't have to. It is also possible to write يا أَيُّها – for greater emphasis.

Here are some examples:

Oh friend!	يا أَيُّها الصَّدِيقُ!
Oh mother!	يا أَيَّتُها الأُمُّ!

Watch out: Sometimes you can delete the vocative-particle, but even then, it will take the same case as if it was there!

Oh Muhammad, oh student! Notice that Muhammad takes only one ضَمَّة	مُحَمَّدُ! أَيُّها الطَّالِبُ!
Oh my friend! It was originally: يا صَدِيقي (Grammatically speaking, we call this تَرْخِيم – see chapter 92)	صَدِيقِ!
Oh lord!	رَبِّ!

92. يا فاطِمَ يا فاطِمَةُ! OR - WHAT IS CORRECT?

Both are correct.

The feminine proper noun فاطِمة is written with a ة at the end, so logically, it should be: يا فاطِمةُ - which is also correct. But يا فاطِمَ is also fine.

In Arabic, this is called التَّرْخِيم which literally means *shortening*. It is usually used for proper nouns that have ة at the end as a sign of feminization, but sometimes also with other feminine proper nouns with other signs of feminization, e.g. ى

When you delete the ة, the word eventually ends with the vowel that was already on top of the letter that preceded the ة - which is by definition always a فَتْحة. But you can also add a single ضَمّة as it would be in the regular form. Both are correct.

meaning	التَّرْخِيم	regular form
Oh Hamza!	يا حَمْزَ! يا حَمْزُ!	يا حَمْزَةُ!
Oh Fatima!	يا فاطِمَ! يا فاطِمُ!	يا فاطِمَةُ!
Oh Marwa!	يا مَرْوَ!	يا مَرْوى!

Even proper nouns that have four or more letters can be shortened for addressing people.

Oh Jaafar!	يا جَعْفَ! يا جَعْفُ!	يا جَعْفَرُ!
Oh Malik!	يا مالِ! يا مالُ!	يا مالِكُ!
Oh Souad!	يا سُعا!	يا سُعاذُ!

93. THE LETTER ج - WHICH PRONUNCIATION IS CORRECT?

There are no rules. It depends on the country and sometimes even on the region. In Egypt, for example, the ج is pronounced as a "g"-sound like in the English word *girl*.

In other countries it is pronounced "j" (like in *job*), sometimes hard (like in *jerry*), sometimes very soft and close to "sh".

Here is a list of the different sounds of the ج

	جيم قُرَشِيّة	جيم قاهِريّة	جيم شامِيّة
Areas	Rest of the Arab world; lit. meaning: of *Quraish*	Egypt, Yemen, Oman, Sudan	Palestine, Syria, Jordan, Lebanon
How to pronounce	"t-sha"	"g"	"d-sha"
	د plus جيم شامِيّة like the English name *Jennifer*	like the English word *girl*	like the English word *germ*

About a hundred years ago, people in Egypt were pronouncing the ج like the قُرَشِيّة-way.

The جيم قاهِريّة comes originally from Yemen.

94. HOW DO YOU SAY: "FOLLOWED BY"?

There are several possibilities. In this chapter, we will have a look at the word: إِثْرَ – which means *immediately after* or *right after*.

But إِثْرَ can also have the meaning: *thereupon, as a result of*. It expresses a consequence, like the expression *one after another*.

The word إِثْرَ is, grammatically speaking, a اِسْم in the مَنْصُوب-case, so called: adverbial accusative (of time). The word which comes after إِثْرَ has to be in the مَجْرُور-case.

Since إِثْرَ is a اِسْم you can also use it together with a preposition, e.g.: عَلَى الإِثْرِ (notice that is takes a كَسْرة then!)

Let us have a look at an example:

The nuclear plant exploded after/followed by an earthquake in Japan.	اِنْفَجَرَتْ مَحَطَّةٌ نَوَويَّةٌ إِثْرَ زِلْزَالٍ كَبِيرٍ فِي الْيَابان.

Here are some other words with a similar meaning:

as soon as; right after; immediately upon. This word has a temporal meaning. Don't put a verb after it. If you want to express *as soon as we arrive*, you should use the مَصْدَر with a personal pronoun: حَالَ وُصُولِنا	حالَ
after; one after another	يَلْوَ
as soon as; immediately after	فَوْرَ
immediately after	عَقِبَ

149

95. WHAT DOES أَيْمَن MEAN?

The root is: ي - م - ن

The literal meaning of the root is *to go to the right*.

- The word أَيْمَن is a صِفة مُشَبَّهة and means: *that which is to the right hand side; right hand; right; on the right; lucky; somebody who does good things*

- The feminine form of the word is يُمْنَى

- The مَصْدَر is الْيُمْن and means *the good; success*

The meaning has to do with the Islamic tradition that right is good and left is bad. For example: You should eat with your right hand – as you use your left hand in the toilet.

The root is also used for directions: شامًا و يَمِينًا for example means *to the north and south*. Since the country Yemen lies south of Mecca in Saudi Arabia, it is said that people once called it: الْيَمَن

96. WHICH VERBS HAVE A PREDICATE?

Every verb that is a sister of كانَ or كادَ (including *verbs of approximation* and *verbs of hope*) has a predicate. Regular sentences, however, have a subject and an object. But watch out: We have to distinguish, if we talk about the original meaning of a verb (we are not dealing with that here) or about verbs meaning *almost; just about to* or *to begin* or *to hope*, etc. Only in the

150

second case, the sentence has a خَبَر which means the predicate (subordinate verb) and the main verb have the same subject and agree to it. We will deal with that in chapter 106. Otherwise, it has the regular structure of a verbal sentence.

Let us have a look at an example:

Soon the winter will be over.	كَادَ الشِّتَاءُ يَنْتَهِي.	١

Here, the word *winter* is not the subject (فَاعِل). Instead, it is called خَبَر كَادَ and it is إِسْم كَادَ and it is مَرْفُوع! The verb is the so called خَبَر كَادَ

The students started studying...	بَدَأَ الطُّلَّابُ يَدْرُسُونَ ...	٢

- The word *students* is the so called إِسْم بَدَأَ
- The verb is the خَبَر بَدَأَ

But watch out:

The students took the book.	أَخَذَ الطُّلَّابُ الْكِتَابَ.

The word *students* in this sentence is the subject (فَاعِل) – as the verb has its original meaning of: *to take*!

Both sentences have the same meaning: *Khalid started to write/writing the letter.*	بَدَأَ خَالِدٌ كِتَابَةَ الرِّسَالَةِ.
	بَدَأَ خَالِدٌ يَكْتُبُ الرِّسَالَةَ.

But there is a grammatical difference:

- In the first sentence with a مَصْدَر, *Khalid* is the regular فَاعِل (subject) – as the خَبَر is not a verb in the present tense!
- In the second sentence, Khalid is the إِسْم بَدَأَ – as the predicate is a verb in the present tense. See chapter 102

97. فِعْل ناقِص - WHAT IS THAT?

First of all, the word فِعْل means *verb*, ناقِص means *incomplete*.
We have already encountered the term فِعْل ناقِص in chapter 11
where we talked about verbs that have a weak letter. But there is
also another application of the term.

In order to understand this, we have to distinguish between

- صَرْف: inflection; forming of nouns, conjugation of
  verbs. We look at the word in an isolated way

- نَحْو: grammar; function and application of a word in a
  sentence.

A	نَحْو	فِعْل ناقِص
	Regarding نَحْو, we are talking about the function of an "incomplete verb" in a sentence: These verbs are incomplete as they cannot give you a sufficient (complete) meaning if you use them alone just with subject (فاعِل) and verb (فِعْل). For example: *You are. Your become.*	
	A sentence with a فِعْل ناقِص has no completed meaning unless you add another word: a predicate (خَبَر).	
	Now comes the grammar part. The regular rules don't work here. That's why these verbs are also called أَفْعال ناسِخة.	
	The root ن - س - خ means *to abrogate; to revoke*. In German: *aufheben*.	
	You need to put the noun into the nominative case (رَفْع الِاسْم) and the predicate into the accusative case (نَصْب الْخَبَر).	

There are two groups:

- كانَ and its sisters
- كادَ and its sisters

To understand the concept behind:

- These verbs are <u>added to a nominal sentence</u> – يَدْخُلُ عَلَى الْجُمْلة الإسْميّة as grammarians say.
- It is called ناقِص as it <u>only points to the time</u> (يَدُلُّ عَلَى الزَّمان فَقَط) – but <u>not to the action</u> (لَا يَدُلُّ عَلَى الْحَدَث) as regular verbs. Since it is not pointing to the action, it does not need a subject (فاعِل). Note: A verb that has a complete meaning is called فِعْل تامّ

Let us have a look at an example:

The weather is nice. This is a nominal sentence (جُمْلة إسْميّة)	الْجَوُّ جَمِيلٌ.
The weather became nice. This is a verbal sentence (جُمْلة فِعْليّة)	أَصْبَحَ الْجَوُّ جَمِيلاً.

فِعْل ماضٍ ناسِخ مَبْنيّ عَلَى الْفَتْح	أَصْبَحَ
إسْم (أَصْبَحَ) مَرْفُوع	الْجَوُّ
خَبَر (أَصْبَحَ) مَنْصُوب	جَمِيلاً

B	صَرْف	فِعْل ناقِص
	Regarding صَرْف, a فِعْل ناقِص is a verb that ends in a weak letter (حَرْف الْعِلّة). See chapter 11.	

98. كانَ - WHAT IS SO TRICKY ABOUT ITS PREDICATE?

The word كانَ is a special verb in Arabic that follows specific grammatical rules.

Especially the predicate (خَبَر) is tricky as the خَبَر has to be مَنصُوب.

Sometimes, however, the predicate is مَنْصُوب – but it doesn't look like that, although grammatically speaking, it is! (see ex. 3)

Let us have a closer look at some problems that might occur:

1	مُفْرَد – the predicate consists of <u>one word</u>	
	The weather was nice.	كانَ الْجَوُّ جَميلاً.

2	جُمْلة فِعْلِيّة – the predicate is a <u>verbal sentence</u>	
	The professor was talking.	كانَ الْأُسْتاذُ يَتَكَلَّمُ.
	The predicate is a sentence with a hidden/implied pronoun! Notice that the verb has a ضَمّة on top of the last letter – but grammatically speaking, it is considered to be مَنْصُوب	

3	جُمْلة إِسْمِيّة في مَحَلّ نَصْب – the predicate is a <u>nominal sen-</u> <u>tence in the state of</u> مَنْصُوب
	كاتتْ الْقِصّةُ أَحْداثُها مُمِلّةٌ.	The events of the story were boring
	Notice the two ضَمّة – the first one on the word *events* and the second one on the predicate for *events*!

4	The predicate is a شِبْه الْجُمْلة
4.1	جار ومَجْرُور – <u>a prepositional sentence</u>
	كاتتْ السَّيارةُ في الْمَوْقِفِ	The car is in its parking lot.
4.2	ظَرْف ومَجْرُور – <u>an adverbial sentence</u>
	كاتتْ السَّيارةُ أَمامَ الْبَيْتِ.	The car is opposite the parking lot.

99. WHAT ARE THE SISTERS OF كانَ (TO BE)?

كانَ (*to be*) is one of the very special and interesting verbs in Arabic.

It is a so called فِعْل ناقِص (see chapter 97) and has many "sisters" which means that these verbs behave grammatically in the same way: They link a subject with a predicate.

The sisters of كانَ (like كانَ) have usually an auxiliary function governing a subordinate verb.

Let us have a closer look at the sisters of كانَ:

translation; explanation	verb
to be (*past tense*)	كانَ
to become; to come to be; original*: to be in the morning* If it is <u>connected with a present tense verb</u> (فِعْل مُضارِع), it usually has the meaning of *to begin* Only when used as a verb in the present (فِعْل مُضارِع) it may have the original meaning of *to begin a new day; to wake up in the morning.* For example: If you wish *good night* in Arabic, you literally say: "*Wake up well!*" – تُصْبِح عَلَى خِير!	أَصْبَحَ
to become; to begin; literal meaning: *between morning and midday*, e.g. 9 o'clock in the morning	أَضْحَى
to become (in the meaning of: <u>to remain;</u> German *bleiben*); to continue	ظَلَّ
to become; to develop to the point of; to come to be Only when used in the present tense (فِعْل مُضارِع) it may have the original meaning of *to be in the evening* or *when it is getting dark.*	أَمْسَى
to become (in the meaning of: <u>to remain;</u> German *bleiben*); time of the night; literal meaning: *to stay overnight.* *Note:* This verb in the meaning of *to stay overnight* is fre- quently used in spoken Arabic.	باتَ
to become; to come to be; to begin	صارَ
not to be; used as negation	لَيْسَ

still; not to cease to be		ما زالَ
still; not to cease; not to stop		ما فَتِئَ
still; not to go away/not to leave	NEGATED	ما بَرَحَ
still		ما أْنْفَكَ
as long as; not to last; not to continue		ما دَامَ

Let us have a look at some examples:

I won't go to the market as long as it is still raining. (Notice: *raining* is مَنْصُوب)	لَنْ أْذْهَبَ إِلَى السُّوقِ مادام المَطَرُ مُتَساقِطًا.
The weather became nice.	أْضْحَى الْجَوُّ جَميلاً.

100. HOW DO YOU SAY: "ALMOST", "JUST ABOUT TO"?

In Arabic you don't use a simple word to express *almost* – you use a verb. These verbs are called: أَفْعال الْمُقارَبة. The best-known example is كادَ. The word مُقارَبة means *approximation*. All these verbs follow the rules of كانَ – but with a difference:

1. The <u>predicate</u> of a verb of approximation is usually <u>a verbal sentence</u> (جُمْلة فِعْلِيّة) in the present tense – فِعْل مُضارِع

2. However, in some cases, the predicate can be linked with أَنْ resulting in a مَصْدَر مُؤَوَّل (أَنْ + verb in the present tense). So when do you use أَنْ؟

* أَنْ is <u>always used</u> with verbs of hope
* أَنْ is <u>used with some</u> verbs of approximation
* أَنْ is <u>never used</u> with verbs of beginning

Grammatically speaking, the predicate is considered to be مَنْصُوب, but since it is a verb, it does not necessarily have to look like that. A hint: Just mark the endings by using the general rules for regular sentences.

The three following verbs describe something, that is very close to happen:

normally used <u>without</u> أَنْ	The choice of the tense (past or present) depends on the view of the narrator, i.e. if he wants to tell something in the past or present	كادَ, يَكادُ
normally used <u>with</u> أَنْ		أَوْشَكَ, يُوشِكُ
normally used <u>without</u> أَنْ	only used in literature	كَرَبَ

Let us have a look at an example:

Soon the winter will be over. Meaning here: *just about to end*. In German you would say *bald vorbei* or *fast vorbei*.	كادَ الشِّتاءُ يَنْتَهي.

Notice the grammatical difference in the following sentences.

They both mean: *The train will move soon.*

You use أَنْ The second verb (after أَنْ) is مَنْصُوب	أَوْشَكَ الْقِطَارُ أَنْ يَتَحَرَّكَ.
Here you don't use أَنْ The second verb is مَرْفُوع	أَوْشَكَ الْقِطَارُ يَتَحَرَّكُ.

Notice that if كَاد is negated, it means *hardly* or *scarcely*! See chapter 124.

101. WHAT ARE THE VERBS OF HOPE?

In Arabic, there are special verbs which are used to express that something is hopefully going to happen.

What is interesting about these verbs:

They are <u>used in the past tense</u> – but the sentence has the <u>meaning of the present or future</u>!

These verbs are called: أَفْعال الرَّجاء. The word رَجاء means *hope*. All the following verbs are usually translated as *I wish; perhaps; it could be that; it is possible that*

This verb is only used in the past. It is a so called فِعْل جامِد – it can't build the imperative nor the present tense.	عَسَى

159

Normally, عَسَى is not conjugated – but it can take a pronoun suffix. <u>This verb needs أَنْ to be connected with the predicate.</u>	
only used in literature; used with أَنْ to be connected with the predicate.	حَرَى
only used in literature; used with أَنْ to be connected with the predicate.	أَخْلَوْلَق

- All the above listed verbs are <u>sisters of كَادَ</u>.

- They have a predicate (خَبَر) which has to be a verb in the present tense (فِعْل مُضارِع). However, the predicate is connected to the "verb of hope" with أَنْ. The added verb has to be مَنْصُوب.

Here are some examples:

I wish (that) the exam will be easy.	عَسَى الْإِمْتِحانُ أَنْ يَكُونَ سَهْلاً.
The (fem.) student wishes to see the teacher.	الطَّالِبَةُ أَخْلَوْلَقَتْ أَنْ تَرَى الْمُدَرِّسَ.
Perhaps you are...?	عَساكَ...؟

102. HOW DO YOU SAY: "TO BEGIN"?

There are a lot of verbs in Arabic which can express that something *starts* or *begins* or *is being started*.

The verbs are called أَفْعال الشُّرُوع.

The word شُرُوع means *attempt; embarking on; engaging in*. So we call these verbs also "verbs of beginning".

The verbs in the following table basically all mean *to start* or *to begin* or *to undertake*.

بَدَأ	أَخَذَ	شَرَعَ	جَعَلَ	راحَ
هَبَّ	أَنْشَأ	قامَ	طَفِقَ	

There are four important things you should know about these verbs:

1. They must be followed by a verb and never by a مَصْدَر

2. The verbs are used in the present tense (الْمُضارِع)

3. Never use أَنْ after these verbs!

   Notice that they belong to كان and its sisters which means: the same rules as for كان / كاد must be applied

4. Since they are a sister of كاد, they have a predicate. The predicate of these verbs (خَبَر) is normally a verb in the present tense (الْمُضارِع)

Let us have a look at an example:

The student starts answering the questions.	يَبْدَأُ الطَّالِبُ يُجِيبُ عَن الأَسْئِلةِ.

103. المُطابَقة - WHAT DOES AGREEMENT MEAN?

In Arabic, there are four different grammatical situations when a word has to correspond with a preceding word and needs agreement – so called المُطابَقة

example	grammatical term	term in Arabic	
الطالِبُ الجَميلُ	attribute, adjunct	نَعْت	1
الطَّالِبان كِلاهُما	emphasis	تَوْكِيد	2
هؤُلاء المُحامُونَ	apposition	بَدَل	3
خالِدٌ ومُحَمَّدٌ	conjunction	عَطْف	4

Remember:

Agreement in Arabic means to adjust four things:

1. definite/indefinite
2. gender (جِنْس)
3. singular/dual/plural
4. case

162

104. WHAT IS THE مَنْصُوب-FORM OF أَنَا - "ME"?

It is the word إِيَّايَ

It is very rare to come across مَنْصُوب and مَجْرُور-forms of personal pronouns, but you might find it in literature, in expressions like: *without me.*

pronoun	explanation			مَنْصُوب
I	Notice the فَتْحة above the last letter ي	*me*		إِيَّايَ
he	Notice the ضَمّة above the last letter ه	*him*		إِيَّاهُ

translation	example	meaning	syntax	pronoun
except me	إِلَّا إِيَّايَ	me	إِيَّايَ	أَنَا
except you	إِلَّا إِيَّاكَ	you	إِيَّاكَ	أَنْتَ

105. إِيَّاكَ نَعْبُدُ - WHAT DOES IT MEAN?

It means: *Thee (alone) we worship.*

It is a line from probably the most famous sura of the Qur'an: الْفَاتِحة - *the opening.*

Grammatically speaking, the word إِيَّاكَ is the personal pronoun *you* in the مَنْصُوب-case (see chapter 104).

163

Since it is preceding the verb, it is a way to emphasize the word *you*, so called أُسلوب الْقَصْر.

In our example, we call this type: التَّقْدِيم والتَّأْخِير

You could even change the word order and still, the meaning would be the same: تَعْبُدُ إِيَّاكَ

If إِيَّا stands at the beginning of a sentence and if a person is addressed, it can mean: *Beware of...* or *don't...*

| (You!) Don't break the glass! | إِيَّاكَ أَلّا تَكْسِرَ الْكُوبَ! |
| Notice that أَلّا = لا + أَنْ | |

One remark: The particle إِيَّا can also mean *with* if it is connected to a و – the so called واو الْمَعِيّة

| We go with her to the room. | نَذْهَبُ وَإِيَّاها إِلَى الْغُرْفةِ. |

106. SOMETIMES YOU DON'T NEED أَنْ - IS THIS TRUE?

Yes, this is true.

Normally, you need the particle أَنْ to connect two verbs. In German, most verbs are connected directly (*Ich möchte gehen*). In English, most verbs are connected with *to* (*I want to go*). Grammatically speaking, we call أَنْ a conjunction.

Notice: أَنْ plus verb has the same meaning as the مَصْدَر – see chapter 80.

However, there are also some verbs that don't need the conjunction أَنْ. These verbs - unlike in English - are directly connected with the second verb.

This has to do with the so called الْحال – since the second verb is describing the first verb and since a حال can be a جُمْلة فِعْلِيّة.

Let us have a look at this sentence:

She let him go.	تَرَكَتْهُ يَذْهَبُ.

Let us check this sentence in detail:

First verb, modified by the subject (*she let*).	تَرَكَتْ	1
The first verb is connected with a personal pronoun (*him*). It is referring to the target person. A remark: If there is no other person involved (if we talk about one person in the entire sentence), there is no need for a pronoun.	هُ	2
The second verb has to be in the present tense (الْمُضارِع) and here, in our example, it means *going*. The second verb has to be conjugated with respect to the preceding pronoun, which means in our case: 3rd person singular (*he*).	يَذْهَبُ	3

A hint: All verbs which have the meaning of *to begin* (أَبَدَ) - verbs of beginning - or *keep on doing* (ما زالَ) or *to be close to do* (كادَ) - verbs of approximation - don't need أَنْ

Here are some examples:

1	to leave	تَرَكَ, يَتْرُكُ
	He let him writing.	تَرَكَهُ يَكْتُبُ.

2	to begin	بَدَأَ, يَبْدَأُ * اِبْتَدَأَ, يَبْتَدِئُ
	He began to work.	اِبْتَدَأَ يَعْمَلُ.
	to begin	صَارَ, يَصِيرُ
	He started to pray.	صَارَ يُصَلِّي.
	to begin	رَاحَ, يَرُوحُ
	He started to laugh.	رَاحَ يَضْحَكُ.
	to begin	قَامَ, يَقُومُ
	He started to work.	قَامَ يَعْمَلُ.

3	to continue	اِسْتَمَرَّ, يَسْتَمِرُّ
	He continued to work.	اِسْتَمَرَ يَعْمَلُ.

4	to hear	سَمِعَ, يَسْمَعُ
	I heard him saying.	سَمِعْتُهُ يَقُولُ.

5	to find	وَجَدَ, يَجِدُ
	I found her sleeping.	وَجَدْتُها تَنامُ.

6	still doing	ما زالَ, لا يَزالُ
	He is still working.	ما زالَ يَعْمَلُ.

7	to do again	عادَ, يَعُودُ
	She is not working again.	ما عادَتْ تَعْمَلُ.

8	to keep doing	بَقِيَ, يَبْقَى
	He kept stopping.	بَقِيَ يَقِفُ.

9	to see	رَأى, يَرَى
	I saw him coming.	رَأَيْتُهُ يَأْتي.

10	to watch	شاهَدَ, يُشاهِدُ
	She watched him going.	شاهَدَتْهُ يَذْهَبُ.

107. AFTER أَنْ - IS IT OKAY TO HAVE A VERB IN THE PAST TENSE?

Yes it is! It is very rare and sometimes used to paraphrase the pluperfect (past perfect). Grammatically speaking, we called it a مَصْدَر مُؤَوَّل

Notice that if you use a verb in the present tense after أَنْ, it has to be مَنْصُوب. However, if you use a verb in the past tense, you don't need a special marker – just use the regular past tense.

For example:

I was happy that you (had) succeeded.	سَرَّنِي أَنْ نَجَحْتَ.
	‎= سَرَّنِي نَجاحُكَ.
مَصْدَر مُؤَوَّل	أَنْ نَجَحْتَ
مَصْدَر صَرِيح	نَجاحُكَ

See chapter 70 for another example.

Watch out: After the words لَمَّا (*when*; *after*) and لَوْ (*if*), you might find the particle أَنْ followed by a past tense verb!

| I swear, if you studied, you would be respected. | أُقْسِمُ أَنْ لَوْ دَرَسْتَ لَاحْتُرِمتَ. |
| | ‎= أُقْسِمُ لَوْ دَرَسْتَ... |

108. "HE HANDS IT OVER TO ME" - HOW DO YOU SAY THAT?

Sounds easy – but it is not. The verb أَعْطَى (*to give, to hand over*) can have two objects. So it can also have two pronominal objects.

- The first one - in our example *me* - is attached to the verb directly.

- The second pronoun - in our example *it* - is detached from the word and is connected with the particle إِيَّا

So it is exactly the opposite compared to English, which is important to keep in mind if you translate.

- The pronoun, which is the indirect object (German: *Dativ*) in an English sentence, is attached directly to the verb.

- The direct object in the English/German sentence is attached to إِيَّا

Here are some examples:

He hands it (masculine) over to me.	يُعْطِينِي إِيَّاهُ.
He hands it (feminine) over to me.	يُعْطِينِي إِيَّاها.
You (fem.) handed it (e.g.: the book**s**) over to him.	أَهْدَيْتِهِ إِيَّاها.
You (fem.) handed it (e.g.: the book) over to her.	أَهْدَيْتِها إِيَّاهُ.

This works for all verbs that take two objects – see chapter 109.

109. ARE THERE VERBS WITH TWO OBJECTS IN ARABIC?

Yes, in Arabic, we can have two objects in one sentence.

This is nothing new, as in English or German, we regularly have a direct and an indirect object in a sentence. So what is so special about it?

The difference to other languages and other Arabic verbs is that you don't use a preposition (*to; with; for* - مَعَ ,لِ) with the second object.

In English, you can't have two direct objects. So watch out as the translation of these verbs into English always contains a direct and an indirect object (connected with a preposition, e.g.: *with, to, as, for*).

Let us have a closer look at verbs with two objects.

There are two groups:

<u>GROUP I:</u> The objects were originally a جُمْلة اِسْمِيّة (nominal sentence) with a subject and a predicate:

I	verbs of preponderance, superiority	أَفْعال الرُّجْحان
	to think; to guess; to suppose	ظَنَّ
		حَسِبَ
		خالَ
	to allege	زَعَمَ

2	verbs of certainty	أَفْعال الْيَقين
	to know	عَلِمَ
	to know; to perceive	رَأَى
	to find	وَجَدَ
	to regard; to deem; to consider	عَدَّ

	transmutative verbs	أَقْعَال التَّخْويل	3
	to take; to take on	إِتَّخَذَ	
	to make; to reduce to	جَعَلَ	

Some examples:

The teacher found the students present.	وَجَدَ الْمُدَرِّسُ الطُّلَّابَ حَاضِرِينَ.	
first object: مَفْعُول بِهِ أَوَّل	الطُّلَّابَ	1
second object: مَفْعُول بِهِ ثانٍ	حَاضِرِينَ	2
The second part was originally a جُمْلة اِسْميّة: *The students are present.*	الطُّلَّابُ حَاضِرونَ	3

The student thinks (that) his colleagues are present.	ظَنَّ الطَّالِبُ الزُّمَلاءَ مَوْجُودِينَ.
The student alleges that the grammar is difficult.	زَعَمَ الطَّالِبُ النَّحْوَ صَعْبًا.
People perceive knowledge as useful.	رَأى النَّاسُ الْعِلْمَ نافِعًا.
The man found the door closed.	وَجَدَ الرَّجُلُ الْبابَ مُغْلَقًا.
The professor considered the answer as correct.	عَدَّ الْأُسْتاذُ الإِجابَةَ صَحِيحَةً.
The goldsmith made a ring from gold.	جَعَلَ الصَّائِغُ الذَّهَبَ خاتَمًا.

GROUP II: Notice here - and this is different to group A - that the two objects did not (could not) form a nominal sentence!

to grant; to donate	مَنَحَ	to dress	أَلْبَسَ
to ask for	سَأَلَ	to give	أَعْطَى

Let us try to understand this better by looking at an example:

The student gave his colleague a book.	أَعْطَى الطَّالِبُ زَمِيلَهُ كِتابًا.
This sentence fragment would not make sense if it stood alone! This is different from all verbs in group A.	زَمِيلُهُ كِتابٌ

Here are some more examples for group B:

The director granted the student a prize.	مَنَحَ الْمُدِيرُ الطَّالِبَ جائِزَةً
The mother dressed her child with his clothes.	أَلْبَسَتِ الْأُمُّ طِفْلَها مَلابِسَهُ.
The student asked his colleague for help.	سَأَلَ الطَّالِبُ زَمِيلَهُ الْمُساعَدَةَ.

110. ARE THERE VERBS WITH THREE OBJECTS?

Yes, there are. In English or German, you would build a subordinate clause (*Nebensatz*) which carries the information of the second and third object.

Let us have a look at the following sentence:

He showed him that the book is nice.	أَرَاهُ الْكِتَابَ جَمِيلَةً.	
him	ه	١
the book	الْكِتَابَ	٢
nice	جَمِيلَةً	٣

Here is another example:

She told him that Karim is lazy.	حَدَّثَتْهُ كَرِيمًا كَسُولًا.

Most of these verbs have the meaning of *to inform; show; to tell*.

to inform	أَنْبَأَ		to show	أَرَى		to tell	حَدَّثَ
to inform	أَخْبَرَ		to let to know	أَعْلَمَ			

111. Is "that" in English always "that" in Arabic?

No, it is not. There are a lot of verbs in English or German which are usually followed by the word *that*. For example: *I assume that... I think that... I claim that... I believe that... I expect that...*

The verbs above are not followed by *that* (أَنَّ) in Arabic. Instead, you use one or two direct objects (مَفْعُول بِهِ)

I thought that he is lazy.	زَعَمْتُهُ كَسُولًا.

173

Did you (f.) think that Fatima is his sister?	هَلْ خِلْتِ فاطِمَةَ أُخْتَهُ؟
I thought that the guy is present.	ظَنَنْتُ الرَّجُلَ مَوْجُودًا.

Here is a list of some verbs that work like this:

to think	ظَنَّ	to proclaim	زَعَمَ	to assume	حَسِبَ
to suppose	خالَ	to deem	حَجا	to find	أَلْفَى

112. CAN AN ARABIC SENTENCE START WITH AN OBJECT?

Yes, it can. Here is an example:

word order	translation	example
verb + subject + object	The professor wrote a letter.	كَتَبَ الأُسْتاذُ الرِّسالةَ
object + verb + subject		الرِّسالةُ كَتَبَها الأُسْتاذُ

Let us have a look at the construction:

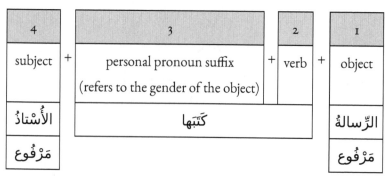

4		3		2		1
subject	+	personal pronoun suffix (refers to the gender of the object)	+	verb	+	object
الأُسْتاذُ		كَتَبَها				الرِّسالةُ
مَرْفُوع						مَرْفُوع

In order to give the listener a hint that the first word is not the subject but the object, it is good to pause for a second after the object – so that the verb, which comes after it, is automatically stressed.

An excursus: You also have to add a pronoun at the end of the verb if you have a construction with a relative pronoun (الَّذِي).

Don't forget the major forms of الَّذِي

	masculine	feminine
singular	الَّذِي	الَّتِي
dual مَرْفُوع	اللَّذانِ	اللَّتانِ
dual مَجْرُور / مَنْصُوب	اللَّذَيْنِ	اللَّتَيْنِ
plural	الَّذِينَ	اللَّوَاتِي or اللَّائِي

For example:

The book that/which I knew...	...الْكِتابُ الَّذِي عَرَفْتُهُ

113. "A MAN WHO WENT..." – HOW IS THAT IN ARABIC?

This sentence leads us to a common mistake which non-native speakers often make: You can not build a relative clause if the word, to which the relative clause is referring to, is <u>indefinite</u>.

Let us have a look at an example:

WRONG! This is not possible in Arabic.	١ ...رَجُلُ الَّذِي ذَهَبَ ...رَجُلُ مَنْ ذَهَبَ
CORRECT! But it means: <u>The</u> man who went...	٢ ...الرَّجُلُ الَّذِي ذَهَبَ

So how do you express the sentence: *A man who went...*?

Answer: رَجُلٌ ذَهَبَ. However, in Arabic - without knowing the context - a sentence like this is not so easy to understand. Here are the possible translations:

١	A man went... or: A man, he went...	رَجُلٌ ذَهَبَ
٢	A man who/that went...	

The problem is that this sentence can mean both – so you have to know the context! Here is another example:

A man, who also went to Austria, called me.	رَجُلٌ ذَهَبَ أَيْضًا إِلَى النِّمْسا اِتَّصَلَ بِي .

114. HOW DO YOU SAY: "ONE"?

In English, the word *one* is a word which always stays the same, no matter what the position or function in the sentence is. In Arabic however, it is a bit tricky as you have to take a look at the gender of the word which is referring to the word *one*. Grammatically speaking, it is a إِضافة

Let us have a look at some examples:

one of the students	وَاحِد + definite plural	وَاحِد مِنْ الشَّباب
one student	أَحَد + definite plural	أَحَد الشَّباب
one girl	إِحْدى + feminine def. plural	إِحْدَى الْبَنات

Notice:

- أَحَد - as a sole word - is <u>only used in a negative sense</u>
- وَاحِد, however, is <u>also used in a positive sense</u>

For example:

There is not a single person (nobody) present.	لَيْسَ أَحَدٌ مَوْجُودًا.	١
There is one present.	وَاحِدٌ مَوْجُودٌ.	٢

In Arabic literature, the word أَحَد is never used in a positive sense – except in the Qur'an with reference to Allah:

Say, He is Allah, [who is] One... سُورة الإِخْلاص (*The sincerity*); 121:1	قُلْ هُوَ اللهُ أَحَدٌ...

However, if you use أَحَد as the first part of a إِضافة meaning *one of...* and you attach a word to it, it can be used in a positive sense.

one of the travellers	أَحَدُ الْمُسافِرِينَ

115. Is there a German „man" in Arabic?

Yes, there is. You can simply use the second person singular - the pronoun *you* (masculine or feminine) - to express the German *man*, the French *on* or the English *one*.

There is also another way. It is not so common, however, it is found in literature and in the Qur'an.

		fem.	masc.
I	*Men* or *women* (in general) The masculine form equals more or less the English *one* or the German *man*.	مَرْأَةٌ الْمَرْأَةُ	مَرْءٌ الْمَرْءُ
	Plural form	نِساء	not used (مَرْءُونَ)
2	If you talk about a *man* or a *woman* in particular	اِمْرَأَةٌ	اِمْرُؤٌ
	Notice: The first letter is a هَمْزة الْوَصْل. You have to write the letter like this (with a هَمْزة) if you start a sentence with one of these words	إِمْرَأَةٌ	إِمْرُؤٌ

Some examples:

One would think....	يَظُنُّ الْمَرْءُ...
Qur'an, 8:24: "Now that God stands between a person (one) and his heart."	وَاعْلَمُوا أَنَّ اللّهَ يَحُولُ بَيْنَ الْمَرْءِ وَقَلْبِهِ.

Qur'an, 70:38: "Does every one of them hope to enter a Garden of bliss?"	أَيَطْمَعُ كُلُّ امْرِئٍ مِّنْهُمْ أَن يُدْخَلَ جَنَّةَ نَعِيمٍ.
Qur'an, 27:23: "I found a woman ruling them."	إِنِّي وَجَدْتُ امْرَأَةً تَمْلِكُهُمْ.

116. HOW DO YOU SAY: "ONE MUST"?

There are several ways to express *one must* (German: *man muss*).

It is a bit tricky in Arabic as you don't use a simple verb.

Let us see how it works:

	مِنَ الْوَاجِبِ (عَلَيْهِ) أَنْ	I
You (one) must write.	مِنَ الْوَاجِبِ عَلَيْكَ أَنْ تَكْتُبَ.	
	مِنَ اللَّازِمِ (عَلَيْهِ) أَنْ	2
You (one) must write.	مِنَ اللَّازِمِ عَلَيْكَ أَنْ تَكْتُبَ.	
	لَا بُدَّ (مِن) أَنْ	3
<ul><li>The word بُدّ means *escape* or *way out*.</li><li>The لا is a so called لا النَّافِية لِلْجِنْس (a complete denial) - so you have to put a فَتْحَة upon بُدّ (see chapter 250).</li><li>لا بُدَّ means *definitely, certainly; by all means*.</li><li>لا بُدَّ مِنْ has the meaning of *it is necessary; inevitable*.</li><li>لا بُدَّ is usually followed by a prepositional phrase (or adverb)</li></ul>		

• The preposition مِنْ can be put between بُدَّ and أَنْ - but is usually omitted • Notice: أَنْ and أَنَّ are sometimes preceded by the conjunction وَ (last example)	
You (one) must write to succeed.	لا بُدَّ (مِن) أَنْ تَكْتُبَ كَيْ تَنْجَحَ.
He simply must do it.	لا بُدَّ لَهُ مِنْهُ.
One must be alert.	لا بُدَّ مِنَ التَّنْبِيهِ.
She must have told him something.	لَا بُدَّ أَنْ تَكُونَ قَدْ قَالَتْ لَهُ شَيْئًا.
No doubt he is here.	لا بُدَّ وَأَنَّهُ مَوْجُودٌ.
يَجِبُ أَنْ	4
You (one) must write.	يَجِبُ عَلَيْكَ أَنْ تَكْتُبَ.

117. خِدْمة - WHAT IS THE PLURAL OF IT?

The word خِدْمة means *service*.

In order to build the plural we need the pattern of a feminine sound plural (جَمْع الْمُؤَنَّث السَّالِم). This is easy. It is the ending ات. Now comes the more difficult part. What about the correct vowels? Is it: خَدَمات or خِدِمات or خِدَمات or خِدْمات؟

In daily life, some Arabs say خَدَمات – but is this form correct? We will see. Let us have a look at the different patterns:

<table>
<tr><td colspan="3">

- **فَعْلة**
- First letter has a فَتْحة
- Second letter (root letter in the middle) has a سُكُون
- Second root letter is not a weak letter

→ The سُكُون is replaced by a فَتْحة in the plural. (Remark: If there is a weak letter, the سُكُون remains.)

</td><td>1</td></tr>
</table>

views	نَظَرات	نَظْرة
ring	حَلَقات	حَلْقة

<table>
<tr><td colspan="3">

- **فِعْلة or فُعْلة**
- First letter has a كَسْرة or ضَمّة
- Second root letter is not a weak letter

→ <u>You can choose:</u> You can put a سُكُون, a فَتْحة or the vowel of the first letter above/under the second letter. Watch out: The <u>vowel of the first letter remains!</u>

</td><td>2</td></tr>
</table>

services	خِدْمات or خِدَمات or خِدِمات	خِدْمة
rooms	حُجْرات or حُجَرات or حُجُرات	حُجْرة

Eventually, it is a matter of taste. You can choose – but don't fall into the trap and say what some people say: خَدَمات! It is wrong.

Remember that a feminine sound plural (definite <u>and</u> indefinite) takes كَسْرة for the مَنْصُوب-ending (never فَتْحة!).

I bought chicken.	اِشْتَرَيْتُ دَجاجاتٍ.

118. HE JUMPED LIKE A TIGER - HOW DO YOU SAY THAT?

If you want to describe how somebody did an action - for example: *he jumped like a tiger* -, you can use a certain paradigm in Arabic.

It is called اِسْم الْهَيْئة and comes from the word هَيْئة which means: *form, shape, condition*. It uses the pattern: فِعْلة

It looks similar to the اِسْم الْمَرّة. So watch out:

The pronunciation is different! It is فِعْلة (fiʒla and not: faʒla)!

He jumped like a tiger.	قَفَزَ اللّاعِبُ قِفْزَةَ النَّمِرِ.
I ate like somebody who is hungry.	أَكَلْتُ إِكْلَةَ الْجائِعِ.
The mother looked at the child with a glance of love.	تَظَهَّرَتْ الأُمُّ إِلَى طِفْلِها نِظْرَةَ الْحُبِّ.

Notice: The اِسْم الْهَيْئة is part of a إِضافة-construction (1st part) and is built only from ثُلاثيّ-verbs (مُجَرَّد) which means that their past tense form consists of only three letters. Therefore, this form is only possible for I-verbs.

119. TO EAT THREE TIMES - HOW DO YOU SAY THIS?

Have a look at these two sentences:

1. قَفَزَ اللّاعِبُ قَفْزًا.

2. قَفَزَ اللّاعِبُ قَفَزَةً.

What is the difference?

The first two words are the same and mean *the player jumped*. So what about the object? First of all, both sentences are correct, but the meaning is slightly different.

In Arabic there is a way to emphasize, if a person has done

a) something in general (الْمَفْعُول الْمُطْلَق):

قَفَزَ اللّاعِبُ قَفْزًا = *the player jumped*

b) something only once or a certain amount of times:

قَفَزَ اللّاعِبُ قَفْزَةً = *the player jumped <u>once</u>*

Let us have a look at some examples:

I ate in this restaurant. (once; exactly one time)	أَكَلْتُ فِي هٰذا الْمَطْعَمِ أَكْلَةً.
I ate in this restaurant. (unknown how often)	أَكَلْتُ فِي هٰذا الْمَطْعَمِ أَكْلاً.
I ate in this restaurant three times.	أَكَلْتُ فِي هٰذا الْمَطْعَمِ ثَلاثَ أَكْلاتٍ.

The player jumped.	قَفَزَ اللّاعِبُ قَفْزًا.
The player jumped once.	قَفَزَ اللّاعِبُ قَفْزَةً.
The player jumped two times. (Dual!)	قَفَزَ اللّاعِبُ قَفْزَتَيْنِ.
The player jumped three times.	قَفَزَ اللّاعِبُ ثَلاثَ قَفَزاتٍ.

The child smiled (one time only).	.اِبْتَسِمَ الطِّفْلُ اِبْتِسامةً
The child smiled (unknown how often).	.اِبْتَسِمَ الطِّفْلُ اِبْتِسامًا

If you use the regular مَصْدَر after a verb to emphasize an action, it means you are saying something in general or that you don't know how often the action was being done.

In Arabic, however, there is a special form to emphasize the <u>amount of times an action</u> was being done.

The form فَعْلة is called اِسْم الْمَرّة and is a form of a مَصْدَر. You can recognize this form easily: It is the مَصْدَر plus a ة. The plural is built by the usual pattern for feminine nouns: ات. Since it has to be the object of a sentence, it has to be مَنْصُوب

One last remark: What happens if the regular مَصْدَر looks like the اِسْم الْمَرّة?

explanation	اِسْم الْمَرّة	verb	
As the regular مَصْدَر of the verb is دَعْوة, you need to add a word (number) to make clear that you emphasize the amount of times.	دَعْوة واحِدة	دَعا	to call
Same here: The regular مَصْدَر of the verb looks like the اِسْم الْمَرّة which is: رَحْمة. You need additional information to indicate that you put the stress on the amount of times.	رَحْمة واحِدة	رَحِمَ	to have mercy

120. WHAT DOES لَسْتُ بِفاهِمٍ MEAN?

The sentence لَسْتُ بِفاهِمٍ means: *I don't understand, really.*

The preposition بِ here is used to emphasize the meaning. Notice that there are two كَسْرة (ِ) under the letter م.

The اِسْم after it is مَجْرُور as it follows the preposition بِ

Let us see the difference:

فاهِمًا is مَنْصُوب as it is the خَبَر of لَيْسَ	لَسْتُ فاهِمًا. ۱
Without the preposition (without emphasizing) the sentence means *I don't understand.*	
Here, it is مَجْرُور because of بِ (explained above)	لَسْتُ بِفاهِمٍ. ۲

121. WHAT IS AN "ABSOLUTE OBJECT"?

Let us check the literal meaning of the grammatical term first before we have a look at it in detail. The word مُطْلَق means *free; unlimited, unrestricted (without exception), absolute (in any respect, under any circumstances); general; stark or perfect.*

This is important to know as the term الْمَفْعُول الْمُطْلَق is usually translated into English as *absolute object.* I guess this expression is not so easy to grasp.

With an *absolute object* you can emphasize an action.

Here is how you use it.

You need two steps:

1. <u>Take the verb and build the مَصْدَر</u>

For example: صَرَبَ - الضَّرْب

2. <u>Add the مَصْدَر as the object of a sentence</u>

You will eventually find the verb and its مَصْدَر in the same sentence. For English speakers, this sounds like a redundancy. But in Arabic, it works perfectly fine to emphasize the meaning this way, and it is used a lot.

By the way: This is also one reason why you sometimes find the مَصْدَر written with أ at the end. It is because the most common form of a مَصْدَر is the مَنْصُوب-form. As seen in chapter 74, a مَصْدَر can't be indefinite if it takes the مَرْفُوع-case.

The الْمَفْعُول الْمُطْلَق occurs only in three forms:

translation	example	type of مَصْدَر	
extraction	مُسْتَخْرَجًا	الْمَصْدَر الْمِيمِيّ	1
thankfulness	شُكْرًا	الْمَصْدَر الأَصْلِيّ	2
shot, strike	ضَرْبَةً	اِسْم الْمَرّة	3

There are two ways to use the الْمَفْعُول الْمُطْلَق for emphasis:

1. <u>For confirmation - تَأْكِيد</u>

I (definitely) hit Carl.	صَرَبْتُ كارل صَرْبًا.

2. For further specification - تَحْدِيد

I hit Carl hard / slightly.	ضَرَبْتُ كَارل ضَرْبًا شَدِيدًا / خَفِيفًا.

Watch out:

Sometimes the original الْمَفْعُـول الْمُطْلَق is substituted by another expression. This means: You don't write the مَصْدَر of the verb as an object but choose something else. The meaning is implicitly understood – and the idea to give emphasis remains.

Let us check some examples of possible representatives/agents of the مَصْدَر.

We call them نَائِب عَن الْمَفْعُول الْمُطْلَق

	original sentence	example of a substitute
1	فَرِحْتُ بِالنَّجاح فَرَحًا.	فَرِحْتُ بِالنَّجاح سُرُورًا.

Meaning: *I am glad/delighted about the success.*

A synonym (مُرَادِف) for *happiness* (سُرُورًا) is used instead of the original فَرَحًا – which is الْمَفْعُول الْمُطْلَق

2	تَكَلَّمَ الْخَطِيبُ تَكَلُّمًا حَسَنًا.	تَكَلَّمَ الْخَطِيبُ كَلَامًا حَسَنًا.

Meaning: *The speaker talked very well.*

Another form of the مَصْدَر - the called اِسْم الْمَصْدَر which is easier to pronounce - is used instead of the original الْمَفْعُول الْمُطْلَق

| | 3 | رَجَعَ الْجَيْشُ رُجُوعَ الْقَهْقَرَى. | رَجَعَ الْجَيْشُ الْقَهْقَرَى. |

Meaning: *The army moved back.*

The word الْقَهْقَرَى already means *backward movement*, so the result is the same (نَوْع مِن أَنْوَاعِهِ).

| | 4 | وَثَبَ الْقِطُّ وُثُوبَ النَّمِرِ. | وَثَبَ الْقِطُّ وِثْبَةَ النَّمِرِ. |

Meaning: *The (male) cat jumped like a tiger.*

Here, we use the اِسْم الْهَيْئة instead of the مَصْدَر to describe how the cat jumped. Notice the difference between the اِسْم الْمَرّة (the first vowel is فَ) and the اِسْم الْهَيْئة (the first vowel is فِ).

| | 5 | فَهِمْتُ الدَّرْسَ فَهْمًا أَيَّ فَهْم. | فَهِمْتُ الدَّرْسَ أَيَّ فَهْمٍ. |

Meaning: *I totally understood the lesson.*

Here, we use a إِضافة-construction with أَيَّ

| | 6 | فَهِمْتُ الدَّرْسَ كُلَّ الْفَهْم. | فَهِمْتُ الدَّرْسَ الْفَهْمَ كُلَّهُ. |

Meaning: *I completely understood the lesson.*

Here, we use a إِضافة-construction with كُلّ

| | 7 | فَهِمْتُ الدَّرْسَ بَعْضَ الْفَهْم. | فَهِمْتُ الدَّرْسَ الْفَهْمَ بَعْضَهُ. |

Meaning: *I understood some parts of the lesson.*

Here, we use a إِضافة-construction with بَعْض

8	فَهِمْتُ الدَّرْسَ فَهْمًا أَحْسَنَ الْفَهْمِ.	فَهِمْتُ الدَّرْسَ أَحْسَنَ الْفَهْمِ.	

Meaning: *I understood the lesson as best as I can.*

Here, we use a special إِضافة-construction: اِسْم التَّفْضِيل

9	فَهِمْتُ الدَّرْسَ فَهْمًا جَيِّدًا.	فَهِمْتُ الدَّرْسَ جَيِّدًا.

Meaning: *I understood the lesson well.* Here, we just use a simple صِفة that was originally attached to the الْمَفْعُول الْمُطْلَق

10	قَفَزَ اللَّاعِبُ قَفَزاتٍ ثَلاثًا.	قَفَزَ اللَّاعِبُ ثَلاثَ قَفَزاتٍ.

Meaning: *The player jumped three times.* Here, we have changed the sentence into a normal sentence with number and noun – عَدَد

11	سَقَيْتُ الظَّمْآنَ سَقْيَ كُوبٍ.	سَقَيْتُ الظَّمْآنَ كُوبًا.

Meaning: *I gave the thirsty person a cup.*

Here, we use the tool or mean that is connected with the absolute object – آلة, وَسِيلة

12	لَيْتَكَ تُعامِلِيني مَعامَلَةً هٰذِهِ الْمُعامَلةِ.	لَيْتَكَ تُعامِلِيني هٰذِهِ الْمُعامَلةِ.

Meaning: *I wish you'd treat me like that.*

Here, we use the اِسْم الْإِشارة without the absolute object.

122. HOW DO YOU SAY: "WHY NOT"?

Let us start with a common mistake:

- Some people translate *why not* with: ‍لِماذا لا ؟
- But in Arabic, you should better ask: ‍لِمَ لا ؟

You only use لِماذا if there is a verb in the sentence, similar to the interrogative particle ماذا (see chapter 25). The word لِماذا is a construction of:

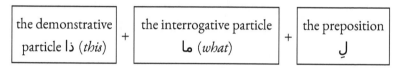

the demonstrative particle ذا (*this*)	+	the interrogative particle ما (*what*)	+	the preposition لِ

Why all this fear?	لِمَ كُلُّ هٰذا الْخَوْفِ؟
Why do you laugh?	لِماذا أَنْتَ تَضْحَكُ؟

The question *why not* can also be introduced by the word هَلَّا. Beware: It can also mean *isn't...* or *doesn't...?* as it is actually built from the expression: هَلْ لا

Why wasn't that possible?	هَلَّا كانَ هٰذا مُمْكِنًا؟
Wouldn't you like to sit down? Used with the second person, هَلَّا can express a polite request.	هَلَّا جَلَسْتَ؟

123.   دَعا (WITH ا) BUT مَشَى (WITH ى) - WHY IS THAT?

The verb مَشَى means *to walk* and دَعا *to call*.

The pronunciation of both last letters is the same: "a". So how can you know the correct spelling of the last letter?

As always, you have to think about the root. For this, you have to build the present tense (الْمُضارِع):

translation	الْمُضارِع	root	verb
to call, invite	يَدْعُو	د - ع - و	دَعا
to walk	يَمْشِي	م - ش - ي	مَشَى

These are the rules:

1. If you have a و in the root – write ا (Alif) at the end

2. If you have a ي – write ى

124.   "BARELY", "HARDLY" - HOW DO YOU SAY IT IN ARABIC?

In most languages, it is often the simple words that are not easy to translate. In Arabic this is true for the words *barely* or *hardly* (German: *kaum*).

There are several possibilities in Arabic to express that.

Let us check some of them:

1		قَلَّما + (verb (any tense
	The directory hardly went to the office.	قَلَّما ذَهَبَ الْمُدِيرُ إِلَى الْمَكْتَبِ.
2		قَلَّما + أَنْ + verb
	I hardly study.	قَلَّما أَنْ أَدْرُسَ.
3		نادِرًا ما + (verb (any tense
	The directory hardly went to the office.	نادِرًا ما ذَهَبَ الْمُدِيرُ إِلَى الْمَكْتَبِ.
4		نادِرًا ما + أَنْ + verb
	I hardly study.	نادِرًا ما أَنْ أَدْرُسَ.
5		لَمْ + يَكَدْ (conjugated) + فِعْل مُضارِع
	I could hardly hear. (see chapter 96)	لَمْ أَكَدْ أَسْمَعُ.

125. HOW MANY THINGS CAN THE LETTER ل MEAN?

Some people say 10, some 12, some claim there are 40!

We will get to know them step by step. During the Abbasid-Caliphate (750 to 1258) somebody had published an entire book in which the function of the letter ل - لام was analysed.

The letter ل is probably the most powerful and sophisticated letter in Arabic. It can mean for example: *to; because; I swear by; in view of; indeed; so that; that; then; with,* etc.

Around half of the applications of the letter ل are pretty common. For example: The ل is used as a short form of إِلَى when talking about directions. It can also be used to express an aim: *in order to* (German: *um zu*):

I went to Egypt to study Arabic.	ذَهَبْتُ إِلَى مِصْرَ لِدِراسةِ اللُّغةِ العَرَبِيّةِ.

It can express possession or the English equivalent of a dative-case. Or it can be used to express astonishment, so called التَّعَجُّب (notice that this ل takes a فَتْحة). But don|t get confused: If a (regular) ل is connected with a pronoun it can also take a فَتْحة, e.g.: لَهُ

Let us have a look at the following sentences:

The pollution is (indeed) harmful.	إِنَّ التَّلَوُّثَ لَمُضِرٌّ.
This man participates (indeed) in the activity.	إِنَّ هذا الرَّجُلَ لَيَعْمَلُ في نَشاطٍ.
You are (indeed) a clever student.	إِنَّكَ لَطالِبٌ زَكِيٌّ.

In the examples above, the letter ل is not a preposition! It is used to emphasize and is called لام التَّأْكِيد

The ل has a فَتْحة on top of it and is pronounced „la". You have to be very careful when reading a text because you might confuse it with a negation! The negation, of course, is written with a long vowel – لا ("laa") The ل is usually not translated, but you could translate it as *indeed* if you want to put stress on something.

What is also important to know:

The ل doesn't change anything regarding cases. The اِسْم after it is مَرْفُوع. A hint: If you have to vowel a sentence, read it as if the letter ل was not there.

It is essential to know the different forms of the ل – or you might run into a mistranslation. Let us have a look at the most important applications. They offer a playground for enthusiasts:

1	ل – meaning of بَعْدَ
Fast when you see it, and stop fasting when you see it.	صُومُوا لِرُؤْيَتِهِ, وَأَفْطِرُوا لِرُؤْيَتِهِ.

2	For strengthening the meaning. This ل is put before the <u>object</u>. Notice that the ل takes a كَسْرة and the word after it is مَجْرُور	التَّقْوية
Mastering your work is your duty.	إِتْقَانُكَ لِلْعَمَلِ وَاجِبٌ عَلَيْكَ.	

3		اللّام الْجازِمة لِلْفِعْل الْمُضارِع
This ل is mostly used in the imperative. Notice: This ل has a كَسْرة and the verb after it is in the مَجْزُوم-case!		لام الطَّلَب لام الْأَمْر
Let us (two) be friends!		لِتَكُنْ صَدِيقَيْنِ!
Watch out: This is better style! If the ل is used after فَ or وَ – then the ل takes a سُكُون		فَلْتَكُنْ صَدِيقَيْنِ!

194

4	In all examples of group 4, the verb is in the مَنْصُوب-mood after the لـ	اللّامُ النّاصِبةُ لِلْفِعْلِ الْمُضارِعِ
	So called *denial* لـ (or لـ *of the impossible*) as it is connected to a negation, with كَسْرة	لام الْجُحُود = لام النَّفْي

Let us see how it works:

1) First of all, you have to use the verb كانَ in a negated form at the beginning of the sentence.

2) The verb which comes after كانَ needs to be a) in the present tense (الْمُضارِع) and b) in the مَنْصُوب-mood.

3) All this together gives the meaning: *something that is totally/really impossible.*

Here is the formula:

5		4		3		2		1
مَنْصُوب	+	verb	+	لِ	+	كانَ	+	ما
أَكْتُبَ				لِ		كُنْتُ		ما
						يَكُنْ		لَمْ

Let us look at some examples for the لام الْجُحُود

I wouldn't have known that.	لَمْ أَكُنْ لِأَعْرِفَ ذَلِكَ.
This student wouldn't neglect his studies.	ما كانَ هذا الطّالِبُ لِيُهْمِلَ دُروسَهُ.
Zaid wouldn't be late at the beginning of the	لَمْ يَكُنْ زَيْدٌ لِيَتَأَخَّرَ عَنْ

lecture.	مَوْعِدِ بَدْءِ الْمُحاضَرَةِ.
Qur'an, 4:137: "...never will Allah forgive them, nor will He guide them to a way."	لَمْ يَكُنِ اللهُ لِيَغْفِرَ لَهُمْ وَلَا لِيَهْدِيَهُمْ سَبِيلًا.
I (indeed, absolutely, truly) didn't neglect my studies. (pronunciation: "liuhmila")	ما كُنْتُ لِأُهْمِلَ دُرُوسِي.
The students were not late indeed. Or: The students didn't miss the deadline.	ما كانَ الطُّلّابُ لِيَتَأَخَّرُوا عَنْ مَوْعِدٍ.
Notice that the ن disappears at the end of the verb and turns into a ا as it is مَنْصُوب	

5	In group (5), we deal with a ل which doesn't change anything (case) what comes after it	لام غَيْرِ الْعامِلَة

5.1	For emphasizing a sentence	لام الْإِبْتِداء

It can precede:

- the subject (مُبْتَدَأ)
- the words بِئْسَ or نِعْمَ
- the noun (= subject) or predicate of إِنَّ (noun or verb in present tense or a شِبْه جُمْلة)
- سَوْفَ or سَ (future tense)

Indeed, Karim is present.	لَكَرِيمٌ حاضِرٌ.
Verily the best character is honesty.	لَنِعْمَ الْخُلُقُ الصِّدْقُ.
Indeed, the students are present.	إِنَّ الطُّلّابَ لَحاضِرُونَ.

Indeed, honesty is beneficial to the honest person.	إِنَّ الصِّدْقَ لَيَنْفَعُ صَاحِبَهُ.
Indeed, success is found in hard work.	إِنَّ النَّجاحَ لَفِي الْعَمَلِ الْجادِّ.
Certainly the ceremony will be magnificent.	لَسَوْفَ يَكُونُ الْحَفْلُ جَمِيلاً.
Indeed, in spring there is beauty.	إِنَّ فِي الرَّبِيعِ لَجَمالاً.

5.2	Literally: *L of the answer or reply* Used to start the main part of a sentence, e.g. the main clause of a conditional sentence.	لام الْجَوَاب

5.2.1	ل – used for an oath	لام الْقَسَم
	Notice: This kind of ل can also be put after قَدْ plus verb in the past tense.	
	By God, Zaid is here!	وَاللهِ لَزَيْدٌ حاضِرٌ!
	By God I indeed/truly worked hard!	وَاللهِ لَأَعْمَلَنَّ بِجِدٍّ!

5.2.2	The ل after a sentence that starts with لَوْ	فِي جَوَاب "لَوْ"
	Notice: It is not used if the answer-sentence is negated with ما or لَمْ	
	If you had listened to the explanation, you would understand.	لَوْ أَنْصَتَّ لِلشَّرْحِ لَفَهِمْتَ.

If people cooperated, they would not fail. (Notice: There is no ل!)	لَوْ تَعَاوَنَ النَّاسُ مَا أَخْفَقُوا.	

5.2.3	This ل is used in the answer of a sentence that starts with لَوْلَا	فِي جَوَابِ "لَوْلَا"
	You can only use the ل if the answer sentence consists of a verb in the past tense – مُثْبِت Don't use the ل if the answer-sentence is negated by ما	
	If it was not for schools, people would have been ignorant.	لَوْلَا الْمَدَارِسُ لَكَانَ النَّاسُ جُهَلَاءَ.
	If it was not for schools, no one would have learned.	لَوْلَا الْمَدَارِسُ مَا تَعَلَّمَ أَحَدٌ.

6	This ل is connected to the indicator of a conditional sentence - normally إِنْ – or after a word of oath.	لَام مُوَطِّئَة
	The ل paves the way to the answer. Notice that the answering sentence also takes a ل and the تَوْكِيد – so called جَوَاب الْقَسَم	
	I swear if you come to visit us, we will be generous to you!	واللّٰهِ لَئِنْ زُرْتَنَا لَنُكْرِمَنَّكَ !

If you are confused about the ending ـَنَّ in some our sentences –
see chapter 155.

126. WHAT IS THE DIFFERENCE BETWEEN 3,000 AND 300,000?

Mathematically, it is obvious. But what about the grammar? Okay, let us get straight to the point: We need to have a look at the plural forms of the word *thousand* – which in Arabic is أَلْف

The word has two main plural-forms: آلاف and أُلُوف

This brings us to the question: When do you use which form?

1. For small numbers (three to ten thousands): آلاف

2. For big numbers (more than ten thousands): أُلُوف

3. Notice: There is a special form which is only applied to three thousands: آلُف

Here are some examples (the numbers refer to the list above):

translation	example	no.
Hundreds of thousand victims	مِئات أُلُوف الضّحايَا	2
Thousands and thousands	أُلُوف مُؤَلَّفة or آلاف مُؤَلَّفة	1 or 2
6,545 people	سِتّة آلاف 545 شخصًا	1
400,000	أَرْبَعمائةِ أَلْفِ	
Be careful about the agreement: If you only say the number 400,000, you have to use the singular form! And take care about the correct endings: The word أَرْبَعمائة really consists of two words. The first word has the case ending that depends on the word's role in the sentence. (So it can never be a سُكُون)		

199

Watch out: The word أَلْف is masculine. So don't mess up the gender-agreement!

three thousand	ثَلاثَةُ آلافٍ
this is one thousand	هٰذا أَلْفٌ وَاحِد

127. شُهُور OR أَشْهُر - WHICH PLURAL IS CORRECT?

Both are correct.

They are both plural-forms of the noun شَهْر which means *month*. The original meaning of the word is: *the new moon, when it appears.*

In Arabic, some words have more than one plural, and so does شَهْر. So how do we know which form is appropriate? Well, it depends on the number it is referring to. In our case: on the amount of months.

Two rules:

1. Normally, the form فُعُول is used for big numbers and is called جَمْع الْكَثْرة (major plural)

2. The form أَفْعُل is used for small numbers (3 to 10) and is called جَمْع الْقِلّة (minor plural)

200

Here are some examples:

translation	plural big numbers	plural small numbers	singular
face	وُجُوه	أَوْجُه	وَجْه
month	شُهُور	أَشْهُر	شَهْر
line	سُطُور	أَسْطُر	سَطْر
star	نُجُوم	أَنْجُم	نَجْم

Let us have a look at some examples:

several months	عِدّة الشُّهُور

four months	أَرْبَعة أَشْهُر

Notice that there are several patterns for the جَمْع الْقِلّة (for things that are between 3 and 10 in number):

translation	plural	singular	pattern	
loafs	أَرْغِفة	رَغِيف	أَفْعِلة	1
pillars	أَعْمِدة	عَمُود		
Normally, this is a <u>masculine</u> اِسْم consisting of <u>4 letters</u> (not root letters; so called رُباعِيّ). There is a long vowel before the last letter.				
months	أَشْهُر	شَهْر	أَفْعُل	2
souls	أَنْفُس	نَفْس		
arms	أَذْرُع	ذِراع		

translation	plural	singular	pattern	
tongue, languages	أَلْسُن	لِسان		

This pattern is usually used for a masculine اِسْم with the singular pattern فَعْل.

In addition to that, normally, this pattern is used for a <u>feminine</u> اِسْم that consists of <u>4 letters</u> (so called رُباعِيّ - not 4 root letters!). It has a long vowel before the last letter, like in the Arabic words *arm* or *tongue* which are being treated as feminine in gender.

A note on لِسان: it can be treated as masculine or feminine.

- If the meaning is *language*, it is mostly treated as masculine.

- If it is *tongue*, it is mostly treated as feminine.

translation	plural	singular	pattern	
young men; juveniles	فِتْية	فَتًى	فِعْلة	3
actions; activities; work	أَعْمال	عَمَل	أَفْعال	4
swords	أَسْياف	سَيْف		

Watch out for the word فتية if it is written without vowels:

youthfulness	فَتِيّة
youthful (feminine); صِفة	فَتِيّة
young men, juveniles; plural of فَتًى	فِتْية

128. WHICH (GREGORIAN) YEAR IS 1435 HIJRI?

The name هِجْرة (*hijrah*) describes the migration of the Islamic prophet Muhammad and his followers from Mecca to Medina in June 622 CE. This also marks the beginning of the Islamic or (lunar) Hijri-calendar, so called التَّقْوِيم الهِجْرِيّ الْقَمَرِيّ

The Muslim calendar is a lunar calendar and doesn't follow a solar system like the Gregorian or Persian calendar. Normally, in Arabic, it is marked by the letter ه. It is written in the form that it has at the beginning of the word (ه) – and not the stand-alone form: ه. I am not sure why; maybe so it is not confused with the number 5. The Gregorian or Christian calendar is marked by the Arabic letter م meaning: مِيلادِيّ, A.D.

So let us come back to our question: Which (Gregorian) year is 1435 Hijri? First of all, one lunar year has about 354 days. We need to convert it. The easiest way is to use a corrective factor (354 divided by 365) ≈ 0.97. This brings us to a formula:

1. If you want to convert a Hijri date to a Gregorian date, you need to multiply the original Hijri year by 0.97 and add 622:

$$\text{Year Gregorian} \approx \text{Year Hijri} \times 0.97 + 622$$

2. If you want to convert a Gregorian date to a Hijri date, you have to subtract 622 from the year and multiply it by 1.03:

$$\text{Year Hijri} \approx (\text{Year Gregorian} - 622) \times 1.03$$

In our example, the result is: 1435 x 0.97 + 622 = 2013.95

It is the year: 2014

129. HOW DO YOU SAY: "...HAS BECOME UNACCEPTABLE"?

If you would like to express that *something has become unaccept-able,* you should watch out. Let us have a look at it:

Bad style! The verb أَصْبَحَ can't have the verb لَيْسَ directly as a predicate – this wouldn't make sense.	أَصْبَحَ لَيْسَ مَقْبُولاً.
This is much better! The predicate of أَصْبَحَ now is a إِضافة – the first part is the word غَيْر	أَصْبَحَ غَيْرَ مَقْبُولٍ.

This also works (depending on the context).	لَمْ يَعُدْ مَقْبُولاً.

Basically, the verb عَادَ / يَعُودُ means to *return* and is therefore usually connected with a preposition, e.g. إِلَى (*to return to*).

But if you don't use a preposition and, instead, attach a direct object, it will change its meaning to: *to become.*

If the verb (without a preposition) is negated, it will mean *to do something no more* or *no longer.*

130. WHAT ASSIMILATIONS DOES THE WORD ما FORM?

The word ما can mean a lot of things. It depends on its function in the sentence (see chapter 133). In this chapter we focus on the interrogative pronoun ما which means *what.*

This type of ما can merge with other words. If it does, it might be even difficult to identify the word ما.

This is especially the case when the preceding word is a preposition. A general rule says that ما doesn't form compounds with words ending with a فَتْحة, like بَعْدَ or قَبْلَ

Let us have a look at the following examples:

meaning; question word	construction	word
about what?	عَن + ما	عَمَّ or عَمَّا
from what?	مِنْ + ما	مِمَّ or مِمَّا
concerning what?	عَلَى + ما	عَلَامَ
to what?	إِلَى + ما	إِلَامَ
concerning what?	فِي + ما	فِيمَ or فِيما
with what?	بِ + ما	بِمَ
why?	لِ + ما	لِمَ or لِما

Here you see the assimilations with ما in action:

And why not?	وَلِما لا؟
How does it concern you?	فِيما يَتَعَلَّقُ بِكَ؟
He asked me about what had happened.	سَأَلَنِي عَمَّا حَصَلَ.
What does the river consist of?	مِمَّ يَتَكَوَّنُ النَّهْرُ؟

Don't mix it up with the following expressions:

- فِيما = الَّذِي: This is a relative pronoun. It means *this* or *that*; *while*; *which*; *during*

- فِيمَ: This is only used for questions. It means: *in what*; *concerning what?*

131. THE NEGATION WITH ما OR لَمْ - SAME MEANING?

It has almost the same meaning.

Let us start with ما.

- The negation ما - and this is important to know - has to stand at the beginning of a sentence.

- ما, if used to negate the past tense, denies the entire matter – it strengthens the meaning of the negation.

- In the present tense, the word ما denies not only the action –but also its possibility.

- In English, we therefore translate ما usually with *not at all*. In German with *gar nicht*.

And what about لَمْ?

- The negation particle لَمْ, which is used to negate the past tense, does not express a complete denial.

Here are some examples:

I didn't get thirsty at all.	ما عَطِشْتُ.	١
I wasn't thirsty.	لَمْ أَعْطَشْ.	
He can't see you at all.	ما يَراكَ.	٢
He can't see you.	لا يَراكَ.	

Watch out:

If you see لا together with a verb in the past tense, it has a different meaning: It can connote a prayer or wish (قَسَم)! Note that the past tense is used for wishes, curses and prayers irrespective of whether it is preceded by لا or no. See also chapter 207.

For example:

May Allah spare you bad things!	لا أراكَ اللهُ مَكْرُوهًا!

132. CAN YOU NEGATE A NOMINAL SENTENCE WITH ما TOO?

Yes, you can. Normally, you negate a جُمْلة اِسْمِيّة with the verb لَيْسَ. However, you could also negate it with ما.

- ما usually precedes the part of the sentence that is to be denied.

- ما can be used with مِن to strengthen the meaning of the negation.

Let us have a look at some examples:

He is not a teacher.	ما هُوَ مُدَرِّسٌ.
Karim is not travelling.	ما كَرِيمٌ مُسافِرٌ.
Karim doesn't understand.	ما كَرِيمٌ فاهِمٌ.
I have nothing.	ما عِنْدِي شَيْءٌ = لَيْسَ عِنْدِي شَيْءٌ = لا شَيْءَ عِنْدِي.
Is there no alternative?	ما مِن بَدِيلٍ؟
Not a single person.	ما مِنْ أَحَدٍ.

In some texts the negative particle ما is used as لَيْسَ which has a grammatical impact: The subject (مُبْتَدَأ) is مَرْفُوع and the predicate (خَبَر) is مَنْصُوب.

This type and application of ما is called ما الْحِجازِيّة – but it is only used in classical Arabic. This is also the reason why it is called الْحِجازِيّة which refers to the أَهْل الْحِجاز. The *Hejaz* is a region in the west of present-day Saudi Arabia.

However, there is one important condition that needs to be fulfilled, if you want to use ما to negate a nominal sentence and put the predicate into the مَنْصُوب-case: The subject must precede the predicate.

The weather is not hot.	ما الجَوُّ حارًّا.
This is not a human being. Qur'an, سُورة يُوسُف (*Yusuf*), 12;31	ما هٰذا بَشَرًا.

208

133. ما - How tricky and various is this word?

ما is used to negate a verb, mainly in the past tense. But there's more to it than that.

ما is a genuine jack-of-all-trades. By throwing this tiny word into a sentence, you can change the meaning dramatically. In my opinion the letter ل and the ما are the key to understanding Arabic properly. It is essential to understand the various meanings of ما.

Here is a list of some possibilities:

1	Negative particle	حَرْف	ما النَّافِية
	Normally ما is used to negate a past tense verb (الْماضِي). Theoretically, however, it is also possible to negate a جُمْلة اِسْمِيّة with ما – see chapter 131. You could even negate the present tense (الْمُضارِع) with ما. This is very rare and occasionally used with the expression: ما يَزالُ (*still*)		
	The students did not show up yesterday.		ما حَضَرَ الطُّلّابُ أَمْسِ.

2	Interrogative pronoun	اِسْم	ما الْإِسْتِفْهامِيّة
	What is your name?		ما اسْمُكَ؟
	What are you thinking about?		فِيمَ تُفَكِّرُ؟

3	Definite conjunctive pronoun	اِسْم	مَا الْمَوْصُولة
	I do understand what you say.		إِنَّني أَفْهَمُ مَا تَقُولُهُ.
	Read what I wrote.		إِقْرَأْ مَا كَتَبْتُهُ.

4	Conditional clause	اِسْم	مَا الشَّرْطِيّة
	Notice the سُكُون at the end of the verb (مَجْزُوم) – it is a شَرْط		
	Whatever good that you do comes back to you.		مَا تَفْعَلْ مِنْ خَيْرٍ تَجِدْ جَاءَهُ.

5	This is used to strengthen the conditional meaning	حَرْف	مَا لِتَأْكِيدِ مَعْنَى الشَّرْط
	If you had worked hard, you would have succeeded. (Notice that it is not a negation!)		إِذَا مَا عَمِلْتَ بِجِدٍّ نَجَحْتَ.

6	Used to introduce a clause equivalent to a مَصْدَر.	حَرْف	مَا الْمَصْدَرِيّة
	It is used like the particle أَنْ and has the same meaning and implications. (See chapter 80)		
	The student came after the lesson had started.		حَضَرَ الطُّلَّابُ بَعْدَ مَا بَدَأَ الدَّرْسُ.

7	Used to introduce a clause equivalent to a مَصْدَر in the adverb of time.	حَرْف	ما الْمَصْدَرِيّة الظَّرْفِيّة
	I will think of you as long as I live.		سَأَظَلُّ أَتَذَكَّرُكَ ما حَيِيْتُ.

8	This ما denotes generality and vagueness		إِسْم	ما الْإِبْهامِيّة
	Notice: In this application ما has to be at the end of the sentence.			
	The man who sat next to me in the plane was reading (a kind of) a book.			كانَ الرَّجُلُ الَّذِي جانِبِي فِي الطَّائِرَةِ يَقْرَأُ كِتابٍ ما.
	some day; sometime in the future			يَوْمًا ما
	I lost something.			أَضَعْتُ شَيْئًا ما.

9	The hindering ما		حَرْف	ما الْكافّة
	In life hope doesn't go away.			إِنَّما الْحَياةُ أَمَلٌ لايَنْتَهِي.

10	ما – as expressive of surprise		إِسْم	ما التَّعَجُّبِيّة
	What a nice spring!			ما أَجْمَلَ الرَّبِيعَ!
	What fortunate I got here!			ما أَسْعَدَنِي بِوُجُودِي هُنا!

134. Is there a one-letter-word in Arabic?

Yes, for example the word for *and*: وَ. But there are other forms too. They are rare and only possible in the imperative (أَمْر) of some verbs. These verbs have two weak letters (حَرْف الْعِلَّة) in the root and only one "strong" consonant. For example:

meaning	verb	pronunciation	imperative
protect!	وَقَى	qi!	قِ !
pay attention!	وَعَى	ʒi!	عِ !
carry out!	وَفَى	fi!	فِ !

It can be difficult to understand these words correctly:

... وَقِنَا عَذَابَ النَّارِ
... and protect us from the punishment of the Fire." (Sura 2:201)

Notice: Generally it is impossible to have a single standalone letter in Arabic. For example: The interrogative particle أَ is always written together with the following word. Other examples are: وَ or ب * ف * ل

135. Because, since and as - In Arabic?

These simple words can lead to problems if you don't know how to use or translate them correctly. Let us check them in detail:

Because, as, since, in so far as – causal clause

1	If the sentence with *because* starts the second part of the sentence	
	because; since, as; in so far as	لِأَنَّ
		إِذْ أَنَّ
		حَيْثُ أَنَّ
	He did not come (show up) <u>be-cause</u> he was lazy.	لَمْ يَحْضُرْ حَيْثُ أَنَّهُ كَانَ كَسُولاً.
	I will go to Egypt <u>since</u> my heart tells me that I love you.	سَأَذْهَبُ إِلَى مِصْرَ إِذْ أَنَّ قَلْبِي يُحَدِّثُنِي أَنَّنِي أُحِبُّكِ.
2	If the sentence starts with the causative part	
	as, since	بِما أَنَّ
	<u>Since</u> I don't like the room I'll move (go) to another hotel.	بِما أَنَّ الغُرْفَةَ لا تُناسِبُنِي سَأَذْهَبُ إِلَى فُنْدُقٍ آخَر.

136. HOW DO YOU SAY: "BECAUSE OF..."?

There are several ways to express *because of; for the sake of*.

It all depends on the context.

- In Egyptian Arabic there is the word عَشان or عَلَشان
- In standard Arabic you could use جَرّاء which is a اِسْم

Here is how you use it:

because of (+ verb); by what; as a result of	جَرّاء ما = بِسَبَبِ ١
because of what happened there	جَرّاء ما لَحِقَ
because of; due to	مِنْ جَرَّاءِ أَنْ ٢

There is another way of writing جَرّاء – the meaning is the same:

because of	مِن جَرَّى
because of you; on your account; for your sake	مِن جَرَّاكَ

I did this for you.	فَعَلْتُ ذلِكَ مِنْ جَرَّائِكَ.
Notice: Both examples on the right mean the same as the sentence above!	فَعَلْتُ ذلِكَ مِن جَرَّائِكَ = وَمِن جَرَّاكَ =ِ من أَجْلِكَ.

137. WHAT DO أَخْرَجَ, عَلَّمَ AND ناقَشَ HAVE IN COMMON?

They are verbs consisting of four letters (<u>not</u> root letters) and are called رُباعِيّ

They have one thing in common: the pronunciation.

In the present tense (الْمُضارِع) the first vowel is a ضَمّة (u) and not a فَتْحة (a) – as it is in all other verb patterns: I and V to X.

Notice the difference:

comparison: verb pattern I		meaning	مُضارِع	وَزْن	
he leaves	يَخْرُجُ	he extracts	"**yu**khriju"	يُخْرِجُ أَفْعَلَ	IV
he paints	يَنْقُشُ	he discusses	"**yu**naaqishu"	يُناقِشُ فاعَلَ	III
he learns	يَعْلَمُ	he teaches	"**yu**ȝallimu"	يُعَلِّمُ فَعَّلَ	II

So every time you see a verb consisting of four letters, you can be sure that the first vowel is "u".

138.   THE مَصْدَر - DOES A WEAK LETTER CAUSE TROUBLE?

Sure it does.

If you have a و or a ي in the root, you have to watch out: Sometimes the weak letter disappears but sometimes it changes into a different letter.

Notice in our examples that the weak letter (حَرْف الْعِلّة) is not always in the same position.

	problem	meaning	مَصْدَر	verb	verb
1	Letter و at the beginning	stopping	إيقاف	أَوْقَفَ	IV
2	Letter ا in the middle	desire; will	إرادة	أَرادَ	IV
3	Letter ء at the beginning plus letter ى at the end	damage; injury	إيذاء	آذى	IV

| 4 | Letter و in the middle and letter ى at the end | takeover; seizure | اسْتِيلاء | اسْتَوْلَى | X |
| 5 | Letter و in the root. The pattern becomes تَفْعِلة instead of تَفْعِيل | education; pedagogy; breeding | تَرْبِية | رَبَّى | II |

Here are the rules that can help you build the الْمَصْدَر:

1. Letter و becomes letter ي

2. Letter ا (Alif) in the middle turns into a ا (Alif) plus ة at the end

3. Letter آ (Alif madda) becomes the letter ي

4. Letter ى at the end becomes a ء

   Exception: ى at the end of a II-verb becomes ية

139. THE WORD اِتِّصال - WHAT DOES THE تّ DO HERE?

The word اِتِّصال is the مَصْدَر of the verb اِتَّصَل and means: *connection; communication; relation.* The root is و - ص - ل

So what about the تّ? Where does it come from?

If a و is the first letter of a root, the و will transform into a ت with a شَدّة in the verb pattern اِفْتَعَل (VIII-verb).

Here are some examples:

meaning	مَصْدَر	verb	root
to be united	إتِّحاد	إتَّحَد	و - ح - د
to agree	إتِّفاق	إتَّفَقَ	و - ف - ق
to get in touch with; be connected	إتِّصال	إتَّصَلَ	و - ص - ل

140. WHY DOES سَماءُ TAKE تَنْوِين - BUT زَرْقاءُ DOESN'T?

The word سَماءُ means *sky*. The word زَرْقاءُ *blue* (fem. form). First of all, we see that both words end with a ء

So why do we use different case endings (تَنْوِين)?

Let us use them both together:

In the blue sky	فِي سَماءٍ زَرقاءَ

We see that سَماءٍ gets تَنْوِين but زَرقاءَ not.

Why is that? Let's check the root:

explanation	root	
ء is part of the root as the و changes into a ء !	س - م - و	سَماء
The ء is additional (زِيادة) and not part of the root. This is the reason why it doesn't take تَنْوِين. The additional هَمْزة leads to a certain pattern which is مَمْنُوع مِن الصَّرْف	ز - ر - ق	زَرْقاء

217

141. مَساءً OR مَساءً - WHAT IS CORRECT?

The expression means *in the evening*. Our question is about the correct spelling of the ending: With an Alif at the end, or not? First of all, it is necessary to write the تَنْوِين above the هَمْزة, but do you also need an additional Alif (ا) after it? Let's have a look at similar examples to understand the problem:

	with Alif?	meaning; explanation	root	ex.
1	yes	*a piece; a portion* If the word functions as a direct object (مَنْصُوب), it is written like this: جُزْءًا For example: *I want a piece.*	ء - ز - ج	جُزْءًا
2	no	*in winter* The root literally means: *to spend the winter.* The ء belongs to the root. It was originally a و that was transformed to a ء	ش - ت - و	شِتاءً
		in the evening	م - س - و	مَساءً

The rules are simple:

1. If there is an <u>Alif before</u> the هَمْزة, you <u>don't write</u> an Alif after the هَمْزة if the word is in the مَنْصُوب-case.

2. If there is <u>no Alif</u> before the هَمْزة, like in the word جُزْء, you <u>write an Alif</u> after it. Why? هَمْزة is part of the root!

218

142. عَظِيمٌ AND رَحِيمٌ - SAME PATTERN, SAME KIND OF WORD?

Although they share the same pattern, they are not of the same kind. Let us first start and have a look at their function:

- In English, we could say that they are both adjectives as رَحِيمٌ means *merciful* and عَظِيمٌ means *great*.

- In Arabic, we call both words (according to their function in the sentence) نَعْت.

What is interesting here is not their function in the sentence. It is the meaning of the type of word and how these words are built from the root. Let's check why they can't be the same type of word. Therefore, we try to build an <u>active participle</u> (إِسْم الْفَاعِل) from the root:

1. The root ر - ح - م means *to have mercy; to have compassion*. An active participle, literally meaning *somebody who is merciful*, <u>makes sense</u>.

2. The root ع - ظ - م means *to become grandiose*. An active participle <u>wouldn't make sense</u>.

Let us have a further look at the words:

الصِّفة الْمُشَبَّهة	صِيغة الْمُبالَغة	إِسْم الْفاعِل	root
---	رَحِيمٌ	راحِم	ر - ح - م
عَظِيمٌ	---	---	ع - ظ - م

219

So what is the difference?

- The صِيغة الْمُبالَغة describes something that is done extensively or often. See chapter 85.

- An active participle (اِسْم الْفاعِل) always points at the occurrence/happening (الْحُدُوث) of an action.

- On the contrary, a صِفة مُشَبَّهة is <u>describing a state or action as natural and permanent</u>!

  The الصِّفة الْمُشَـبَّهة - which literally means *similar quality; verbal adjective; assimilate epithet* - belongs to the derived nouns: (so called: اِسْم مُشْتَقّ)

  The الصِّفة الْمُشَبَّهة can only be built from a so called فِعْل ثُلاثِيّ لازِم. This type of verb cannot carry a direct object. The active participle of it wouldn't make sense.

- Since some roots can't build an active participle, but only a صِفة مُشَبَّهة, we could say that the الصِّفة الْمُشَبَّهة is a substitute for the non-existing (اِسْم الْفاعِل).

As a general rule we could say:

- You <u>cannot</u> build the اِسْم الْفاعِل of a I-verb if it has a ضَمّة on the <u>second</u> root letter in the past tense. These verbs do not have a اِسْم الْفاعِل. This gap is filled by the الصِّفة الْمُشَبَّهة

- Notice: For verbs with كَسْرة under the second root letter, this is sometimes also the case (but not always!)

Here are some examples:

translation	الصّفة الْمُشَبَّهة	اِسْم الْفاعِل	verb	root
a lot	كَثِيرٌ	---	كَثُرَ	ك - ث - ر
big	كَبِيرٌ	---	كَبُرَ	ك - ب - ر
small	صَغِيرٌ	---	صَغُرَ	ص - غ - ر
generous	كَرِيمٌ	---	كَرُمَ	ك - ر - م
brave	شُجاعٌ	---	شَجُعَ	ش - ج - ع

Let us now check both verb forms in detail:

A	Verbs having a كَسْرة under the second root letter, following the pattern: فَعِل Note: Some forms are مَمْنُوع مِن الصَّرْف and don't take تَنْوِين

meaning	الصّفة الْمُشَبَّهة	I-verb	pattern	
happy	فَرِحٌ	فَرِحَ	فَعِلٌ	١
lame	أَعْرَجُ - عَرْجاءُ	عَرِجَ	أَفْعَلُ - فَعْلاءُ	٢
green	أَخْضَرُ - خَضْراءُ	خَضِرَ		
thirsty	عَطْشانُ - عَطْشَى	عَطِشَ	فَعْلانُ - فَعْلَى	٣

221

meaning	الصِّفة الْمُشَبَّهة	I-verb	pattern	
noble	شَرِيفٌ	شَرُفَ	فَعِيلٌ	1
clean	نَظِيفٌ	نَظُفَ		
difficult	صَعْبٌ	صَعُبَ	فَعْلٌ	2
easy	سَهْلٌ	سَهُلَ		
brave	شُجاعٌ	شَجُعَ	فُعالٌ	3
coward(ly)	جَبانٌ	جَبُنَ	فَعالٌ	4
brave, heroic	بَطَلٌ	بَطُلَ	فَعَلٌ	5
beautiful	حَسَنٌ	حَسُنَ		
hard; solid	صُلْبٌ	صَلُبَ	فُعْلٌ	6
sweet	حُلْوٌ	حَلُوَ		

143. ‏السَّيارَةُ الْجَمِيلُ لوْنُها...‏ - IS THERE A MISTAKE?

No, there isn't!

If you thought that the word ‏الْجَمِيل‏ should be written with a ة, you might have misunderstood the meaning of the sentence. The second part of the sentence is a so called *causative description* (‏نَعْت سَبَبِيّ‏).

The sentence ...السيارةُ الجميلُ لوْنُها means: *The car whose colour is beautiful*. Or: *The car with the **beautiful colour***. Watch out! The sentence doesn't mean: *The colour of the **nice car**...*

Let us make the difference clear:

نَعْت حَقيقيّ	The successful student.	الطَّالِبُ النَّاجِحُ.
نَعْت سَبَبيّ	The student whose sister is successful	الطَّالِبُ النَّاجِحَةُ أُخْتُهُ

Let us check the different parts of the النَّعْت السَّبَبيّ

نَعْت مُؤَنَّث	Although it is a نَعْت, it doesn't describe what precedes, but what comes after it. The word *sister* (أُخْت) is the thing being described (مَوْصُوف) because it is not the (male) *student*, who is successful.	النَّاجِحَةُ
فاعِل	Subject; the thing which is being described.	أُخْتُهُ

Don't get confused: The sentence does not start with a verb.

So it is a جُمْلة اِسْميّة, and الطَّالِبُ is the مُبْتَدَأ (subject) as the مُبْتَدَأ has to stand at the beginning of a sentence.

So what about أُخْتُهُ? Why do we say it is the الْفاعِل? Well, grammarians regard it as الْفاعِل. That might sound strange. But it is a tricky construction (two sentences combined).

The word النَّاجِحَةُ does the job of a verb here. It is the اِسْم الْفاعِل (active participle). In Arabic, we say: تَعْمَلُ عَمَلَ فِعْلِها.

223

Still difficult? This is how you could re-write our example by using a اِسْم إِشارة (relative clause).	الطَّالِبُ الَّذِي نَجَحَتْ أُخْتُهُ

Here are some more examples:

The students with the following names succeeded. Or: The students whose names follow (are listed below) succeeded.	الطُّلَّابُ الْآتِيةُ أَسْماؤُهُم نَجَحُوا.
This is how you could rewrite the sentence for easier understanding.	الطُّلَّابُ الَّذينَ أَتَتْ أَسْماؤُهُم نَجَحُوا.
نَعْت	الآتِيةُ
فاعِل	أَسْماؤُهُم

The car whose colour is nice...	السَّيَّارةُ الْجَميلُ لَوْنُها...
This is how you could rewrite the sentence (easier to understand).	السَّيَّارةُ الَّتِي (تَكُونُ) لَوْنُها جَميلٌ...
نَعْت	الْجَميلُ
فاعِل	لَوْنُها

This is a man whose mother is standing.	هٰذا رَجُلٌ قائِمَةٌ أُمُّهُ.
نَعْت	قائِمَةٌ
فاعِل	أُمُّهُ

These are the rules for the النَّعْت السَّبَبِيّ:

1	The النَّعْت السَّبَبِيّ is always <u>singular</u> and comes <u>before</u> the subject of the sentence (فاعِل) which is a اِسْم مَرْفُوع
2	It agrees with the <u>preceding</u> اِسْم in: * definite/indefinite form (تَعْرِيف/تَنْكِير) * إِعْراب
3	It agrees with the <u>following</u> اِسْم - which is the فاعِل - in: * gender (masculine/feminine) (تَذْكِير/ تَأْنِيث)
4	The noun after it (فاعِل) takes the <u>pronoun which refers to the first subject</u> in the sentence! Notice: the فاعِل is always مَرْفُوع

Let us have a look at some examples to understand the rules:

The man whose brother is honourable came.	جاءَ الرَّجُلُ الْفاضِلُ أَخُوهُ.
The man whose two brothers are honourable came.	جاءَ الرَّجُلُ الْفاضِلُ أَخَواهُ.
Two men whose two brothers are honourable came.	جاءَ رَجُلانِ فاضِلٌ أَخَواهُما.
The two men whose sisters are honourable came.	جاءَ الرَّجُلانِ الْفاضِلَةُ أَخَواتُهُما.
Ladies whose sisters are honourable came.	جاءَتْ سَيِّداتٌ فاضِلَةٌ أَخَواتُهُنَّ.

225

A summary:

- The النَّعْت الْحَقِيقِيّ always comes <u>after the noun</u> which it describes. It follows the noun in gender, negated/not negated, case and singular/dual/plural.

- The النَّعْت السَّبَبِيّ always <u>comes before the thing</u> which it describes. It is <u>always singular</u>!

144. WHAT IS THE اِسْم الْفَاعِل OF أَتَى (TO COME)?

If you have a closer look at the verb أَتَى, you will encounter two difficulties:

1. The first root letter is a هَمْزة

2. The last root letter is a ى

So, the regular rules don't work here. For the active participle (*coming*) we need the pattern: فاعِل

Let us first deal with the هَمْزة. The rule is: آ = ا + ء

Now let us check the letter ى at the end. In the indefinite form, the ى is omitted and you have to add تَنْوِين under the second root letter, which all results in: ٍ. If the word is definite, the letter ى will turn into a ي.

Finally, we get:

definite	الآتِي		indefinite; pronounced "aatin"	آتٍ

226

145. أَفْعَلُ - THIS IS THE COMPARATIVE PATTERN, ISN'T IT?

Yes and no. The form أَفْعَلُ is used for 2 different types of words:

1. اِسْم التَّفْضِيل (comparative or superlative) and
2. الصِّفة الْمُشَبَّهة

What is important here:

1. They both share the same pattern for the <u>masculine form</u>. So watch out to identify the correct meaning.

2. The <u>feminine form</u>, however, looks <u>different.</u>

Let us check both patterns:

meaning	feminine pattern	feminine form	اِسْم التَّفْضِيل
bigger	فُعْلى	كُبْرى	أَكْبَرُ
smaller		صُغْرى	أَصْغَرُ

meaning	feminine pattern	feminine form	الصِّفة الْمُشَبَّهة
shining	فَعْلاءُ	زَهْراءُ	أَزْهَرُ
red	used for colours and handicaps	حَمْراءُ	أَحْمَرُ
blind		عَمْياءُ	أَعْمى

146. دُنْيا - WHAT DOES THIS WORD MEAN?

The word دُنْيا is usually translated into English as *world*. The meaning is correct – but the literal translation is totally different. Let us check the root for this word: د - ن - و

The literal meaning of الدُّنْيا is *the lowest* or *the closest* or *the nearest* – and not *world*.

Grammatically speaking, the word دُنْيا is the feminine form of the pattern أَفْعَلُ. It is the comparative or superlative (elative) form, so called اِسْم التَّفْضِيل. The word دُنْيا is generally used in its definite form: الدُّنْيا. The plural of دُنْيا is دُنْيَيات

Let us check this pattern in detail:

meaning	comparative feminine form	comparative masculine form	root
closer; closest	دُنْيا	أَدْنَى	د - ن - و
higher; highest	عُلْيا	أَعْلَى	ع - ل - ى
further; furthest	قُصْوَى	أَقْصَى	ق - ص - و
	Notice the feminine form in the last example! It is different, because in the root, there is a و		

The meaning of دُنْيا is similar to أَقْرَبُ – meaning: *closer*.

A long time ago, people were using the term الْحَياةُ الدُّنْيا for describing the life which is closest to us (namely: life in this world)

228

– because the afterlife/the hereafter (الْحَياة الْآخِرة) is something we don't know. After some time, the word الْحَياة was deleted.

The expression الدُّنْيا is already found in the Qur'an, e.g. 16;30, سُورة النَّحْل (*The bee*)

> ... لِلَّذِينَ أَحْسَنُوا فِي هٰذِهِ الدُّنْيَا حَسَنَةٌ وَلَدَارُ الْآخِرَةِ خَيْرٌ ...
>
> ...for those who do good is a reward in this present world, but the abode of the Hereafter is far better...

A remark: The most famous mosque in Jerusalem, which is also one of the most important in Islam, is called *al-Aqsa-Mosque*. It is called الْأَقْصَى as in old times it was the mosque that was the furthest from Mecca. الْأَقْصَى literally means *the furthest*.

147. الدُّنْيا - HOW DO YOU MARK THE مَجْرُور - CASE HERE?

Just do nothing.

The Alif at the end of the word الدُّنْيا - meaning *the world* or *the nearest* - doesn't change in any case. It is always an Alif.

The word الدُّنْيا is a so called اِسْم مَقْصُور. Grammatically speaking, it can be مَرْفُوع, or مَجْرُور, or مَنْصُوب. However, in any case the case marker is hidden (مُقَدَّرة - a presumptive vowel). This means two things:

1. The case marker it is not pronounced
2. The word looks always the same

Here is an example:

king of the world	مَلِكُ الدُّنْيا

148. WHY IS عُلْيا WRITTEN WITH AN ALIF - BUT كُبْرَى NOT?

First of all, عُلْيا means *higher* and كُبْرَى *larger/greater*. Both words are a so called اِسْم تَفْضيل in the feminine form. But they have something else in common: They are also a so called اِسْم مَقْصُور which means that their last letter is pronounced as an Alif, as a long a-sound.

But how do you know if the last letter is ا (Alif) or ى (Ya)?

This rule might help you: <u>If you see an Alif at the end, it means that there is a و in the root and not a ي</u> !

meaning	root	example
stick	ع - ص - و	عَصا
young man	ف - ت - ي	فَتَى

Now let us go back again to our initial question:

explanation	feminine comparative
Before the last letter, there is a ى in the root. So you have to write an Alif at the end.	عُلْيا, دُنْيا

230

Before the last letter, there is a ر There is no weak letter in the root. So you have to write the letter ى, pronounced as an Alif ("aa"-sound).	كُبْرَى

149. HOW DO YOU SAY "STILL"?

The word *still* refers to the fact that an action is not yet over or something or somebody has not changed its status/shape. It is translated into German with *(immer) noch sein* or *solange*.

In Arabic, unfortunately, there is no simple word for *still*.

You have to express *still* by a negated verb. The verbs that are used to express *still* follow the same rules as كانَ وَأَخَواتُها.

Let us quickly remember the special rules of كانَ by looking at an example: كانَ الْجَوُّ جَميلاً - *The weather was nice.*

The subject (إِسْم كان) is مَرْفُوع and the predicate (خَبَر كان) is مَنْصُوب.

Now let us go back to *still*. It is important to know that you can use the verbs in the following table in the present or past tense – the meaning in Arabic is the same.

But don't forget:

- the present tense (الْمُضارِع) is negated with لا
- the past tense (الْماضِي) with: لَمْ or ما

Here are some possibilities to express the meaning of *still*.

Notice that you can use a فِعْل or a اِسْم directly after the verbs.

جِذْر: ز- و- ل	ما زالَ / لا يَزالُ
Meaning: *still; yet.* German: *noch; noch immer* Literally the verb - if not negated - means: *to come to an end; to vanish; to abandon*	
He is still sick.	ما زالَ مَريضًا.
She is still sitting.	لا تَزالُ جالِسةً.
He still needs it.	لا يَزالُ فِي حاجةٍ إِلَيْهِ.
He is still a student.	ما زالَ طالِبًا.

جذر: ف - ك - ك	ما اِنْفَكَّ = لَمْ يَنْفَكَّ / لا يَنْفَكُّ
Meaning: *not stop doing; keep doing.* German: *nicht aufhören zu tun.* It has the verb pattern اِنْفَعَلَ If not negated, it means *to be separated; be disconnected; be undone.* In its root-form, فَكَّ means *to separate; disjoin; disconnect.*	
The man is still writing.	ما اِنْفَكَّ الرَّجُلُ كاتِبًا.

جِذْر: ف - ت - ء	ما فَتِئَ = لَمْ يَفْتَأْ / لا يَفْتَأُ
Meaning: *not to cease to be.* German: *nicht aufhören zu sein*	

Without negation, the verb means *to desist, refrain or stop.*	
He is still doing...	...مَا فَتِئَ يَفْعَلُ
He is still thinking about her.	مَا فَتِئَ يَذْكُرُها.
He always will be.	لَنْ يَفْتَأَ.
Khalid is always trying to travel.	مَا فَتِئَ خَالِدٌ يُحَأْوِلُ السَّفَرَ.

جِذْر: ب - ر - ح	مَا بَرِحَ, لَم يَبْرَحْ / لَا يَبْرَحُ
Meaning: *to continue to be.* German: *nicht aufhören zu sein.*	
If not negated, the meaning is *to leave; to depart.*	
He is still rich.	مَا بَرِحَ غَنِيًّا.
They are still in London.	مَا بَرِحوا فِي لَنْدَن.

150. HOW DO YOU SAY "NOT YET"?

This is more difficult in Arabic than in English or German. In Egyptian Arabic, for instance, you can use the word لِسَّه – meaning *still* or *not yet* – see chapter 151.

But in standard Arabic? In this chapter, we will have a look at a group of expressions that are somehow related to each other: *still; yet; not yet; not any more.*

Here are the general forms:

1.1	(2) بَعْدُ + negated verb (1)	not yet

- Notice: The word بَعْدُ is an <u>adverb of time</u>, and as such <u>can theoretically appear anywhere</u> in the sentence. However, in verbal sentences, it sounds more natural at the end of a sentence (and not between the verb and the direct object).
- Watch out: It is possible to use بَعْدُ without a negation.
- Notice the difference: بَعْدَ with a فَتْحة means *after*. See chapter 221

He has not written the letter yet.	لَمْ يَكْتُبْ بَعْدُ الْجَوابَ.
	ما كَتَبَ الْجَوابَ بَعْدُ.

Notice: It is usually better to put بَعْدُ at the end of the sentence. But right after the verb is also correct.

He had not written the letter yet.	لَمْ يَكُنْ قَدْ كَتَبَ بَعْدُ الْجَوابَ.
	ما كانَ قَدْ كَتَبَ بَعْدُ الْجَوابَ.
He will not have written the letter yet.	كانَ لَنْ يَكْتُبَ بَعْدُ الْجَوابَ.
	كانَ سَوْفَ لا يَكْتُبُ بَعْدُ الْجَوابَ.

1.2	بَعْدُ	not any more
Same as 1.1. The meaning depends on the context.		
Nobody else came then.		لَمْ يَأْتِ أَحَدٌ بَعْدُ.
She doesn't write any more.		هِيَ لا تَكْتُبُ بَعْدُ.

2	لَمَّا + فِعْل مَجْزُوم	not yet
	He has not written the letter yet.	لَمَّا يَكْتُبْ الْجَوابَ.

3	*عادَ / يَعُودُ + فِعْل مُضارِع * negated with ما or لا, لَمْ	not any more
	The director did not go to the office any more.	لَمْ يَعُدْ الْمُديرُ يَذْهَبُ إِلَى الْمَكْتَبِ.
		ما عادَ الْمُديرُ يَذْهَبُ إِلَى الْمَكْتَبِ.
	The director doesn't go to the office any more.	لا يَعُودُ الْمُديرُ يَذْهَبُ إِلَى الْمَكْتَبِ.

Watch out: A negation particle can change the meaning (or not):

not yet; not longer; not any more	لَيْسَ بَعْدُ
She is still young. (She is only a small girl.) Notice here that we don't use the negation.	هِيَ بَعْدُ صَغِيرَةٌ.
He is yet to come.	سَيَأْتِي بَعْدُ.
He has not come yet.	لَمْ يَأْتِ بَعْدُ.

151. THE EGYPTIAN WORD لِسَّه – IS IT "STILL" OR "YET"?

It can mean both: *still* or *yet*.

It depends on the context if لِسّه (pronounced "lissa") has the meaning of *still* or *(not) yet*. It is a common expression in Egyptian Arabic and pretty often used in Arabic movies or TV-shows. Apart from the meaning of *still* and *(not) yet*, لِسّه can also describe that something has happened just now.

Let us have a look at some examples (inspired by the dictionary of Martin Hinds; A Dictionary of Egyptian Arabic; 1987):

1. <u>Meaning *still* or *yet*</u>

She is still young.	هِيَ لِسّه صُغَيَّرة.
Haven't you gone yet?	إنتَ لِسّه مارُحْتِش؟
Still three dollars (to go; owing).	لِسّه ثلاثة دولار.
It is not yet a month since he has left.	سافِر لِسّه مافيش شَهْر.
I've still to read the magazine.	لِسّه هأقْرَأ الْمَجَلّة.
Has he come yet or not?	جاء ولّا لِسّه؟
Have you seen the student? - Not yet.	شُفْت الطّالِب؟ - لِسّه
You haven't seen anything yet!	هُوَ إنْتَ لِسّه شُفْت حاجة!
It is still early (still plenty of time)	لِسّه بَدْري.

2. <u>Meaning of *just*: *just now*; *only recently*</u>

She was standing next to me just a second ago.	دي لِسّه كانِت واقِفة جنبي من ثانية.	١

The lady who had just come from the doctor...	٢ السِتّ اللّي كانِت لِسّه جايّة مِن عَنْد الدُّكْتُور...

152. مَتْحَف OR مُتْحَف - WHAT IS THE WORD FOR "MUSEUM"?

Speaking in dialects, most Arab people call a *museum* مَتْحَف – pronounced with a فَتْحة at the beginning. Although there is only a slight difference, it is strictly speaking wrong although the *Academy of the Arabic Language* in Cairo has approved it.

The root is: ت - ح - ف. It primarily means *to present; to show.* But the root is only used in the verb pattern أَفْعَل

If we want to build the اِسْم الْمَكان - the place where something is being displayed - we have to watch out:

meaning	verb	pattern	اِسْم الْمَكان
museum	أَتْحَفَ	أَفْعَل	مُتْحَف

The word is pronounced with a ضَمّة at the beginning: مُتْحَف. So what is مَتْحَف then?

مَتْحَف would be the اِسْم الْمَكان for a I-verb (ثُلاثيّ مُجَرَّد). But this form is not used. The I-verb تَحَفَ basically doesn't exist.

This brings us to a general rule:

If you want to build the اِسْم الْمَكان from verb-forms II to X, you make use of the same pattern as for the اِسْم الْمَفْعُول.

Don't mix them up in a sentence as they look exactly the same. Take for example the word مُبْتَعَثٌ:

It can mean *source* (اِسْم الْمَكان) or *sent* (اِسْم الْمَفْعُول).

Here are some examples:

form	verb	meaning	اِسْم الْمَكان	meaning
II	صَلَّى	to pray	مُصَلَّى	place of prayer
IV	أَتْحَفَ	to present	مُتْحَف	museum
VII	اِنْبَعَثَ	to originate	مُنْبَعَثٌ	place of origin; source
VIII	اِجْتَمَعَ	to gather together	مُجْتَمَعٌ	gathering place
X	اِشْتَفَى	to seek a cure	مُسْتَشْفًى	hospital

153. مُبْتَدَأ - WHAT IS THAT?

You might know that a مُبْتَدَأ is the subject of a nominal sentence. That is correct. But have you ever thought about what مُبْتَدَأ literally means? Well, let's have a look.

The root is ب - د - ء. From this root, we build a VIII-form-verb following the pattern: اِفْتَعَلَ. So we get the verb: اِبْتَدَأ. This verb means: *to begin; to start; to bring out sth.*

Let's come back to our word: مُبْتَدَأ.

It can mean two things:

1. It can be the اِسْم الْمَفْعُول of the verb اِبْتَدَأ which would mean: *begun*

2. It can also be the اِسْم الْمَكَان which would mean: *the place where it* (the sentence) *begins*

Why is that?

The اِسْم الْمَفْعُول and اِسْم الْمَكَان may share the same pattern as shown in chapter 172. If we are talking about the subject of a nominal sentence, we basically mean the first word. I also use the word subject in the book. But it is a good idea to think about the literal meaning of grammar terms when studying grammar.

Let us now go back to the grammatical features of the الْمُبْتَدَأ:

- The subject of a nominal sentence cannot be a verb, or a prepositional or adverbial phrase (شِبْه الْجُمْلة).

- If a sentence starts with a preposition or an adverb, it is the predicate, so called: خَبَر مُقَدَّم (used for emphasis)

The الْخَبَر (predicate) of a nominal sentence can consist of:

- a single noun

- a verbal or nominal sentence

- a quasi-sentence (شِبْه الْجُمْلة)

Now have a look at these two sentences:

239

جُمْلة فِعْلِيَّة	١ ذَهَبَ مُحَمَّدٌ إِلَى الْمَدِينةِ.
جُمْلة اِسْمِيّة	٢ مُحَمَّدٌ ذَهَبَ إِلَى الْمَدِينةِ.

Both mean exactly the same: *Muhammad went to the city*. But grammatically, there is a big difference. Let us analyse it:

In the <u>first sentence</u>, مُحَمَّدٌ is the subject of a verbal sentence, so called الْفاعِل. If we only used the first word of this sentence – the verb ذَهَبَ -, it would be enough to form a sentence, even without the word Muhammad. So we would get: ذَهَبَ. This is a complete sentence. The hidden pronoun in ذَهَبَ - which is "*he*" (the ending of the verb!) - would be the الْفاعِل (subject).

In the <u>second sentence</u>, مُحَمَّدٌ is the subject of a nominal sentence or so called: الْمُبْتَدَأ. If we only used the first word - Muhammad -, it would not be enough to form a sentence.

The <u>subject of a nominal sentence needs a predicate</u>. The predicate completes the meaning. What is the function of the verb in a nominal sentence? It is the predicate!

So we have a full sentence within the predicate itself (a compound structure).

first sentence	ذَهَبَ إِلَى الْمَدِينةِ.	+	مُحَمَّدٌ
	predicate: <u>a verbal sentence</u>!		subject
second sentence	It is a full sentence itself: *He went to the city.*		

154. HOW CAN YOU GIVE SPECIAL EMPHASIS?

In Arabic, there are a lot of possibilities to give special emphasis,
so called: تَأْكِيد or تَوْكِيد. In this chapter, we will have a look at a
very sophisticated way – by using the letter ل:

1	الإِبْتِداء literally means *the beginning*.	لام الإبْتِداء
	The ل for emphasizing is never combined with a verb! It always precedes the المُبْتَدَأ (subject in a nominal sentence).	
	You are (truly, indeed) a faithful friend.	لَأَنْتَ صَدِيقٌ وَفِيٌّ.

2	*What a wonderful... what a bad...!*	نِعْمَ / بِئْسَ
	Expressions like these two can be connected with a ل in order to make the meaning even stronger. See chapter 183 for more details.	
	The best thing a person can do is to seek knowledge.	لَنِعْمَ ما يَفْعَلُهُ الإِنْسانُ طَلَبُ الْعِلْمِ.
	The worst character is lying.	لَبِئْسَ خُلُقًا الْكَذِبُ.

3	ل plus far future with سَوْفَ	لَسَوْفَ
	I will (definitely) attend the party.	لَسَوْفَ أَحْضُرُ الْحَفْلَ.

4	ل used in the second part of a if-clause with لَوْ or لَوْلا	لام الْواقِع
	If there was no doctor, the situation of	لَوْلا الطَّبِيبُ لَساءَتْ

	the patient would become bad.	حالة الْمَرِيض.

5	ل before the predicate of إِنَّ	خَبَر إِنَّ
	The satisfaction of people is difficult in-deed.	إِنَّ رِضا النَّاسِ لَصَعْبٌ.

6	ل before the noun of إِنَّ	اِسْم إِنَّ
	There is (indeed) benefit in travelling.	إِنَّ فِي السَّفَرِ لَمَنافِعَ.

For other possibilities to give emphasis, see chapters 155, 157, 159.

155. CAN YOU USE AN ADDITIONAL ن TO GIVE EMPHASIS?

Yes. The letter ن is a more complicated possibility to give emphasis. There is a "light" and a "strong" form.

You can use the نُون التَّوْكِيد (emphasis with the letter ن) with the <u>present tense</u> (الْمُضارِع) and the <u>imperative</u> (أَمْر) – but you cannot use it with the past (الْماضِي).

Here is how it works:

A	The <u>light</u> ن It is formed by adding a ن with a سُكُون	ن خَفِيفة ساكِنة
	Obey your parents!	أَطِيعَنْ والِدَّيْكَ!

B	The <u>strong/heavy</u> ن This form is more common. Here is how you build it:	ن ثَقِيلة

1.	Delete the ضمّة on the verb (marker for present tense) or delete the final ن if the verb-form belongs to the so called الْأَفْعال الْخَمْسة ("five verbs")
2.	<u>Add a</u> فَتْحة (ˉ) <u>on the last letter</u>
3.	Finally, add نّ → Note: do the same for the imperative

Do you (really) help your friend?	هَلْ تُساعِدَنَّ زَمِيلَكَ؟

Let us analyse the "heavy" ن in detail:

1.	نّ – used to express a demand or inquiry	مُضارِع جائِز

1.1	Used with the imperative. Notice that you have to use the لام الطَّلَب, namely لِ, before the imperative. See chapter 125.	أَمْر
	Beware of overeating!	لِتَحْذَرَنَّ الإِفْراطَ فِي الطَّعامِ!

1.2	Used to express warnings or prohibitions	نَهْي
	Don't think that success in life is easy!	لاَ تَحْسَبَنَّ النَّجاحَ فِي الْحَياةِ سَهْلاً!

1.3	Used with questions to express a request	إِسْتِفْهام
	Could you help your colleague?	هَلْ تُساعِدَنَّ زَمِيلَكَ؟

1.4	Used to give advice/offer	عَرْض
	Shouldn't you certainly help your colleague!	أَلا تُساعِدَنَّ زَمِيلَكَ!

1.5	Used to goad somebody	تَحْضِيض
	Would you stop lying!	هَلَّا تَتْرُكَنَّ الْكَذِبَ!

1.6	Used to express a wish, hope or desire	تَمَنٍّ
	I wish that you would do good deeds!	لَيْتَكَ تَعْمَلَنَّ طَيِّبًا!

2	After the negation with لا → to put stress on the thing you won't do or accept
	I like honesty and I won't tolerate lying. أُحِبُّ الصِّدْقَ وَلا أَرْضَيَنَّ الْكَذِبَ.

3	After the word إِمَّا used in a conditional sentence – شَرْطِيَّة Notice the سُكُون in the second part of the sentence as the verb has to be مَجْزُوم

244

If you really work hard you will certainly succeed in your life.	إِمَّا تَعْمَلَنَّ بِجِدٍّ تَنْجَحْ فِي حَيَاتِكَ.

4	After an oath – الْمُضَارِع الْوَاجِب التَّوْكِيد The verb gives the details why you swear and what you promise, so called جَوَاب قَسَم. It is not negated and although the verb is in the present tense, it has a future meaning. Notice: After an oath you (normally) need a لَ – see chapter 206.

	I swear I will definitely work hard!	وَاللَّهِ لَأَعْمَلَنَّ بِجِدٍّ!
4.1	I swear I write the letter now!	وَاللَّهِ لَأَكْتُبُ رِسَالَةَ الْآنَ!
	If there is no conditional meaning involved, you don't use the ن	

156. WHAT ARE THE PARTICLES FOR ATTENTION?

Particles which are used to call somebody's attention to something or somebody are called أَحْرُف التَّنْبِيه.

There are several words that can be used to give emphasis on parts of a sentence. It is important to identify them correctly.

The common ones are:

particles for attention - أَحْرُف التَّنْبِيه		
This is called الْاِسْتِفْتَاحِيّة which literally means *the beginning*. It is a particle of inauguration that is often found in the	أَلَا	1

Qur'an.

This particle is an intensifying interjection introducing sentences: *verily; truly; indeed; oh yes,* ...

It is with knowledge that nations advance.	أَلا بِالْعِلْمِ تَتَقَدَّمُ الْأُمَمُ.
"Unquestionably, it is Allah who is the Forgiving, the Merciful." (Qur'an, سُورة الشُّورى (*The consultation*), 42;5)	أَلا إِنَّ اللهَ هُوَ الْغَفُورُ الرَّحِيمُ.

	أَما	2
Same meaning as أَلا – but watch out: أَما is usually combined with an oath.		
I swear he is truly honest!	أَما وَاللهِ إِنَّهُ لَصَادِقٌ!	

	ها	3
The particle ها has an emphatic meaning. It can be connected with other words. It basically just means: *look here, oh*		
Here I am.	هَأَنَذا حاضِرٌ.	
Here	هاهُنا	
and so forth (and so on)	وَهَكَذا	
Hey you there!	ها أَنْتَ ذا!	
Hey you (fem.) there!	ها أَنْتِ ذي!	
Here, take it! There you are! There you have!	هاكَ / هاكُم (pl.)	

246

157. CAN YOU USE بِ AND مِنْ TO EMPHASIZE?

Yes, this is possible. Both - بِ or مِنْ - can be used to give emphasis, so called أَحْرُف الزِّيادة (additional letters). Notice that the word which comes after بِ or مِنْ has to be مَجْرُور:

1	The letter بِ
Travelling is not difficult at all.	لَيْسَ السَّفَرُ بِصَعْبٍ.
Knowledge is sufficient (an enough way) to advance.	كَفَى بِالْعِلْمِ وَسِيلَةً لِلتَّقَدُّمِ.
Allah is the best protector!	كَفَى بِاللهِ وَكِيلاً.
Note: The verb كَفَى basically means *to be enough*. However, it can also mean *to protect*; *to spare*. It is used <u>without</u> a preposition. The preposition بِ here is used to give emphasis.	
2	The preposition مِنْ There has to be a singular noun (اِسْم نَكِرة) after it. Notice that there is no difference in meaning whether the sentence is written with or without مِنْ – it is just the emphasis!
Nobody came to me.	ما جاءَنِي مِنْ أَحَدٍ.

158. WHAT DOES A (SOLO) PERSONAL PRONOUN EXPRESS?

It can be used to give emphasis. You can easily emphasize a اِسْم by just adding the corresponding personal pronoun in its normal form after the اِسْم which you want to focus on.

This form is called صَمِير الْفَصْل – as it separates the subject from the predicate and provides some space in between.

Let us have a look at some examples:

It is <u>Khalid</u> who sits there.	خالِدٌ هُوَ الْجالِسُ هُناكَ.
The <u>engineers</u> were the ones responsible for the success of the project.	كانَ الْمُهَنْدِسُونَ هُم الْمَسْؤُولِينَ عَنْ نَجاحِ الْمَشْرُوعِ.
<u>I</u> have done my duty.	قُمْتُ أَنا بِالْواجِبِ.
<u>He</u> wrote the lesson himself.	كَتَبَ هُوَ الدَّرْسَ.

159. DO YOU KNOW EXPRESSIONS THAT ARE USED FOR EMPHASIS?

If you want to place emphasis on something, you can use particles, words – or expressions. Let us check some of them. Notice the ending (فَتْحة) of the word after لا – see chapter 250.

doubtless; not doubt	لا رَيْبَ فِي
doubtless; without doubt	لا شَكَّ
indisputably	لا جِدالَ
unquestionable	لا مِراءَ
I say firmly...	أَقُولُ جازِمًا...
I say for sure...	أَقُولُ عَنْ يَقِينٍ...

248

160. WHEN DO YOU USE A PRONOUN IN A RELATIVE SENTENCE?

You never (visibly) decline the relative pronoun (إِسْم الْمَوْصُول) in Arabic. For example: الَّذِي stays the same in all cases, no matter if it means *which, who* or *whom*. (The only exception is the dual! See chapter 112.) In German, however, you decline the relative pronoun, e.g. *welch - welcher - welche – welches*.

So what happens in Arabic? Let's check it step by step:

Without a possessive pronoun (مَرْفُوع)	A
The lazy man. = The man who is lazy.	الرَّجُلُ الْكَسُولُ. = الرَّجُلُ الَّذِي هُوَ كَسُولٌ.
Here, the relative pronoun would be in the <u>nominative case</u> in English or German (not declined). The information in the relative clause has the same case as the subject. You could rewrite the sentence and it would keep the same meaning.	
The man who came...	الرَّجُلُ الَّذِي جَاءَ.
You wouldn't decline the relative pronoun in English. Imagine the sentence <u>without the relative pronoun</u> (*The man came*): This perfectly makes sense – so you don't need a possessive pronoun.	
With a possessive pronoun	B
The man whom I knew.... (attached to a verb)	الرَّجُلُ الَّذِي عَرَفْتُ**هُ**...
Have you found the keys that you lost? (attached to a verb)	هَلْ وَجَدْتَ الْمَفَاتِيحَ الَّتِي فَقَدْتَ**هَا**؟

249

This is the pen that you asked for. (attached to a preposition)	هذا الْقَلَمُ الَّذِي سَأَلْتَ عَنْهُ.
This is the professor whose book I read. (attached to a noun)	هذا هُوَ الْأُسْتاذُ الَّذِي قَرَأْتُ كِتابَهُ.

Try to imagine these sentences (B) without the relative pronoun – they wouldn't make sense. In all these examples, the relative pronoun would be declined in English (*whom*) or in German (*Der Mann, den...*).

In Arabic, however, the word الَّذِي is مَبْنِيّ. Although it doesn't change its form, we still say that it is فِي مَحَلّ رَفْع (*nominative*) or نَصْب (*accusative*) or جَرّ (*genitive*).

If the information, which precedes the relative pronoun, is referred to as an object, or as having a preposition, or as being a genitive attribute, it has to be resumed by a <u>suffix possessive pronoun in the second part of the sentence</u> (after the relative pronoun). Which means: The pronoun has to be attached to the verb, to a preposition, or a noun.

This back-referring suffix pronoun is called الْعائِد which literally means *the returner*.

161. الَّذِي AND مَنْ - WHEN DO YOU USE WHICH WORD?

First of all, both express the meaning of a relative pronoun (اِسْم الْمَوْصُول): *this; that; the one; which; whom; who*.

regarding a specific person	الَّذِي	1
for a general statement	مَنْ	2

I like the professor who cares about his students.	أُحِبُّ الْأُسْتَاذَ الَّذِي يَهْتَمُّ بِطُلَّابِهِ.	1
I like (one) who cares about students.	أُحِبُّ مَنْ يَهْتَمُّ بِطُلَّابٍ.	2

This is similar to ما which is also used for general statements:

I like the (two) dresses that my (two) friends have bought.	أُحِبُّ الْفُسْتَانَيْنِ اللَّتَيْنِ اِشْتَرَتْهُما صَدِيقَتَي.	1
I like what I bought.	أُحِبُّ ما اِشْتَرَيْتُهُ.	2
But watch out: You don't use ها at the end of the second sentence. It is ه – as in general statements, the masculine pronoun is used!		

162. EXACTLY 20 OR MORE THAN TWENTY – HOW DO YOU KNOW?

In Arabic, there is a nice way of expressing that you are talking about an exact amount of people/things or only about an approximate amount.

Look at these two examples:

exactly 20	قَابَلْتُ عِشْرِينَ طَالِبًا
about/more than twenty	قَابَلْتُ عِشْرِينَ مِن الطُّلَّابِ

So if we use the construction مِنْ plus the plural form of a noun, we can indicate that we are not talking about an exact number.

163. TRANSITIVE OR INTRANSITIVE – WHAT IS THE DIFFERENCE?

For a better understanding of verbs it is useful to understand the difference between a transitive and an intransitive verb.

- A verb is called <u>intransitive</u> if it <u>can't have a direct object</u>. It can only have a subject – which is the one who carries out the action. In Arabic, an intransitive verb is called: فِعْل لازِم

Let us have a look at an example:

The child sat down.	جَلَسَ الْوَلَدُ.
The child broke the cup. Notice: The verb needs an object. Otherwise, the sentence would not work.	كَسَرَ الطِّفْلُ الْكُوبَ.
The player runs. Notice: There is no object.	جَرَى اللَّاعِبُ.

It is impossible to use a direct object with the verb *to sit*, as the action can only be done by the doer – but the doer can't do it to a thing or an object.

Contrary to this, a transitive verb (فِعْل مُتَعَدٍّ) can carry an object. The object is the answer to the question: *what?*

In Arabic, there are verbs that can have two, even three objects.

- If a verb can carry only one object, it is called:

مُتَعَدٍّ إِلَى مَفْعُول واحِد

- If a verb can carry two objects (direct and indirect):

مُتَعَدٍّ إِلَى مَفْعُولَيْنِ - see chapter 109 for more details.

164.   WHY DO WE SAY: "TALIBAN"?

The word *Taliban,* which is the name of a hardline Islamic movement in Afghanistan and Pakistan, is not an Arabic word. It is commonly mistaken that طالِبان is the Arabic dual and therefore describes *two students.*

- The Arabic plural of طالِب is طُلّاب.

- The plural for طالِب in the Pashto language is طالِبان. The meaning is the same as طُلّاب: students.

165.   تاريخ - WHAT IS THE ROOT OF THIS WORD?

The word تاريخ means *history.* The root is ء - ر - خ.

It is worth digging deeper into this root. The corresponding verb for history is أَرَّخَ, a II-verb following the paradigm فَعَّلَ.

As the مَصْدَر of these verbs follows the pattern تَفْعِيل, the مَصْدَر of the verb أَرَّخَ is تَأْرِيخ – notice the هَمْزة on top of the Alif. تَأْرِيخ describes the *process of writing down history or dates.*

253

The one, who is writing down the history (إِسْم الْفَاعِل), is the مُؤَرِّخ. The result of تَأْرِيخ is تَارِيخ = *history*. Notice that the Alif doesn't take a هَمْزة!

تَارِيخ is a إِسْم which describes a result. Whereas the مَصْدَر of the verb is describing the process of reaching the goal of the action, the so called هَدَف – it describes the process, and not the result.

A remark:

ء - ر - خ is probably not an Arabic root. The original root is w – r – kh. In Accadian and Hebrew it means *moon* and *month*, from which the idea of a *calendar* and *date* arose.

166. HOW DO YOU CONVERT TRANSITIVE VERBS INTO INTRANSITIVE?

Every verb has a subject – but not every verb has an object.

A verb which can carry an object is a transitive verb or فِعْل مُتَعَدٍّ.

A verb which can't carry an object and therefore only has a subject is called intransitive verb or فِعْل لَازِم.

A single letter – either added or deleted – can convert a transitive verb into an intransitive verb or vice versa.

There are several ways to convert <u>transitive into intransitive</u> verbs. Let's see how it works:

translation	transitive	translation	intransitive
I	أَفْعَلَ ->		فَعَلَ
The policeman threw the thief out of the house.	أَخْرَجَ الشُّرْطِيُّ اللِّصَ مِنَ الْبَيْتِ.	The thief got out of the house.	خَرَجَ اللِّصُّ مِنَ الْبَيْتِ.
2	فَاعَلَ ->		فَعَلَ
Muhammad sat with the guest.	جَالَسَ مُحَمَّدٌ الضَّيْفَ.	The guest sat.	جَلَسَ الضَّيْفُ.
3	اِسْتَفْعَلَ ->		فَعِلَ
The company brought tourists to Egypt.	اِسْتَقْدَمَتِ الشَّرِكَةُ السُّيَّاحَ إِلَى مِصْرَ.	The tourists came to Egypt.	قَدِمَ السُّيَّاحُ إِلَى مِصْرَ.
4	فَعَّلَ ->		فَعُلَ
The student improved his handwriting.	حَسَّنَ الطَّالِبُ خَطَّهُ.	The handwriting of the student is nice.	حَسُنَ خَطُّ الطَّالِبِ.

255

There are also possibilities to convert <u>intransitive</u> verbs (without an object) into <u>transitive</u> verbs:

	translation	intransitive	translation	<u>transitive</u>
I		اِنْفَعَلَ, تَفَعَّلَ <-		فَعَلَ
	The cup got broken.	اِنْكَسَرَ الْكُوبُ.	The child broke the cup.	كَسَرَ الطَّفْلُ الْكُوبَ.
	The cup broke into pieces.	تَكَسَّرَ الْكُوبُ.		

		افْتَعَلَ <-		فَعَلَ
2				
	The cup is full with water.	اِمْتَلَأَ الْكُوبُ بِالْماءِ.	The child filled the cup with water.	مَلَأَ الطَّفْلُ الْكُوبَ بِالْماءِ.

167. WHAT IS SO SPECIAL ABOUT "A KILOGRAM OF SUGAR"?

It is the grammar. When you say *I buy a kilo, a litre* or *a hectare* it is a pretty vague information because you don't say what kind of good you are actually buying.

The sentence becomes clear as soon as you add a specification – which is called تَمْيِيز in Arabic. It will give you an answer to the question: *what?* (ماذا؟)

However, there are several grammatical problems involved. Let us first check the grammar terms:

You give me a litre (of) milk.	.تُعْطِينِي لِتْرًا لَبَنًا
This is called *the specification*: التَّمْيِيز	لِتْرًا
This is called *the distinguished*: الْمُمَيَّز	لَبَنًا

If you want to express *a kilo (of) sugar*, you can choose between three different possibilities which all mean exactly the same. However, the case markers might be different:

Add the word *sugar* directly	.اِشْتَرَيْتُ كِيلُو سُكَّرًا	1
Notice that the الْمُمَيَّز - in our example *sugar* - has to be مَنْصُوب		
Use a إضافة-construction	.اِشْتَرَيْتُ كِيلُو سُكَّرٍ	2
Notice that الْمُمَيَّز is the second part of the إضافة and therefore has to be مَجْرُور		
Construction with مِن	.اِشْتَرَيْتُ كِيلُو مِن سُكَّرٍ	3
The الْمُمَيَّز follows a preposition and therefore has to be مَجْرُور		

The specification doesn't have to be a classical unit like *kg*, *litre*, etc. It can also be of other type (no measurement):

I bought (a bouquet) of flowers.	.اِشْتَرَيْتُ بَاقَةً زَهْرًا
I bought a sack of tea.	.اِشْتَرَيْتُ كِيسًا شَايًا

Even most of the numbers are a form of تَمْيِيز

	grammar	translation	example
3-10	جَمْع مَجْرُور	In the room are 7 students.	فِي الْغُرْفةِ سَبْعةُ طُلّابٍ.
11 - 99	مُفْرَد مَنْصُوب	In the room are 11 students.	فِي الْغُرْفةِ أَحَدَ عَشَرَ طالِبًا.
100	مُفْرَد مَجْرُور	The faculty has 100 professors.	فِي كُلِّيَّةِ مِئَةُ أُسْتاذٍ.
1000	مُفْرَد مَجْرُور	The faculty has 4000 students.	فِي كُلِّيَّةِ أَرْبَعةُ آلافِ طالِبٍ.

There is only one exception: The numbers 1 and 2 are not a تَمْيِيز

In the office, there is one (male) employee and two (female) employees.	فِي الْمَكْتَبِ مُوَظَّفٌ واحِدٌ, وَمُوَظَّفَتانِ اثْنَتانِ.
Notice: The number comes after the noun! It is a صِفة and needs agreement with the preceding اِسْم	

One last remark: Also a comparison can be a form of التَّمْيِيز

Cairo is more crowded than Alexandria.	الْقاهِرةُ أَكْثَرُ اِزِدِحامًا مِن الإِسْكَنْدَرِيّةِ.
In this example, the word اِزِدِحامًا is the الْمُمَيَّز. It makes clear what you are talking about – without it, the sentence wouldn't make sense.	

168.‎ يَخْتَلِفُ النَّاسُ ثَقافةً‎ - WHAT DOES IT MEAN?

Before we move on to the translation we should have a look at the construction of the sentence: ‎يَخْتَلِفُ النَّاسُ ثَقافةً‎

We have to deal with a sentence that has changed its word order.

In Arabic grammar, sentences like these are called ‎تَمْيِيز الْجُمْلة‎ or ‎تَمْيِيز الْنِسْبة‎ which literally means: *specification of the sentence* or *specification of the relation*.

In principle, you could also just say ‎يَخْتَلِفُ النَّاسُ‎ – and it would perfectly make sense: *people differ*. It would be a general saying as you have removed the additional information which made it specific – the so called ‎التَّمْيِيز‎. However, they could differ in thinking, in talking, etc.

That is the reason why in our given example, the additional information - the thing that determines why people differ: the word *culture* - is noticeable (‎الْمُمَيِّز مَلْحُوظ‎).

The culture of the people differs. This was the original sentence, formed by using a ‎إضافة‎-construction.	‎تَخْتَلِفُ ثَقافةُ النَّاسِ.‎
This is how the sentence got restructured by keeping the same meaning. Notice two things: 1) the different form of the verb (here it is masculine; above: feminine) 2) the word *culture* has the ‎مَنْصُوب‎-case because it is a ‎تَمْيِيز‎	‎يَخْتَلِفُ النَّاسُ ثَقافةً.‎

What we have seen above can be applied to different parts of a sentence. Notice that the following examples - original sentence and التَّمْيِيز - mean the same. (A remark: I didn't use the proper helping vowels - e.g. in اِشْتَعَلَتْ - to make the difference clearer.)

what has changed	التَّمْيِيز	original sentence	
subject	اِشْتَعَلَ الْبَيْتُ نَارًا.	اِشْتَعَلَتِ النَّارُ فِي الْبَيْتِ.	١
	The house caught fire.		
object	نَظَّمَ الْقَائِدُ الْجُنُودَ صُفُوفًا.	نَظَّمَ الْقَائِدُ صُفُوفَ الْجُنُودِ.	٢
	The leader organized the soldiers to stand in a line.		
	Notice: You have to change the order of the إِضَافة and delete the definite article.		
comparative, superlative	هذا الطَّالِبُ أَشَدُّ ذَكَاءً.	---	٣
	This student is the most intelligent.		

169. دَعَا - WHAT IS THE اِسْم الْمَفْعُول OF THIS VERB?

The verb دَعَا means *to call, to invite*.

The passive participle (اِسْم الْمَفْعُول) has the pattern مَفْعُول.

But if you deal with a verb whose root contains either a و or ي (حَرْف الْعِلّة), you have to watch out.

Let us first examine some examples that follow the regular rules:

translation	إسْم الْمَفْعُول	verb
to understand - *understood*	مَفْهُومٌ	فَهِمَ
to read - *was read*	مَقْرُوءٌ	قَرَأَ
to break - *broken*	مَكْسُورٌ	كَسَرَ

Remember that the هَمْزة is not a weak letter!

The verb قَرَأَ (*to read*) follows the regular rules, except that you have to pay attention how to write the هَمْزة correctly: مَقْرُوءٌ

So how about verbs that contain weak letters?

translation	إسْم الْمَفْعُول	verb
to invite or call - *invited* or *called*	مَدْعُوٌّ	دَعَا - يَدْعُو
to say - *said*	مَقُولٌ	قَالَ - يَقُولُ
to sell - *sold*	مَبِيعٌ	بَاعَ - يَبِيعُ
to forget - *forgotten*	مَنْسِيٌّ	نَسَى - يَنْسَى
to throw - *thrown*	مَرْمِيٌّ	رَمَى - يَرْمِي

So we have the <u>answer to our question</u>: مَدْعُوٌّ

Verbs that have a weak letter in the middle (مُعْتَلّ الْوَسَط) are called أَجْوَف which literally means: *hollow*. For example: قَالَ

Verbs which have a weak letter at the end (مُعْتَلّ الآخِر) are called نَاقِص which literally means *missing*. See also chapter 152.

In order to get the correct (middle or last) letter for a passive participle check the present tense (الْمُضَارِع) first. The الْمُضَارِع shows you how the weak letter changes. This means:

- If the present tense verb ends in a و or ى, the passive participle will have a شَدّة on the last letter.

The اِسْم الْمَفْعُول for verbs with more than three letters (not root letters!) is easily formed: <u>You just add مُ to the verb in the past-tense stem.</u> If it starts with ا, delete the ا. Unfortunately, the اِسْم الْفَاعِل (active participle) looks exactly the same if the vowels are not written. The only spelling difference is in a vowel. Let's take for example اِخْتَرَمَ

اِسْم الْمَفْعُول	*respected*	مُخْتَرَمٌ	1
	The vowel on the second root letter is a فَتْحة		
اِسْم الْفَاعِل	*the one who respects*	مُخْتَرِمٌ	2
	The vowel of the second root letter is a كَسْرة		

A remark on the plural:

the invited students	الطُّلَّابُ الْمَدْعُوُّونَ
Notice: you have to write two و	

170. اِسْم الْمَكان - HOW DO YOU BUILD IT?

In Arabic, it is easy to build a word for the place where the action happens. It is called اِسْم الْمَكان (noun of place) and belongs to the الْمُشْتَقّات. For a I-verb (ثُلاثِيّ) there are two patterns:

A. The pattern مَفْعَل

It is used

  1. if the verb has a weak letter at the end

  2. if the present tense (2nd stem) has a فَتْحة or ضَمّة

translation	اِسْم الْمَكان	translation	verb	
principle; basis	مَبْدَأ	to begin	يبدَأ	بَدَأ
playground	مَلْعَب	to play	يلعَب	لَعِب
amusement centre	مَلْهَى	to be amused	يلهُو	لَهَا

Here are some exceptions that are not following this pattern:

translation	اِسْم الْمَكان	translation	verb	
school	مَدْرَسةٌ	to learn	يدرُس	دَرَسَ
farm	مَزْرَعةٌ	to plant	يزرَع	زَرَعَ
place of sunset*	مَغْرِب	to depart	يغرُب	غَرَبَ
mosque*	مَسْجِدٌ	to bow down	يسجُد	سَجَدَ

* Notice: According to the rules it should be مَسْجَدٌ and مَغْرَبٌ

263

B. The pattern مَفْعِل

It is used

1. if the verb starts with a weak letter

2. if the present tense (2nd stem) has a كَسْرة

translation	إِسْم الْمَكان	translation	verb	
position, station	مَوْقِفٌ	to stop	يَقِف	وَقَّفَ
appointment	مَوْعِدٌ	to promise	يَعِد	وَعَدَ
birthplace	مَوْلِدُ	to give birth to	يَلِد	وَلَدَ
native country	مَوْطِنٌ	to settle down	يَطِن	وَطَنَ
runway	مَهْبِطٌ	to descend	يَهْبِط	هَبَطَ
place of retreat	مَرْجِعٌ	to return	يَرْجِع	رَجَعَ
residence	مَنْزِلٌ	to stay	يَنْزِل	نَزَّلَ

Here is a well-known exception:

airport*	مَطارٌ	to fly	يطير	طَارَ

* Notice: According to the rules it should be مَطِيرٌ

If you want to know how to build the إِسْم الْمَكان for other verb forms (II to X), have a look at chapter 172.

264

171. مَوْلِد - Does it Mean "Birthday" or "Birthplace"?

It can mean both.

Depending on the context, the اِسْم الْمَكان can function as the اِسْم الزَّمان (noun of time). The اِسْم الزَّمان describes the time when the action happens. So the اِسْم الْمَكان and the اِسْم الزَّمان look exactly the same. Moreover, they can even mean approximately the same sometimes.

Let us have a look at an example:

اِسْم الزَّمان	My birthday is in October.	مَوْلِدي في شَهْرِ أكْتوبر.
اِسْم الْمَكان	My birthplace is in London.	مَوْلِدي في مَدِينَةِ لَنْدُن.

172. What do Verbs with More than Three Letters Share?

First of all, when we say "more than three letters", we mean that we deal with verb forms from II to X.

Let us take an example and have a look at the verb اِلْتَقَى which means *to meet*. It is a VIII-verb following the pattern اِفْتَعَلَ

What happens if we derive some nouns from this verb? For example: the passive participle, the noun of place or time, etc.

Well, it is getting a bit complicated as some الْمُشْتَقّات (derived nouns) look exactly the same – but mean different things depending on the function in the sentence:

I	اِسْم الْمَكَان	The centre is the meeting point for the students.	الْمَرْكَزُ مُلْتَقَى الطُّلَّابِ.
2	اِسْم الزَّمان	The students meet at 9 o'clock.	السَّاعَةُ التَّاسِعة مُلْتَقَى الطُّلَّابِ.
3	اِسْم الْمَفْعُول	The students have met.	الطُّلَّابُ مُلْتَقَى بِهِم.
4	الْمَصْدَر الْمِيمِيّ	The meeting of the students was nice. Notice: The original الْمَصْدَر الأَصْلِيّ would be: اِلْتِقاء	كانَ مُلْتَقَى الطُّلَّابِ جَميلاً.

Let's summarize the most important points:

- The اِسْم الْمَكَان and اِسْم الزَّمان as well as the اِسْم الْمَفْعُول share the same pattern! This is true for all derived verb forms (II to X), so called غَيْر ثُلاثِيّ

- Only a I-verb has special patterns for the اِسْم الزَّمان and اِسْم الْمَكَان. They share them (مِفْعَل or مَفْعَل) and therefore look the same.

Let us now check the other verb forms:

اِسْم الْمَفْعُول	passive verb	meaning	verb	
مُغْلَقٌ	أُغْلِقَ	to close; to shut	أَغْلَقَ	IV
مُدَرِّسٌ	دُرِّسَ	to teach	دَرَّسَ	II
مُراعًى	رُوعِيَ	to supervise; to control	راعَى	III

مُسْتَخْرَجٌ	أُسْتُخْرِجَ	to take out; extract	اِسْتَخْرَجَ	X
مُتَّهَمٌ	اُتُّهِمَ	to accuse	اِتَّهَمَ	VIII

173. مُسْتَشْفَى - WHAT IS THE ROOT FOR THIS WORD?

The word means *hospital* and is the اِسْم الْمَكان of a verb. It literally describes *the place to seek cure.*

The source for this derived noun - اِسْم مُشْتَقّ - is a X-verb following the pattern اِسْتَفْعَلَ. It has the root: ش - ف - ى

So the verb looks like this: اِسْتَشْفَى

If you want to build the place where an action happens - the place where somebody seeks cure - you need the اِسْم الْمَكان

Remember:

There is something special about the verb forms II to X: The اِسْم الْمَكان and the اِسْم الْمَفْعُول share the same pattern!

translation	اِسْم الْمَكان
meeting place	مُلْتَقًى
hospital	مُسْتَشْفًى
society	مُجْتَمَعٌ

translation	verb
to meet	اِلْتَقَى
to seek a cure	اِسْتَشْفَى
to meet	اِجْتَمَعَ

If you are not sure, whether the word مُسْتَشْفًى is masculine or feminine, have a look at chapter 174.

174. مُسْتَشْفَى - IS IT MASCULINE OR FEMININE?

The word means *hospital*. And it is masculine.

This might look strange as there is a ى at the end which is usually an indicator for a feminine word. As a general rule, we could say: In most cases, the اِسْم الْمَكان is masculine.

So how about the agreement? It has to be masculine!

Let us have a look at two examples:

| a nightclub | مَلْهًى لَيْلِيّ (NOT لَيْلِيّة) |
| a big hospital | مُسْتَشْفًى كَبِيرٌ |

175. اِسْم الْآلة - HOW DO YOU BUILD THE WORDS FOR TOOLS?

Scissors, spoon or car – it is very easy to form a word for a tool with which the action (the verb) is being done: the اِسْم الْآلة

It is a اِسْم مُشْتَقّ. There are special patterns to build it:

			مِفْعَل
translation	اِسْم الْآلة	translation	I-verb
microscope	مِجْهَرٌ	to come out	جَهَرَ
scissors	مِقَصٌّ	to cut	قَصَّ

		مِفْعَلة	
translation	اِسْم الْآلة	translation	I-verb
sweeper	مِكْنَسةٌ	to sweep	كَنَسَ
spoon	مِلْعَقةٌ	to lick	لَعِقَ

		مِفْعال	
translation	اِسْم الْآلة	translation	I-verb
key	مِفْتاحٌ	to open	فَتَحَ
weight scales	مِيْزانٌ	to weigh; balance	وَزَنَ

		فَعّالة	
translation	اِسْم الْآلة	translation	I-verb
eyeglasses	نَظّارةٌ	to see	نَظَرَ
car; vehicle	سَيّارةٌ	to ride; move on	سارَ

Sometimes the active participle is used for describing tools:

		اِسْم الْفاعِل		
translation	اِسْم الْآلة	translation	verb	
air plane	طائِرةٌ	to fly	طارَ	I
air conditioner	مُكَيِّفةٌ	to adjust; fit	كَيَّفَ	II

269

Watch out! Not all words for tools are derived from roots. These words are called اِسْم جامِد. It literally means *hard, solid*. In grammar, it means *defective*.

Here are some examples:

			اِسْم جامِد
translation	example	translation	example
pen	قَلَمٌ	sword	سَيْفٌ
knife	سِكِّينٌ	spear	رُمْحٌ

176. مِئْذَنة OR مَأْذَنة - WHAT IS THE WORD FOR MINARET?

This is a question about the correct first vowel. Nowadays, the common word for *minaret* is مَأْذَنة with فَتْحة on the first letter. In the early times of Islam, however, the spelling was مِئْذَنة – with كَسْرة

Old dictionaries like *Lane's dictionary* even call the word مَأْذَنة a *vulgar word*, although nowadays, this is the most common pronunciation. Let's have a closer look now at the word.

The root is ع - ذ - ن and mainly means *to hear*.

- The II-verb أَذَّنَ means *to call to prayer*. A side note: it can also mean *to crow* (rooster).

- The IV-verb آذَنَ means: *to make public; to announce*

Now let's make the difference between مِئْذَنة and مَأْذَنة clear:

1. The word مِئْذَنة is a derived noun: the اِسْم الآلة
2. The word مَأْذَنة is a derived noun: the اِسْم الْمَكان

→ مِئْذَنة is an instrument to do the call to prayer.

If we take that seriously, it could probably mean that the مِئْذَنة was originally a structure small enough justifiably to be called an instrument.

By the way: Other words for minaret are: مَنارة (*lighthouse*) or صَوْمَعة which has the original meaning of *hermitage*.

177. "WRITE!" - HOW CAN YOU EXPRESS THIS?

You can simply use the imperative: ! أُكْتُبْ. The imperative (أَمْر) is the most common way. But there are other possibilities which basically all mean the same. The following examples all mean: *write!* Notice that all verbs end with a سُكُون

pronunciation	imperative	prefix
"uktub"	أُكْتُبْ!	--
"litaktub" Notice the لِ with كَسرة – so called لام الطَّلَب	لِتَكْتُبْ!	لِ
"waltaktub" Notice the سُكُون above the لـ which is due to the combining of the و with the other parts.	وَلْتَكْتُبْ!	وَلْ

178. ذٰلِكُم الْكِتابُ مُفِيدٌ يا أَصْدِقائي – **ANY MISTAKE?**

No, there isn't. But let us check why.

First of all, the sentence means: *That book is useful, my friends!*

But the first two words in the Arabic sentence - ذٰلِكُمْ - might look strange. Since the meaning is *that book* - why is it not just: ذٰلِكَ الْكِتاب؟

For English speakers, it is not logical that the <u>demonstrative pronoun</u> (اِسْم الْإِشارة) <u>agrees</u> in gender and singular/plural <u>with the one you call</u>. In our example with: *my friends!*

In Arabic, this is only true if you use the كاف الْخِطاب (*K of allocution; pronominal K*). It is normally used in two situations:

Used with a verb			1
He met you.	قابَلَكَ.	The ك here serves as an object (مَفْعُول بِهِ) and is, grammatically speaking, مَنْصُوب (although there is no change in vowels).	
Used with a إضافة-construction			2
your book	كِتابُكَ.	The ك here is, grammatically speaking, مُضاف إلَيْهِ مَجْرُور as it serves as a	

Let us check some other examples:

Hey Karim, that notebook is useful!	ذٰلِكَ الدَّفْتَرُ مُفِيدٌ يا كَرِيمُ!

Hey my (two) friends, that notebook is useful!	ذٰلِكُمَا الدَّفْتَرُ مُفِيدٌ يا صَدِيقَيَّ!
Hey my friends, that notebook is useful!	ذٰلِكُمْ الدَّفْتَرُ مُفِيدٌ يا أَصْدِقائِي!
Hey (my)ladies, that notebook is useful!	ذٰلِكُنَّ الدَّفْتَرُ مُفِيدٌ يا سَيِّداتِي!

179. WHAT DOES إِمَّا MEAN?

The word إِمَّا could be translated as: *either.... (or)*.

Generally speaking, the word *either* is used when there are two possibilities only. So how do you use it in Arabic?

1	If there is doubt	الشَّكّ
	This man is either stupid or insane.	هٰذا الرَّجُلُ إِمَّا أَحْمَقُ وَإِمَّا مَجْنُونٌ.
2	Letting choose	التَّخْيِير
	You have to meet either the director or the secretary.	يَجِبُ عَلَيْكَ أَنْ تُقابِلَ إِمَّا الْمُدِيرَ وَإِمَّا السِّكْرِتِيرَ.

Notice that you have to use إِمَّا twice – and in the second part, you have to connect it with وَ

180. لَيْسَ - WHAT KIND OF WORD IS THAT?

The word لَيْسَ literally means: *not to be; not to exist*. It is a verb and used to negate a nominal sentence – a sentence that has no other verb, in Arabic called جُمْلة اِسْمِيّة

It is a special verb because it only exists in the past tense. There is no imperative (أَمْر) and no present tense (مُضارِع).

- In Arabic, verbs like لَيْسَ which are only used in the past tense are called فِعْل جامِد. Another example is the verb عَسَى which means: *to wish*

- All other verbs are called: فِعْل مُتَصَرِّف

لَيْسَ is also a sister of كانَ. This implies that the subject (it is called اِسْم لَيْسَ) is in the مَرْفُوع-case and the predicate (خَبَر لَيْسَ) is مَنْصُوب

<u>Although</u> لَيْسَ <u>is only used in the past tense, it has the meaning of the present tense!</u> Only in very few cases, when the context is clear, you could translate the verb with a past tense meaning.

Since لَيْسَ is a verb, you don't need to add a certain personal pronoun (أنا, هُوَ, ...) as it is defined by the ending of the verb – by the الضَّمِير الْمُسْتَتِر (hidden/implied pronoun).

Note that there are other options to express a negation meaning more or less the same. Let's take the sentence: *She is not generous.*

Here, the predicate has to be مَنْصُوب because it is the خَبَر of لَيْسَ – similar to the خَبَر كان	لَيْسَتْ كَرِيمةً	1
Here, we use a construction with بِ to emphasize	لَيْسَتْ بِكَرِيمةٍ	2

274

the negation, sometimes in addition with the definite article. Watch out: You have to treat the predicate like all other nouns after a preposition! This means it has to be مَجْرُور and takes كَسْرة		
Here, we use a construction with غَيْر instead of لَيْسَ – notice that this is a إِضافة	هِيَ غَيْرُ كَرِيمةٍ	3

The preposition مِنْ can be used to accentuate the negation:

No one knows everything.	لَيْسَ مِنْ إِنْسانٍ يَعْرِفُ كُلَّ شَيْءٍ.

181. لَيْسَ لَدَيْهِ سَيّارةٌ - IS THERE A MISTAKE?

No, there isn't. The sentence means: *He doesn't have a car.*

If you translate it into English, you might not find a mistake anyway as the subject is *he* and the predicate is *car*.

But take a closer look at the construction of the sentence:

The underline verb لَيْسَ has to agree with the subject (اِسْم لَيْسَ).

You can easily identify the subject in a sentence with لَيْسَ by the مَرْفُوع-marker, namely two ضَمّة here. So the subject is: *car*!

But *car* is feminine and لَيْسَ is used in the 3rd person singular masculine. So what happened?

The feminine subject *car* is separated from the other parts of the sentence. That is why the verb لَيْسَ can have the masculine form. This is pretty common in Arabic scripts.

Notice: The خَبَر لَيْسَ (predicate) here is لَدَيْهِ (a prepositional phrase, so called جَارّ وَمَجْرُور). The predicate of لَيْسَ is often mistaken as the subject, especially in sentences that express possession which is due to the inverted word order. Let us remember what inverted word order means:

He has a book.	عِنْدَهُ كِتابٌ.
This is the predicate: شِبْه جُمْلة خَبَر مُقَدَّم (adverbial phrase) Here, the predicate comes first which is usually the position for the subject = inverted word order.	عِنْدَهُ
مُبْتَدَأ (subject of a nominal sentence; جُمْلة اِسْمِيّة)	كِتابٌ

He does not have a book	لَيْسَ عِنْدَهُ كِتابٌ.
Here, عِنْدَهُ is the predicate of the sentence and is مَنْصُوب – but you don't see that it is مَنْصُوب because the predicate is an adverbial phrase which stays the same in any case.	
Notice: The masculine singular form is also used to negate just parts of a sentence or an adverbial phrase. For example the phrase: not from here	لَيْسَ مِنْ هُنا.

The verb لَيْسَ is usually put before the predicate (the part of the sentence it denies): The اِسْم لَيْسَ ("subject") comes at the end.

3		2		1
"subject"	+	predicate	+	لَيْسَ
سَيّارةٌ		لَدَيْهِ		لَيْسَ

276

Let us go back to our example and change the word order to see
what the problem is:

wrong	If you rearrange the sentence like this, it suddenly looks wrong – and it is wrong!	لَيْسَ سَيَّارةٌ لَدَيْهِ.	١
correct	This is a correct sentence because the "subject" is <u>not separated</u> from لَيْسَ	لَيْسَتْ سَيَّارةٌ لَدَيْهِ.	٢
correct	This looks correct and most scholars say it is, although the verb here doesn't agree with the "subject".	لَيْسَ لَدَيْهِ سَيَّارةٌ.	٣
	There is another part of the sentence (لَدَيْهِ) between the اِسْم لَيْسَ ("subject") and the verb لَيْسَ, so you can do it.		

It can be tricky to identify the اِسْم لَيْسَ. Without the vowel
markers, both sentences in this example would look the same!

The professor is not in this school. Here, the word *professor* is the "subject" (اِسْم لَيْسَ).	لَيْسَ الأُسْتاذُ فِي هٰذِهِ الْمَدْرَسة.
He is not the professor in this school. Here, a hidden pronoun (هُوَ) is the "subject" (اِسْم لَيْسَ). The word *professor* is the predicate!	لَيْسَ الأُسْتاذَ فِي هٰذِهِ الْمَدْرَسة.

182. لَسْتُ أَدْرِي - IS THAT CORRECT?

Yes, it is. The expression لَسْتُ أَدْرِي means: *I don't know.*

Normally, we use the verb لَيْسَ only to negate a جُمْلة اِسْمِيّة (nominal sentence).

But here we have a verb after لَيْسَ. It is دَرَى and means *to know; to be aware.*

You might also hear لَسْتُ أَذْكُرُ occasionally which means: *I don't remember.* This, too, is grammatically correct. But why?

The خَبَر of لَيْسَ here is a verb. This is usually found in the first person singular (*I*) and used to negate the present tense. It is not very common and only found in two or three examples like the ones we showed in this chapter.

183. نِعْمَ / بِئْسَ - ARE THESE WORDS SUPERB OR MISERABLE?

Actually, they are both. These two words (verbs!) are used to describe an emphatic meaning.

In Arabic, this is called: أُسْلُوب الْمَدْح والذَّم – which literally means: *praise* and *criticism.*

Let us have a look at the main two verbs:

what a good / superb / perfect / wonderful / truly excellent ...	نِعْمَ
what bad / miserable ...	بِئْسَ

Both verbs are a so called فِعْل جامِد (like the verb لَيْسَ) which means: These verbs are not used in the present tense (الْمُضارِع) and do not form an imperative (أَمْر).

- Moreover, these two verbs never change their form. They are invariable.

- The word which follows (the word being qualified) has to be a <u>definite noun</u> and is مَرْفُوع (nominative).

- The feminine forms are rarely used: نِعْمَت / بِئْسَت

Let us have a look at some examples:

What an excellent man Karim is! Notice: The لَ at the beginning is used to intensify the meaning.	لَنِعْمَ الرَّجُلُ كَرِيمُ!
He is a wonderful friend indeed. Notice: The particle إِنَّ is used to emphasize.	إِنَّهُ نِعْمَ الْخَلِيلُ.
What bad men you both are!	لَبِئْسَ الرَّجُلانِ أَنْتُما!

Both words can be connected with a اِسْم الْمَوْصُول, namely: ما or مَن. Merged with the particle ما, the meaning is slightly different and normally translated as *indeed* (German: *gar*).

Indeed bad things you did! In German: *Gar Schlechtes hast du getan!*	بِئْسَما صَنَعْتَ!

There are other words in Arabic that follow the same rules (invariable and connected to a noun in the nominative case) and are also used emphatically:

what/how a great..., monumental...	جَلَّ
	شَدَّ
	عَزَّ
	هَدَّ
what a big...	كَبُرَ
what a bad..., wicked...	ساءَ
what a nice..., beautiful...	حَسُنَ - حُسْنَ - حَسْنَ
what a great..., powerful...	عَظُمَ - عُظْمَ - عَظْمَ
how lovely..., what lovely...	حَبَّ + ذا
how terrible, bad...	لا حَبَّ + ذا

Here are some examples:

How lovely you are!	حَبَّذا أَنْتَ!
How dear/strong you loved her!	لَشَدَّ ما أَحْبَبْتَها!
What big/bad word comes out of your mouth! Notice here that we used the feminine form. But this is optional! You could also use just كَبُرَ. If you want to say "your mouth" (singular) it is either فِيكَ or فِيكَ (مَجْرُور if فِيكَ). The word فَم is tricky!	كَبُرَتْ كَلِمَةً تَخْرُجُ مِن أَفْواهِكُمْ.

280

Let us analyse a sentence:

What an annoying hypocrisy!	لا حَبَّذا النِّفاقُ!
حَرْف نَفْي	لا
فِعْل ماضٍ جامِد	حَبَّ
اِسْم إِشْارة مَبْنِيّ فِي مَحَلّ رَفْع	ذا
الْمَخْصُوص بِالذَّم مُبْتَدَأ مَرْفُوع	النِّفاق

Some remarks:

- The verb حَبَّ is used as a فِعْل جامِد which is merged with a demonstrative pronoun (اِسْم إِشارة)

- The demonstrative pronoun اذ is the subject! In Arabic, we say: فِي مَحَلّ رَفْع فاعِل

- For criticism – use the negation: لا حَبَّذا

184. WHEN DOES A VERB NEED THE مَنْصُوب-MOOD?

There are certain words after which a verb must be put into the مَنْصُوب-mood. The مَنْصُوب-mood is often translated as *verb in the direct case*; as *subjunctive* (German: *Konjunktiv*); also as: *verb with open ending*.

So what does مَنْصُوب mean in practical terms? There are several meanings, e.g. it expresses the subjunctive mood, it expresses a state or act that you would like to have, that you could do. The subjunctive can't be used on its own. It is connected to a possibility, to a wish or a duty (which normally stands at the beginning of a sentence). Here is a list of words after which you have to put the verb into the مَنْصُوب-mood:

translation	grammatical term	
that	الْمَصْدَرِيّة	أَنْ
not to		أَنْ لا = أَلَّا
in order to/that; so that; so	لام التَّعْلِيل (justification)	لِ
so that	فاء السَّبَبِيّة	فَ
in order to	كاف التَّعْلِيل	كَيْ / لِكَيْ
in order not to		كَيْ لا = كَيْلا لِكَيْ لا = لِكَيْلا
until; so that	الْغاية (purpose) or التَّعْلِيل (justification)	حَتَّى
will not	النَّفْي فِي الْمُسْتَقْبَل	لَنْ
therefore; so; then	تكُونُ فِي جَواب كَلام قَبْلَها	إِذَن
so that...		فَ
Used if there is a preceding word indication a wish, a command, a question or a prohibition.		
(emphasis)	لام الجُحُود - (denial لام)	لِ
After a denied form of كان, this لِ is used to emphasize the negation. This is not a preposition!		

An example for فَ

Don't be lazy, so you (will) win.	لا تَكُنْ كَسُولاً فَتَكْسِبَ.

Watch out if the <u>last root letter</u> is a و or a ي (weak letter) and you have to make this verb مَنْصُوب. The important thing is the vowel on the second root-letter:

example		What is the مَنْصُوب-ending?	last letter	verb	
he won't be pleased	لَنْ يَرْضَى	hidden "a"	ى	يَرْضَى	١
he won't complain	لَنْ يَشْكُوَ	فَتْحة on top of و	و	يَشْكُو	٢
he won't throw	لَنْ يَرْمِيَ	فَتْحة on top of ي	ي	يَرْمِي	٣

185. زَهْر جَميلة OR زَهْر جَميل - WHAT IS CORRECT?

The expression means: *nice flowers.*

The word زَهْر is the collective plural for *flowers*. The singular form is زَهْرة which means *a flower* or *blossom*. In Arabic, we call the collective plural اِسْم الْجِنْس الْجَمْعِيّ

Collective nouns don't describe a specific group, but species. For example: شَجَر (*trees*) or عِلْم الشَّجَر (*dendrology; the science of trees;*). Another example: لَحْم الْبَقَر (*beef; meat*). Collective nouns, in comparison to English, tend to have a distinction

283

between being collective and being countable, often related to elements in nature.

The difference between شَجَر and أَشْجار is like the difference between *Gebirge* (species) and *Berge* in German. Both mean mountains. Regarding *Gebirge,* you are thinking of the mountains as one entity; regarding *Berge,* you are thinking of them as individual entities. Unfortunately, there is no collective plural in Arabic for *mountains.*

Now let us go back to our initial question: If you want to say *nice flowers,* you should say: زَهْر جَمِيل

This is because <u>collective plurals take a masculine singular adjective</u> – and not, as usual in Arabic, the feminine form. Here is another example: شَجَر طَوِيل – which means *tall trees.*

Notice: There is another plural form for زَهْرة. It is: أَزْهار

It is used to describe a small amount of flowers, like a bouquet or a bunch of. In this case the adjective agrees with the regular rules for plurals: أَزْهار جَمِيلة

186. HOW DO YOU SAY "NOT AT ALL" IN ARABIC?

The expression *not at all* is used if you want to stress on the fact that you have not done anything or that you have never done a certain thing.

Let us have a look at possible ways to express *not at all* in Arabic:

with negation: *not at all; never; by no means*	غَيْرَ مَرّةٍ 1
never; not at any point; in any respect	مُطْلَقًا 2
by no means	عَلَى الإِطْلاقِ

Some examples:

It will not be accepted at all.	لَنْ يُقبَلَ مُطْلَقًا.
I've seen him more than once.	رَأَيْتُهُ غَيْرَ مَرّةٍ.

187. "THE GIRL IS BIGGER THAN..." - HOW IS IT IN ARABIC?

For the translation of this sentence, we need to form a comparative. This is usually done by using the pattern أَفْعَل.

For example: أَكْبَر which means *bigger*. This is the masculine form. But in the sentence *The girl is bigger than...* we are talking about a girl. So do we have to use the feminine form of *bigger*, which is كُبْرَى? Well, we will see.

There are several possibilities for the translation of our example. Let's have a look at them. Pay attention to the vowels at the end!

1	Comparative meaning (*bigger than*)
	It is always أَكْبَرُ مِن
	What is important to know about this construction:
	• No definite article. It is only أَكْبَر and not الأَكْبَر

> - This isn't a إضافة-construction: There is the preposition مِن after the word أَكْبَر

English translation	example		
This boy is bigger than his brothers.	إِخْوَتِهِ	أَكْبَرُ مِن	هٰذا الْوَلَدُ
This girl is bigger than her sisters.	أَخَواتِها	أَكْبَرُ مِن	هٰذِهِ الْبِنْتُ
These two boys are bigger than their brothers.	إِخْوَتِهِما	أَكْبَرُ مِن	هٰذانِ الْوَلَدانِ
These two girls are bigger than their sisters.	أَخَواتِهِما	أَكْبَرُ مِن	هاتانِ الْبِنْتانِ
These boys are bigger than their brothers.	إِخْوَتِهِم	أَكْبَرُ مِن	هٰؤُلاء الْأَوْلادُ
These girls are bigger than their sisters.	أَخَواتِهِنَّ	أَكْبَرُ مِن	هٰؤُلاء الْبَناتُ

Notice that أَكْبَرُ مِن stays the same in every sentence!

There is no feminine form, nor a plural form, and there is no agreement! It <u>always</u> has the same form: <u>masculine and singular</u>.

Don't forget: It doesn't take تَنْوين as it is مَمْنُوع مَن الصَّرْف

So the answer is: الْبِنْتُ أَكْبَرُ مِن

Before we move on to the next possibility, let us first understand some grammatical terms (the examples are taken from above):

286

explanation	grammar term	word
Lit. meaning: *The preferred.* The thing which has more of it.	الْمُفَضَّل	الْوَلَدُ
The thing which has less of it. The person/thing which is inferior.	الْمُفَضَّل عَلَيْهِ	إِخْوَتِهِ

2	Superlative meaning (*the biggest*)
	The word أَكْبَر changes and has a definite article.
	What is important to know about this construction: • The الْمُفَضَّل needs a definite article!

English translation	اِسْم التَّفْضِيل	الْمُفَضَّل	
This is the biggest boy.	الأَكْبَر	أَلْوَلَدُ	هٰذا هُوَ
This is the biggest girl.	الْكُبْرى	الْبِنْتُ	هٰذِهِ هِيَ
These two are the biggest (two) boys.	الأَكْبَرانِ	الْوَلَدانِ	هٰذانِ هُما
These two are the biggest (two) girls.	الْكُبْرَيانِ	الْبِنْتانِ	هاتانِ هُما
These boys are the biggest.	الأَكْبَرُونَ or الأَكْبَر	الأَوْلادُ	هٰؤُلاءِ هُمْ
These girls are the biggest.	الْكُبْرَيات or الْكُبَر	الْبَناتُ	هٰؤُلاءِ هُنَّ

287

Notice:

- The اِسْم التَّفْضِيل has to follow the الْمُفَضَّل in terms of agreement.

- If you have a feminine dual, you have to write a ي and not a ت – as there is a ى at the end of the feminine form! For example: الْكُبْرَيانِ

Be careful if the اِسْم التَّفْضِيل is the object of a sentence – it has to be مَنْصُوب! For example:

I saw the two big (biggest) girls.	شاهَدْتُ الْبِنْتَينِ الْكُبْرَيَيْنِ.

3	Superlative meaning (*the biggest*)
	Again, it is only أَكْبَر
	- The الْمُفَضَّل has an indefinite article
	- The اِسْم التَّفْضِيل is <u>always</u> masculine and singular

English translation	الْمُفَضَّل عَلَيْهِ	اِسْم التَّفْضِيل		الْمُفَضَّل
This is the biggest boy.	وَلَدٍ	أَكْبَر	هوَ	هذا
This is the biggest girl.	بِنْتٍ	أَكْبَر	هِيَ	هذِهِ
These two are the biggest boys.	وَلَدَيْنِ	أَكْبَر	هُما	هذانِ
These two are the biggest girls.	بِنْتَيْنِ	أَكْبَر	هُما	هاتانِ

هٰؤلاءِ	هُمَ	أَكْبَر	أَوْلادٍ	These are the biggest boys.
هٰؤلاءِ	هُنَّ	أَكْبَر	بَناتٍ	These are the biggest girls.

4	Superlative meaning (*the biggest*)
	You can choose: أَكْبَر or another form

- The الْمُفَضَّل has a definite article
- Regarding the form of the اِسْم التَّفْضِيل, you have the choice between two equal forms:
  1. Indefinite and masculine: أَكْبَر
  2. Or match with the الْمُفَضَّل

الْمُفَضَّل		اِسْم التَّفْضِيل	مُفَضَّل عَلَيْهِ	English translation
هٰذا	هو	أَكْبَر	الأَوْلادِ	This is the biggest boy.
هٰذه	هِيَ	أَكْبَر - كُبْرى	الْبَناتِ	This is the biggest girl.
هٰذانِ	هُما	أَكْبَر - أَكْبَرا	الأَوْلادِ	These two are the biggest boys.
هاتانِ	هُما	أَكْبَر - أَكْبَريا	الْبَناتِ	These two are the biggest girls.
هٰؤلاءِ	هُمْ	أَكْبَر - أَكْبَروا	الأَوْلادِ	These are the biggest boys.
هٰؤلاءِ	هُنَّ	أَكْبَر - كُبْرَيات	الْبَناتِ	These are the biggest girls.

<u>So is there a difference in meaning?</u> Basically: no.

Most sentences are translated in the same way. But you have to watch out to spot the nuances:

It is not clear if we are talking about only two children in total (which are being compared) or a lot.	هٰذا هُوَ أَكْبَرُ الأَوْلادِ. ١
It could mean that there are only two children (which are being compared) in total. This is the only difference.	هٰذا هُوَ أَكْبَرُ وَلَدٍ. ٢

188. اِطْمَأَنَّ - CAN YOU RECOGNIZE THE VERB FORM?

The verb means *to be reassured*. It is a IV-verb – but there is something special about it:

The root has 4 letters and is: ط - م - ء - ن

What is the paradigm for a IV-verb with 4 root letters?

It is pretty simple:

You add a هَمْزة at the beginning of the root and double the last radical. In Arabic this is called مَزيد الرُّباعِيّ بِحَرْفَينِ

Notice that the conjugation of a IV-verb (based on a four-letter-root) is similar to a IX-verb, e.g. اِحْمَرَّ. IV-verbs with a four-letter-root are reflexive in meaning and don't form the passive tense, nor a passive participle (اِسْم الْمَفْعُول).

290

meaning	type	pattern		
he was reassured	الْماضِي	اِفْعَلَلَّ	اِطْمَأَنَّ	١
he is reassured	الْمُضارِع	يَفْعَلِلُّ	يَطْمَئِنُّ	٢
tranquillity; serenity	الْمَصْدَر	اِفْعِعْلالٌ	اِطْمِئْنان	٣
be reassured!	الْأَمْر	masculine	اِطْمَأْنِنْ	٤
		feminine	اِطْمَئِنِّي	
		plural	اِطْمَئِنُّوا	
calm	اِسْم الْفاعِل	مُفْعَلِلٌّ	مُطْمَئِنٌّ	٥

189. HOW DO YOU SAY: "MORE CROWDED"?

This is not so easy in Arabic, as you can't use the word *crowded* directly for a comparative (*more crowded*). You have to change the form of the word. We will explain this step by step.

Adjectives in Arabic don't function in the same way as we are used to in English or German. They are derived from the root and have different shapes, patterns and grammatical origins.

So how do we translate expressions like: *more respected; more crowded; more intense red; feeling more not like going to school?*

First of all, we will start with the conditions which have to be fulfilled in order to build a comparative or superlative form in Arabic. This is pretty similar to English:

1. The underlying verb is of form I and has a triliteral root: فِعْل ثُلاثِيّ

2. It isn't a صِفة مُشَبَّهة

3. Active voice, not passive: أَنْ يَكُونَ الْفِعْلُ مَبْنِيّاً لِلْمَعْلُوم

4. The verb isn't negated: أَنْ يَكُونَ الْفِعْلُ مُثْبَتًا, لَيْسَ مَنْفِيًّا

5. The verb has a subject: أَنْ يَكُونَ الْفِعْلُ تامًّا, لَهُ فاعِل

6. The verb can be conjugated in all tenses: أَنْ يَكُونَ الفِعْلُ مُتَصَرِّفًا

7. You can make a comparison: أَنْ يَكُونَ الْفِعْلُ قابِلاً لِلتَّفاوُت

But what happens if our conditions are not fulfilled?

Let's see

CASE 1: It is not a I-verb and its pattern has more than three letters.	possible

This brings us to a construction called: أُسلُوب التَّفْضِيل

Let us take the verb for *to get jammed, to be crowded*: اِزْدَحَمَ

How would you say: *Cairo is more crowded than Beirut.*

Here is a step by step guide:

1. Build the مَصْدَر

The root of the verb is زَحَمَ. Notice that the letter د is not part of the root, as it should actually be a ت following the pattern: اِفْتَعَلَ. It was replaced by a د to make pronunciation easier.

The مَصْدَر is اِزْدِحامًا The

2. Choose a helping word

Now, you should choose a helping word, for example:

more; bigger	أَكْثَر		more; more intense	أَشَدّ
less	أَقَلّ			

3. Combine the two words

Cairo is more crowded than Beirut.	الْقاهِرةُ أَكْثَرُ اِزْدِحامًا مِن بَيْروتَ.
Notice: The expression *more crowded* itself is called أُسْلُوب التَّفْضيل For the correct تَنْوين (nunation) use the rules for a اِسْم التَّفْضيل	

CASE 2: Comparison of a الصِّفة الْمُشَبَّهة	possible

We will deal with these two forms of the الصِّفة الْمُشَبَّهة:

1	أَفْعَل	masculine
2	فَعْلاء	feminine

293

Notice in number 2 the فَتْحة above the first letter! If it was a ضَمّة, it would be a regular comparative form and not a صِفة مُشَبَّهة! For example the feminine form of *bigger*: كُبْرى

Here are some examples:

meaning	feminine form	masculine form	root
red	حَمْراء	أَحْمَر	حَمِرَ
blind	عَمْياء	أَعْمى	عَمِىَ

A صِفة مُشَبَّهة doesn't have a comparative form in Arabic. We need a helping construction.

<u>Here is a step by step guide:</u>

1. Build the مَصْدَر

Let us take a look at these examples:

meaning	مَصْدَر	root / I-verb
redness; red colour	حُمْرة	حَمِرَ
blueness; blue colour	زُرْقة	زَرِقَ

Watch out – there are two exceptions:

meaning	مَصْدَر	root / I-verb
whiteness; white colour	بَيَاض	باضَ - بيض
blackness; black colour	سَواد	سود

294

2. Choose a helping word

more; bigger	أَكْثَر
less	أَقَلّ

more; more intense	أَشَدّ

This is the final result:

The flower has more redness than the other flower.	الْوَرْدةُ أَشَدُّ حُمْرةً مِن الْوَرْدةِ الْأُخْرى.
For the correct تَنْوِين (nunation) use the rules for a اِسْم التَّفْضِيل	

CASE 3: Comparison of a passive voice	possible (with a helping construction)

In Arabic, you can't build a comparative form by using the passive voice itself (see also CASE 1). For example: *more respected*.

First of all, watch out for the difference:

active (past tense) form of the root: *to listen*	سَمِعَ
passive (past tense) form of the root: *to listen*	سُمِعَ

meaning	passive, present tense	past tense	pattern	root
is respected	يُحْتَرَمُ	اِحْتَرَمَ	اِفْتَعَلَ	حَرِمَ

Here is a step by step guide:

1. Build the الْمَصْدَر الْمُؤَوَّل

This is very easy:

الْمَصْدَر الْمُؤَوَّل	الْمَصْدَر الأَصْلِيّ
أَنْ يُحْتَرَمَ	اِحْتِرامٌ

2. Choose a helping word – اِسْم التَّفْضِيل

The following words mean basically the same, you can choose any of them:

meaning	اِسْم التَّفْضِيل	root
worthier; more deserving	أَحَقُّ	حَقَّ
more appropriate, suitable, deserving	أَوْلَى	وَلَى
worthier; more suitable	أَجْدَر	جَدُرَ

Watch out for the ending!

The words don't take تَنْوِين.

They are so called diptotes (مَمْنُوع مِن الصَّرْف)

3. Combine the two things - here is the result:

The father is more respected.	الأَبُّ أَحَقُّ أَنْ يُحْتَرَمَ.

CASE 4: The verb is negated	possible

So what can we do if we have the verb: لا يَعْرِفُ؟

Here we are following the same procedure as explained for case 3, but we have to watch out for the negation.

<u>A step by step guide:</u>

1. Build the الْمَصْدَر الْمُؤَوَّل

أَلَّا يَعْرِفَ	=	يَعْرِفُ	+	لا	+	أَنْ
Notice that أَنْ plus لا merges to: أَلَّا						

2. Choose a helping word – اِسْم التَّفْضِيل

As explained above, the following words mean basically the same, you can choose any of them: أَحَقُّ - أَوْلَى - أَجْدَرُ

3. Combine it

It is better for humans not to lie.	الإِنْسانُ أَجْدَرُ أَلَّا يَعْرِفَ الْكِذْبَ.
My colleague deserves not to go.	زَمِيلِي أَحَقُّ أَلَّا يَذْهَبَ.

CASE 5: The verb has no subject	impossible

There are verbs in Arabic which need more than a subject. They do not give you a complete meaning – using unless you add something. They are called: فِعْل ناقِص. A well-known example is the verb to be: كانَ.

For example:

The weather was nice.	كانَ الْجَوُّ جَميلاً.

If you have كانَ, there is no way to express a comparison. This is pretty logical, because what should be the comparative of *to be?*

CASE 6: The verb can't be conjugated in all tenses	impossible

There are verbs in Arabic which can't be conjugated in all tenses. For example: لَيْسَ

This verb can only be used in the past tense (الْماضي). There is no present tense (الْمُضارِع) and no imperative.

Verbs like this are called فِعْل جامِد.

RULE: Regarding لَيْسَ, there is no way to express the comparison.

CASE 7: You can't make a real comparison	possible (in a certain sense)

If someone is dead, he is dead. You can't be *more dead*. But what if it is meant in the meaning of time? For example: *he has died before...* Or: *he has been sitting on the chair longer than...*

Yes, a comparative in this way is possible – but only in the meaning of time (the amount of time; length).

<u>Here is a step by step guide:</u>

Let us take the word *to sit*: جَلَسَ

1. Build the الْمَصْدَر الأَصْلِيّ in the مَنْصُوب-mood

This is easy: جُلُوسًا

2. Choose a helping word – اِسْم التَّفْضِيل

Here we need another root (one that is connected with time):

meaning	اِسْم التَّفْضِيل	root
previous; former; earlier	أَسْبَق	سَبَقَ

3. Combine it

Meaning: The child sat down before the teacher.	الطِّفْلُ أَسْبَقُ جُلُوسًا مِن الْمُدَرِّس.
Abd el-Nasser died earlier than el-Sadat.	عَبْد النَّاصِر أَسْبَقُ مَوْتًا مِن السَّدات.

299

190. WHY SHOULDN'T YOU SAY: "I BUY A QUR'AN"?

The root for الْقُرْآن is ق - ر - ء which describes the action of *to read* or *to recite*.

According to *Lane's dictionary*, some scholars say that the word الْقُرْآن was originally the اِسْم الْمَصْدَر (infinitive noun) of the expression: قَرَأْتُ الشَّيْءَ which means *I collected together the thing* or of قَرَأْتُ الْكِتَابَ which means *I read, or recited, the book, or scripture*. It was later conventionally applied *to signify the Book of God that was revealed to Muhammad*.

Precisely speaking, the word قُرْآن describes all the words that are in the book. So it doesn't make a lot of sense to use this term if you want to say that you have or want a copy of the Qur'an.

Instead, it is better to use the expression الْمُصْحَف with the definite article (= الْمُصْحَف الشَّرِيف) which means *volume* or *binder*; German: *Einband*. The plural of مُصْحَف is مَصَاحِف.

Let us have a look at the sentence: *I bought a Qur'an.*

This is understandable – but poor style.	اِشْتَرَيْتُ قُرْآنًا.
This is much better.	اِشْتَرَيْتُ مُصْحَفًا.

191. عَسَى - WHAT IS SO SPECIAL ABOUT THIS VERB?

The original meaning of the verb عَسَى is *to be possible*.

It belongs to a special group of verbs. It is a so called فِعْل جَامِد. This means it can only be used in the past tense (الْمَاضِي).

Present tense, future tense, the imperative simply don't exist. And it is used in the third person masculine singular only! So basically, it is never conjugated – it is always عَسَى

The verb is usually followed by أَنْ plus verb in the present tense (مَنْصُوب). It can be followed by the subject of a sentence which has to be مَنْصُوب – because عَسَى follows the same rules as كَادَ. Remember that the predicate has to be مَرْفُوع.

The verb عَسَى can be connected to a personal pronoun suffix to drive a connection to a person: *perhaps you; perhaps we, ...*

Let's have a look at some examples:

عَسَى: *It could be; it was possible; wishfully; maybe*	
It expresses a wish or rhetorical question	
What should I do?	مَاذَا عَسَى أَنْ أَفْعَلَ؟
What could he say?	مَاذَا عَسَاهُ يَقُولَ؟
The weather should be nice.	عَسَى الْجَوُّ يَكُونَ جَمِيلاً.
Perhaps you are lazy?	عَسَاكَ كَسُولٌ؟
Perhaps I... (notice the ن)	عَسَانِي
Maybe Allah (مَنْصُوب) will...	عَسَى اللهَ أَنْ...

192. HOW DO YOU SAY: "DARK/DEEP RED"?

This construction is actually pretty similar to English or German – but a bit tricky. You can use the word دَاكِن which means *dark* or *blackish*. As it is used as an adjective (صِفَة), it comes <u>after the colour</u>. So the usual way to say "*dark red*" would be أَحْمَر دَاكِن

However, like any other صِفَة, it can be put into a so called إِضافة غَيْر حَقيقِيّة – which means that the الصّفة <u>precedes</u> the noun. Here is how it works:

What we call an adjective in English (in Arabic, this could be a صِفة مُشَبَّهة or, اِسْم الْمَفْعُول a, اِسْم الْفاعِل) can be put as the first part of an إِضافة. Normally, a إِضافة should only exist of what we call nouns in English (similar to a genitive construction with 's). For example:

| Karim is good hearted. | كَرِيمٌ طَيِّبُ الْقَلْبِ. |

Watch out: An adjective has to agree in definiteness with the pre-ceding noun it modifies. This means: <u>When the modified noun is definite, the adjective has to be definite too.</u> This is normally not possible in a إِضافة!

| The delicious tasting food. | الْأَكْلُ اللَّذِيذُ الطَّعْمِ. |

<u>Notice</u>: What we showed above has nothing to do with an <u>inver-ted word-order</u> which means that the predicate precedes the sub-ject in a nominal sentence.

For example:

Smoking is forbidden.	مَمْنُوعٌ التَّدْخِينُ.
خَبَر مُقَدَّم مَرْفُوع بالضَّمَّة	مَمْنُوعٌ - "un"
مُبْتَدَأ مُؤَخَّر مَرْفُوع بالضَّمَّة	التَّدْخِينُ

Let's continue with our topic: *dark blue*.

Here is how it works:

dark red	دَاكِنُ الْحُمْرِةِ
dark black	دَاكِنُ السَّوَادِ
dark green	دَاكِنُ الْخُضْرِةِ
dark blue	دَاكِنُ الزُّرْقَةِ

Notice: There is common mistake. The Arabic phrases that are in the following table cannot exist – as the second part of a إضافة must be a noun ("*redness*", "*blueness*") and <u>not</u> an adjective ("*red*", "*blue*").

dark black	دَاكِنُ السُّوداءِ (WRONG)
dark red, deeply red	دَاكِنُ الأَحْمَرِ (WRONG)

193. بَيْتًا OR بَيْتاً - WHERE DO YOU ADD THE TWO LINES AT THE END?

In this chapter, we will deal with the writing of the تَنْوِين if you have to deal with an indefinite اِسْم in the مَنْصُوب-case.

What is correct? On top of the Alif (بَيْتاً) or before the Alif (بَيْتًا)? You will see both versions in books, in movie subtitles, in newspapers, etc. This is a debating topic especially as you find both variations in calligraphies.

Most grammarians argue that the تَنْوِين should be written on the last letter <u>before the Alif</u>. This is also applied in this book.

The reason is simple: The Alif is a so called حَرْف ساكِن and therefore can't take any vowel!

<u>There is only one exception:</u>

If a word ends with a ل, it will become لا in مَنْصُوب. In this situation, don't put the تَنْوِين before the last letter because the تَنْوِين would separate the Alif from the ل. Instead, write the تَنْوِين on top of the Alif. The result is: لًا

Let's have a look at an example: كَسُول (lazy)

wrong	كَسُوًلا
correct	كَسُولًا

But watch out: This is not the case for the ى which is also pronounced as Alif.

An example: the word for *meaning*

304

wrong	معنىً
correct	معنّى

Remember that there are four situations in which you don't add an Alif after the last letter in the مَنْصُوب-case.

Therefore, the تَنْوِين will be on the last letter – except when the last letter is already a "long Alif" like in no. 2 in the following examples:

اِنْتِهاءً, ماءً	هَمْزة		1
مُصْطَفَى, عَصًا	أَلِف مَقْصُورة	as last letter	2
مَكْتَبةً	ة - تاء تَأْنِيث		3
مَلْجَأً	هَمْزة (أ)		4

An excursus:

However, there is a theoretical discussion going on claiming that the Alif is not a "silent letter" (حَرْف ساكِن) but rather a "long vowel", a so called حَرْف مَدّ

The latter (حَرْف مَدّ) explains the rule why the "long vowel" in a verb has to be elided if the verb is مَجْزُوم – because it is theoretically impossible to have two سُكُون in a row.

Here is an example:

لَمْ يَقُلْ is correct and works, but لَمْ يَقُوْل doesn't work whereas theoretically, يَقُوْلُ does. If you are interested in these theoretical discussions, try to search for this term: اِلْتِقاء ساكِنَيْن

305

194. أَجْمَلَ - WHAT KIND OF WORD IS THAT?

It depends on the meaning. Theoretically it could be the اِسْم التَّفْضيل and would therefore mean: *more beautiful*.

But there is another possibility:

It can be an example for the so called أُسْلُوب التَّعَجُّب. In this case, the word أَجْمَلَ would be a <u>verb</u>, a so called: فِعْل التَّعَجُّب. This structure is used to express *surprise* or *admiration*.

Here is an example:

What a beautiful view of the sea!	ما أَجْمَلَ مَنْظَرَ الْبَحْرِ!

There are two patterns and they are used for ثُلاثيّ-verbs (I-verb), for example with: جَمُلَ – عَذُبَ – عَظُمَ – صَدَقَ – كَثُرَ – كَبُرَ

I	ما ... أَفْعَلَ	ما + فِعْل ماضٍ عَلَى وَزْن أَفْعَلَ + اِسْم مَنْصُوب

What a beautiful sky!	ما أَجْمَلَ السَّماءَ!

ما	اِسْم نَكِرة فِي مَحَلّ رَفْع مُبْتَدَأً It has the implicit meaning of *something great*.
أَجْمَلَ	Past tense verb; the subject (الْفاعِل) is substituted by a hidden/implied pronoun. It is the predicate (خَبَر) of ما
السَّماء	Direct object of the verb in the مَنْصُوب-case

فِعْل ماضٍ عَلَى وَزْن أَفْعِلْ + ب + إِسْم مَجْرُور	أَفْعِلْ ... بِ	2

What a beautiful sky!	أَجْمِلْ بِالسَّماءِ!

Past tense verb; following the pattern of the imperative	أَجْمِلْ
The ب is a حَرْف جَرّ (preposition) and the word for *sky* is the فاعِل مَرْفُوع with a supposed or presumptive vowel, a so called ضَمَّة مُقَدَّرة over the هَمْزة	بِالسَّماء

If you are dealing with other verb forms (II to X) or a negation or passive construction, the أُسْلُوب التَّعَجُّب is still possible, but tricky. Let us have a look at some examples.

They are similar to the اِسْم التَّفْضِيل regarding the non-ثُلاثيّ-verbs. (For special cases see chapter 205)

فِعْل ناقِص:كانَ		1
The rain was heavy.	كانَ الْمَطَرُ شَدِيدًا.	
What a heavy rain! Construction: describing word + مَصْدَر	ما أَصْعَبَ كَوْنَ الْمَطَرِ شَدِيدًا!	
What a heavy rain! Construction: instead of a مَصْدَر, use the الْمَصْدَر الْمُؤَوَّل	ما أَصْعَبَ أَنْ يَكُونَ الْمَطَرُ شَدِيدًا!	

	2 الْفِعْل غَيْرُ ثُلاثِيّ
What an effort of the professor! Construction: describing word + مَصْدَر	ما أحْسَنَ اِجْتِهادَ الأُسْتاذِ!
What an effort of the professor! Construction: instead of the regular مَصْدَر, use the الْمَصْدَر الْمُؤَوَّل	ما أحْسَنَ أَنْ يَجْتَهِدَ الأُسْتاذُ!

195. WHAT'S CORRECT? - الْمَدِينة قَرطاج OR مَدِينة قَرطاج

They both mean *city of Carthage* – and they are both correct. But the grammatical construction is different – and the تَنْوِين!

Let us check the differences:

Here, *Carthage* is an apposition (بَدَل) and takes the same case as *city*. It literally means: *the city Carthage*	الْمَدِينةُ قَرطاجُ
Here, *Carthage* is the second part of a إضافة Please don't forget that foreign names of cities are مَمْنُوع مِن الصَّرْف. It literally means: *the city of Carthage*	مَدِينةُ قَرطاجَ

196. WHY DO WE COUNT NUMBERS FROM LEFT TO RIGHT?

Arabic is written from right to left. But numbers are usually written (and spoken) from left to right. This has to do with contemporary Arabic, basically with the influence of the West. However, Ibn Abbas, the cousin of the prophet Muhammad one of the early Qur'an scholars, is said to have already used the numbers from left to right (for instance his speech in Basra).

Actually, you can choose as both reading directions are regarded as correct. For example: the year 1997

7+90+ 900+ 1000	فِي عامِ سَبْعةٍ وَتِسْعِينَ وَتِسْعِ مئةٍ وَأَلْفٍ
1000+900+7+90	فِي عامِ أَلْفٍ وَتِسْعِ مِئةٍ وَسَبْعةٍ وَتِسْعِينَ

Notice: The word *hundred* is usually merged and written with long Alif before the Hamza: (=تِسْعِمائةٍ)

197. WHY IS THERE AN "AN"-ENDING IN "AHLAN WA SAHLAN"?

There are words in Arabic which are indefinite and end with تَنْوِين in the مَنْصُوب-case. These words were originally part of a whole sentence, but the verbs in that sentence were deleted – and the only thing that remained was a مَصْدَر in the مَنْصُوب-case. Grammatically speaking, this is the الْمَفْعُول الْمُطْلَق

So words like شُكْرًا or أَهْلاً are actually a مَفْعُول مُطْلَق. For more information on the الْمَفْعُول الْمُطْلَق see chapter 121.

	expression	original sentence
1	أَهْلاً وَسَهْلاً	حَلَلْتُم أَهْلاً وَنَزَلْتُم سَهْلاً .
2	شُكْرًا	أَشْكُرُكَ شُكْرًا.

In everyday speech, these nouns function as exclamations! Notice the exclamation mark (!) in the following examples:

welcome!	مَرْحَبًا	thanks!	شُكْرًا
welcome!	أَهْلاً وَسَهْلاً	blessings!	نَعِيمًا
naturally! of course!	طَبْعًا		

Only some adjectives (صِفة) may lose their case-ending as they are not a مَصْدَر and therefore not used as a مَفْعُول مُطْلَق.

Notice the سُكُوت at the end!

congratulations!	مَبْرُوكْ!	wonderful!	عَظِيمْ!
إِسْم الْمَفْعُول of بَرَكَ		This is the الصِّفة الْمُشَبَّهة of عَظُمَ	

198. النَّوْمَ, النَّوْمَ - WHY IS THERE A فَتْحة AT THE END?

There is a special form in Arabic if you want to warn or instigate somebody. It is called أُسْلُوب التَّحْذِير والْإِغْراء which literally means: *warning and instigation*.

النَّوْمَ, النَّوْمَ... so what does it mean?

When somebody is sitting in class and almost falls asleep, the teacher can warn the person by saying النَّوْمَ, النَّوْمَ – which means: *Beware of sleep!*

The tricky thing about this construction is that the word (also the repetition) is مَنْصُوب!

Let us have a look at some examples:

All three sentences mean the same: *beware of fire!*	إِيَّاكَ النَّارَ! 1
	إِيَّاكَ والنَّارَ! 2
	إِيَّاكَ مِن النَّارِ! 3
Notice three things here: 1) The whole sentence with إِيَّاكَ is مَنْصُوب 2) The pronoun ك is a حَرْف خِطاب 3) If the fire is confirmed, repeat the vocative: إِيَّاكَ إِيَّاكَ النَّارَ!	

Fire!	النَّارَ!
Fire and drowning!	النَّارَ والْغَرَقَ!

199. THOUGH, ALTHOUGH; EVEN IF; HOWEVER - IN ARABIC?

These words start a so called concessive clause which expresses an idea that suggests the opposite of the main part of the sentence. In Arabic the construction is a bit more difficult than in English.

Let us have a look at it:

1	These words can stand <u>at the beginning of a sentence or after</u> the main sentence. They always precede a جُمْلة اِسْمِيّة	
	although; even though	رَغْمَ أَنَّ
		بِالرَّغْمِ مِنْ أَنَّ
		عَلَى الرَّغْمِ مِنْ أَنَّ
		مَعَ أَنَّ
	although; nevertheless; however; whereas; but	بَيْدَ أَنَّ
		غَيْرَ أَنَّ
	He showed up <u>although</u> he was lazy.	حَضَرَ مَعَ أَنَّهُ كَانَ كَسُولاً.

2	The construction إِلَّا أَنَّ is common in the combination with رَغْم or other prepositions which were shown above.	
	despite; in spite of; although	إِلَّا أَنَّ
	<u>Despite</u> the hotel was nice it nevertheless had no toilet.	مَعَ أَنَّ الْفُنْدُقَ كَانَ جَمِيلاً إِلَّا أَنَّهُ يَخْلُو مِنْ دَوْرَةِ مِياهٍ.

3	Used in between two sentences or after a main sentence	
	even if; though	وَإِنْ
	even if	وَلَوْ
	Call me, <u>even if</u> you are on the train!	كَلِّمْني بِالْمَحْمُولِ وَلَوْ كُنْتَ فِي الْقِطارِ!

312

You will visit Cairo again <u>even if</u> you have visited Cairo before	أَنْتَ - وَإِنْ زُرْتَ الْقَاهِرَةَ مِنْ قَبْلُ - سَوْفَ تَزورُها مَرَّةً أُخْرَى.

200. DO YOU KNOW HOW TO USE ADVERBIAL EXPRESSIONS?

Tiny words like *after, later* or *earlier* - generally speaking: adverbs of time or place - but also expressions like *as much as* can be difficult to translate. Here are common expressions:

1	after; later; in the future	فِيما بَعْدُ
	He came later.	جاءَ فِيما بَعْدُ.

2	before; earlier; in the past	فِيما مَضَى

3	whenever; as soon as	عِنْدَما + present tense verb

4	as much as; to the same extent as	بِقَدْرِ ما
	You are as free as I am.	أَنْتَ حُرٌّ بِقَدْرِ ما أَنا حُرٌّ.

5.1	every time when; whenever	كُلَّما
	Sometimes used with the past tense – but with a present tense meaning.	
	Whenever (every time) he studies, he is happy.	كُلَّما دَرَسَ فَرِحَ.

5.2	the more... the more	كُلَّما + verb... كُلَّما + verb
	The more the girl refuses to meet the more I want to meet her.	كُلَّما رَفَضَتِ الْبِنْتُ اللِّقاءَ كُلَّما أَرَدْتُ أَنْ أُقابِلَها.

6	maybe; possibly; perhaps	رُبَّما
	Sometimes, it may be introduced by the emphatic particle لَ	
	Perhaps he has escaped.	لَرُبَّما نَجا.

7	as soon as	حالَما + past tense verb

8	as soon as; the moment when	أَوَّلَ ما

9	often; frequently	طالَما + past tense verb
	Literally: *as long as.* it comes from the verb طالَ - *to be long*	
	that occurred often	طالَما حَدَثَ ذلِكَ

10	until; while; as long as	رَيْثَما

11	especially; in particular; mainly	لا سِيَّما
	Notice that this is a compound (absolute negation + noun سِيٌّ)	

12	mostly; largely; generally	غالِباً ما

13	seldom; rarely	قَليلاً ما

201. "SO THAT..." - HOW IS IT IN ARABIC?

Sentences that include *so that...* or in German *so dass...* - so called subordinate clauses - are common in any language. They give a cause or result.

In Arabic, there are several possibilities to express that. Let us have a look at three main constructions:

so that; to the point where; in such a manner that Usually a جُمْلة فِعْليّة (present or past tense) follows. Sometimes, it can be followed by أَنّ and a جُمْلة اِسْميّة	بِحَيْثُ	1
You had a lot of money, so that you could travel to Germany.	كانَ لَدَيْكَ مالٌ كَثيرٌ بِحَيْثُ اسْتَطَعْتُ أَنْ تُسافِرَ إِلى أَلْمانيا.	

فَ can also have the meaning of *so that* and expresses a wish, a command, maybe a question – note that you have to put the verb into the مَنْصُوب-mood.	فَ	2
He hoped/wished to see me so that we could discuss the topic.	تَمَنّى لَوْ رَآني فَنُناقِشَ الْمَوْضُوعَ.	

حَتّى is usually translated into English as *until*. Sometimes, it can also be translated as *so that*. If the situation which you describe in your sentence is still ongoing, use the present tense. If the action is already over, you should use the past tense after حَتّى	حَتّى	3

202. HOW DO YOU RECOGNIZE A REPORTED (INDIRECT) SPEECH?

In Arabic, the reported speech (كَلام مَنْقُول, غَيْر مُباشِر) is not different from the direct speech – regarding tense or word order. You don't have to change words like in English, e.g. *yesterday* which becomes *the day before*. In German, the reported speech is easy to recognize as you have to use the *Konjunktiv I*.

So what happens in Arabic?

Let us have a look at an example:

1	Direct speech	
	He said: "I wrote you a letter."	.قالَ: "(إِنَّنِي) كَتَبْتُ لَكَ رِسالةً"

2	Reported speech	
	He said that he had written me a letter. (Both mean the same.)	.قالَ إِنَّهُ كَتَبَ لِي رِسالةً
		.قالَ بِأَنَّهُ كَتَبَ لِي رِسالةً
	Notice the فَتْحة on top of the Alif in the word بِأَنَّ	
	After the preposition بـ, we don't have to use the particle إِنَّ – for more information about إِنَّ see chapter 231)	

A hint: If you want to make clear that a sentence is a reported speech you should use بِأَنَّ = *that* after قالَ !

203. HOW DO YOU BUILD REPORTED QUESTIONS?

The reported speech is easy in Arabic. But how about a reported question or situation? For example: *He asked me whether/if...* This is a bit more difficult. Let us first have a look at how to translate *whether/if*:

whether / if...	إنْ + كانَ ...	I
	إذا + كانَ (ما) ...	2
If you have a verb with a preposition: e.g. سَأَلَ عَن (*to ask about*)	ما إذا + عَن عَمّا إذا	3
	ما إذا + فِي فِيما إذا	

Now let us check the tenses:

	direct question	reported question
present tense	الْمُضارِع	الْماضِي or كانَ + الْمُضارِع
past tense	الْماضِي	كانَ + قَدْ + الْماضِي
future tense	الْمُسْتَقْبَل	كانَ + الْمُسْتَقْبَل
nominal sentence	جُمْلة اِسْمِيّة	كانَ + خَبَر

Here are some examples:

	direct question	reported question
1	لا أَعْرِفُ: "هَلْ ذَهَبَ أَمْ لا؟"	لا أَعْرِفُ ما إذا (=إنْ) كانَ قَدْ ذَهَبَ أَمْ لا

I don't know: "Did he go or not?"	I don't know if he had gone or not.	
سَأَلْتُهُ: "هَلْ تُحِبُّ الْقَهْوَةَ أَمْ الشَّايَ؟"	سَأَلْتُهُ **إِنْ (= عَمَّا إِذا)** كانَ يُحِبُّ الْقَهْوَةَ أَمْ الشَّايَ.	2
I asked him: "Do you like coffee or tea?"	I asked him if he liked coffee or tea.	

204. HOW DO YOU SAY: "ONE DAY" OR "ONE NIGHT"?

We can translate it directly which works perfectly fine. But since we are using a number - *one* - we have to watch out for the gender and the correct agreement.

1	one day	أَحَدُ الْأَيَّامِ
	As *day* is masculine, we have to use the masculine form of *one*.	
2	one night	إِحْدَى اللَّيالِي
	As *night* is feminine, we have to use the feminine form of *one*.	

205. لَبَّيْكَ سُبْحانَ اللهِ OR - WHAT FORM IS THAT?

The Arabic expression سُبْحانَ اللهِ is used as an exclamation of surprise. It is used a lot in daily life of Muslims. It means: *Praise Allah!* Or: *God be praised!*

It is a special form of the أُسْلُوب النَّعَجُّب because it doesn't fol-low the main patterns (see chapter 194).

Grammatically speaking, سُبْحانَ is a so called اِسْم مَصْدَر and is used as a مَفْعُول مُطْلَق (since it is used as a surprise or exaggera-tion). Actually there is no other application: سُبْحانَ is only used as a مَفْعُول مُطْلَق.

If you wonder why there is only one فَتْحة at the end, well this pattern is مَمْنُوع مِن الصَّرْف, it doesn't take nunation. There are other مَصادِر which are only used for the مَفْعُول مُطْلَق. You will find some examples at the end of this chapter.

<u>Let us go now to the other expression:</u> لَبَّيْكَ

لَبَّيْكَ اللّٰهُمَّ لَبَّيْكَ is said during the pilgrimage before the pilgrims enter Mecca and means: *Here I am! At your service!* The expres-sion is pretty tricky. Let us check the construction:

<u>1. The root:</u> It is ل - ب - ى. This root is only used as a II-verb and means *to follow, to obey* (*a call, an invitation*).

<u>2. The مَصْدَر:</u> The مَصْدَر of لَبَّى – which is a II-verb (فَعَّل) - would be تَلْبِية. But we don't use this word for our expression. Instead, we use لَبٌّ which is the اِسْم الْمَصْدَر of the verb لَبَّى. (See chapter 81).

<u>3. Form the dual:</u> لَبٌّ is put into the dual form for the sake of corroboration (emphasis) meaning *"answer after answer"*, *"say-ing after saying"* (إلبابًا بَعْدَ إلبابٍ ، وإجابةً بَعْدَ إجابة). The dual is مَجْـرُور or مَنْصُوب if لَبَّيْنِ or مَرْفُوع if لَبَّانِ (genitive, accusative).

319

4. Put the word into in مَنْصُوب: This expression is used as an exclamation of surprise – a special form of the أُسْلُوب التَّعَجُّب. So we need لَبَّيِن for our example.

5. Add the personal pronoun: Since we like to add the personal pronoun *you* (*you* refers to Allah) and since we use the word as a مَفْعُول مُطْلَق, the ن is elided because it is connected to a personal pronoun (إِضافة).

6. Result: Finally, we get: لَبَّيْكَ

There is a bunch of expressions that are similarly constructed using a مَفْعُول مُطْلَق (sometimes in dual form, e.g.: سَعْدَيْكَ).

meaning	original meaning	expression
Praise God!	أُسَبِّحُ اللّهَ تَسْبِيحًا.	سُبْحانَ اللّهِ!
God forbid! God save (protect) me (us) from that!	أَعُوذُ بِاللّهِ مَعاذًا.	مَعاذَ اللّهِ!
Here I am! At your service!	أُلَبِّيكَ تَلْبِية بَعْدَ تَلْبِية أي أُلَبِّيكَ كَثِيرًا.	لَبَّيْكَ!
And all good is in your hands.	أُسْعَدُّكَ إِسعادًا بَعْدَ إِسعادٍ.	سَعْدَيْكَ!

Some other expressions using the أُسْلُوب التَّعَجُّب:

Literally: *His achievement is due to God.* Meaning: *how capable, how good, how excellent he is!*	لِلّهِ دَرُّهُ !
What a hero!	يالَهُ مِنْ بَطَلٍ!

An excursus: Why do we use اللّٰهُمَّ ("allahumma") for God?

The word اللّٰهُمَّ is used in the Qur'an about five times. The origin of the expression is not entirely clear. Muslim scholars argue that it just means يا اللّٰه (*O God!*). The م, they say, was added to compensate the omission/suppression of the vocative particle يا

Other scholars say that it is just a short form for: يا اللّٰهُ أُمَّنا بِخَيْرٍ which means *O God! Bring us good!* Or: *O God! Instruct us in righteousness!*

Other scholars say it comes from biblical Hebrew because one word for *God* is אֱלֹהִים which is pronounced "ĕlohīm". However, Muslim scholars say, God's name in Hebrew is the plural form which is true.

אֱלֹהִים is grammatically speaking the plural of אֱלוֹהַ or אֱלַהּ (*Eloah*). Jewish scholars reply that אֱלֹהִים is grammatically singular (it governs a singular verb or adjective) when referring to the Hebrew God, but grammatically plural (taking a plural verb or adjective) when used of pagan divinities. Another explanation is that the plurality is a "plural of respect" (*pluralis excellentiae*).

And what do secular biblical scholars say? They attribute the plural אֱלֹהִים to a polytheistic origin of the Israelite religion.

206. وَاللّٰهِ - WHY DO YOU HAVE TO BE CAREFUL IF YOU SWEAR?

At least, because the grammar is a bit tricky. In Arabic, the word for oath is قَسَم.

The principle meaning of the root is *to share, to part*; but also *to destine*. From this root, the IV-verb أَقْسَمَ بِ عَلَى is used to express the English verb *to swear*. The preposition بِ means *by*.

One of the most common oaths is وَاللّٰه which literally means: *by God!* It is usually translated as *I swear*. Grammatically speaking, the important thing is that the word which comes after it (the person or thing you swear on; الْمُقْسَم بِهِ) is مَجْرُور

The helping letters which introduce an oath - أَدَوات الْقَسَم - are the following three:

1. وَ

2. بِ

3. تَ – the تَ is exclusively used with Allah

The words that can be sworn on are for example:

وَأَيْمُنُ - عُمْر - هِيَ – اللّٰه

I swear by God!	وَأَيْمُنُ اللّٰهِ!
By my life! Notice the first vowel above the word عمر. Normally it is a ضَمّة as the word for *life* is عُمْرٌ. But if you swear on it, the vowel turns into a فَتْحة	لَعَمْري!

Let us check more grammatical implications:

1. If the sentence after the oath is a جُمْلة اِسْمِيّة (nominal sentence), you'll have to use either إِنَّ or أَنَّ combined with لِ

I swear that indeed life is a struggle!	وَاللّهِ إِنَّ الْحَياةَ كِفاحٌ!
I swear that indeed life is a struggle! In this sentence we use the preposition لِ. The meaning is the same.	وَاللّهِ إِنَّ الْحَياةَ لَكِفاحٍ!

2. If the sentence after it is a جُمْلة فِعْلِيّة (verbal sentence) in the past tense, you'll have to use قَدْ or لَقَدْ

By Allah, I have obeyed your command!	تَاللّهِ لَقَدْ أَطَعْتُ أَمْرَكَ!
By Allah, I obeyed your command!	تَاللّهِ قَدْ أَطَعْتُ أَمْرَكَ!

3. If the sentence after it is a جُمْلة فِعْلِيّة in the present tense, you'll have to add the letter لَ after the oath and us the letter ن for emphasis – the so called نُون التَّوْكِيد (see chapter 155).

In short: you put a فَتْحة at the end of a verb and add نَّ.

I swear, I will punish the negligent!	وَاللّهِ لَأُحاسِبَنَّ الْمُقَصِّرَ!

4. If the sentence after it is negated, you won't have to use any form of تَوْكِيد

Your right to success is only by persistence!	وَحَقِّكَ نَجاحُ إِلّا بِالْمُثابَرِةِ!
Notice that the sentence after the oath is a (negated) جُمْلة اِسْمِيّة	

I swear, your effort will not be in vain!	وَاللهِ ما يَضيعُ مَجْهودُكَ!
Notice that the sentence after the oath is a (negated) جُمْلة فِعْلِيّة	

207. IF WE CURSE IN THE NAME OF GOD - DO WE USE THE PAST?

Yes, we do. When we curse in the name of God, we use a past tense verb to express the present tense. The same goes for wishes that refer to God.

Let us see some examples (notice the past tense):

God kill them!	قَتَلَهُم اللهُ!	١
May God not make you prosper!	لا أَصْلَحَكَ اللهُ!	٢
Notice: If you want to negate a verb (and want to express a curse or wish), you use لا plus past tense (الْماضي). This is a rare exception as normally, you only negate the present tense (الْمُضارِع) with لا		
May God protect you from diseases!	حَماكَ اللهُ مِن الأمْراض!	٣
God assist you!	نَصَرَكَ اللهُ!	٤

208. مَنْ - CAN THIS WORD START A CONDITIONAL SENTENCE?

Yes, it can. In literature or formal Arabic, you can choose of a variety of words to start a conditional sentence (*if, when*).

The word مَنْ generally means *who* but it can also be used for an (indefinite) conditional sentence meaning: *whoever; whatever; wherever; however.* مَنْ is used for general assumptions like in the sentence: *Whatever you do, you will be my friend.*

If you use مَنْ, you have to watch out for the correct mood of the verbs.

Look at these 2 examples and pay attention to the endings:

| 1 | Whoever strives, succeeds in life. | مَنْ يَجْتَهِدْ يَنْجَحْ فِي حَيَاتِهِ. |

Here, يَنْجَحْ ends in a سُكُون as it is just a regular verb and therefore follows the regular rules.

| 2 | Whoever visits Egypt meets a friend. | مَنْ يَزُرْ مِصْرَ يَلْقَ صَدِيقًا. |

The verb يَزُور turns into يَزُرْ (with سُكُون at the end) – but يَلْقَ ends with a فَتْحَة because the original form is يَلْقَى. Notice the difference to يُلْقِي which means: *to throw, to arrest* (IV-verb)

So why do we write يَلْقَ? This is true for all verbs which have a و or a ي as the final root letter and follow the past tense pattern فَعِلَ – in our case: لَقِيَ

In the مَجْزُوم-mood, the weak letter is dropped and the vowel on top of the second (and now last letter) is a فَتْحَة. Same would happen to: بَقِيَ, رَضِيَ, نَسِيَ

In our sentence we eventually get: يَلْقَ

209. أَلَّا AND إِلَّا - WHAT IS THE DIFFERENCE?

These two words almost look the same. Let's focus on the difference: the هَمْزة. It is written either on top or at the bottom. The position is decisive for the meaning:

- إِلَّا is a particle. It means *except* (see chapter 215)
- أَلَّا is a combination of two words and means *not to*

أَلَّا has a فَتْحة upon the هَمْزة. It means *that not; unless; if not* and is the result of a grammatical construction:

3		2		1
أَلَّا	=	لَا	+	أَنْ

Notice that the verb which comes after it has to be مَنْصُوب as it is actually preceded by أَنْ. Here are some examples:

...that you don't travel...	أَنْ لا تُسافِر = أَلَّا تُسافِرَ
Give me your money and I won't kill you (or I will kill you!) Notice the past tense after أَنْ. This is theoretically possible - see chapter 107.	أَعْطِيني نُقُودَكَ وَأَلَّا قَتَلْتُكَ!
If you don't (didn't) do it...	أَلَّا تَفْعَلَهُ...
I think that he didn't drink.	أَظُنُّ أَلَّا يَشْرَبَ.
The child didn't want to go to school.	أَرادَ الطِّفْلُ أَلَّا يَذْهَبَ إِلَى الْمَدْرَسةِ.

Let us have a look at a sentence in which you find both words:

He decided not to take anything with him except the book.	قَرَّرَ أَلَّا يَأْخُذَ مَعَهُ إِلَّا الْكِتَابَ.

After أَنْ the verb is مَنْصُوب, so the verb has to be يَأْخُذَ with a فَتْحة at the end ز	أَنْ + لا = أَلَّا
But why has the word الْكِتَابَ a فَتْحة at the end? Here, the word إِلَّا means *except*. The grammatical construction is called أُسْلُوب الْقَصْر and follows certain rules. If you don't remember them, have a look at chapter 216.	إِلَّا

A hint: If you want to vowel the sentence, just delete the negation in your mind and you will get: يَأْخُذ الْكِتَابَ

The word الْكِتَاب is the مَفْعُول بِهِ – and has to be مَنْصُوب

210. بَدَل - WHAT IS IT AND WHAT IS ITS FUNCTION IN A SENTENCE?

Literally, the word بَدَل means: *substitute*. It has the meaning of to *stand in for someone*. In English grammar, we would call it an apposition. An apposition is (normally) a noun that describes a subject or an object more precise. What is important here: An apposition takes the same case as the word it is accompanying.

Let us have a look at the grammar terms:

- The first part is called: مُبْدَل مِنْه (*substituted for*)

327

- The second part: بَدَل (apposition)

Let us dig a bit deeper to grasp the meaning of the الْبَدَل

Karim, the driver, was in the house.	كانَ السّائِقُ كَرِيمٌ فِي الْبَيْتِ.
This is actually the origin of the above sentence!	كانَ السّائِقُ ,كانَ كَرِيمٌ, فِي الْبَيْتِ.

What about the position of the الْبَدَل in a sentence?

1. The بَدَل follows the subject of a sentence

This student came.		جاءَ هٰذا الطّالِبُ.
The word *this* is the subject of the sentence.	فاعِل / مُبْدَل مِنْهُ	هٰذا
The word *the student* is <u>not</u> the subject of the sentence. It is an apposition.	بَدَل	الطّالِبُ

2. The بَدَل follows the object of a sentence

I met this student.		قابَلْتُ هٰذا الطّالِبَ.
Object of the sentence. Notice: The word هٰذا never changes its shape, whatever the position in the sentence is.	مَفْعُول بِهِ مُبْدَل مِنْهُ	هٰذا
The student is <u>not the object</u> of the sentence! It is an apposition and needs agreement. That is why you have to add a فَتْحة at the end.	بَدَل	الطّالِبَ

328

Let us check another example where the بَدَل has an attributive meaning. In this situation you could actually understand the sentence even without the بَدَل

The doctor healed the leg of the patient.	عالَجَ الطَّبِيبُ الْمَرِيضَ رِجْلَهُ.

Direct object (مَفْعُول بِهِ)	الْمَرِيض
Apposition; so called بَدَل بَعْض مِن كُل	رِجْلَهُ
This pronoun always ends in a ضَمّة as it is مَبْنِيّ (fixed). Grammatically speaking, the pronoun is a مُضاف إِلَيْهِ	ه

211. اِطَّلَعَ - WHAT IS THE ROOT?

The word means *to examine*; *to study*; *to check*. It is VIII-verb following the pattern اِفْتَعَلَ. The root of the verb is: ط - ل - ع

So watch out: According to the verb pattern the verb should be: اِطْتَلَع. As this would be a bit difficult to pronounce, the ت and the ط merge to a double ط

Watch out for two things:

- The الْمَصْدَر of the verb is اِطِّلاع and means *inspection*; *examination*

- Notice that the IV-verb looks almost the same: أَطْلَعَ But it doesn't have a شَدّة and starts with a ع (on top of the Alif). The IV-form means: *to teach*

212. فَ, وَ AND ثُمَّ - HOW DO YOU USE THEM?

They all three are found between two words which have the same case. فَ, وَ and ثُمَّ are so called حُرُوف الْعَطْف

In other words: The word which comes after it and the preceding word take the same agreement. That's for the grammar part. Now let's focus on the meaning: These three words are used to describe a chronological sequence.

- فَ could be translated as: *and; and so; then*. It implies a closer relationship, some development or logical order between the words or sentences.

- ثُمَّ could be translated as: *then; after that; thereupon*. It shows that one event is over, and that a new thing starts.

Let us look at an example:

Ahmad and Khalid came. We don't know who came first or if they came at the same time. The chronological sequence doesn't matter.	جَاءَ أَحْمَدُ وَخَالِدٌ. ١
Ahmad came, and right after (immediately after) him, Khalid.	جَاءَ أَحْمَدُ فَخَالِدٌ. ٢
Eventually (later), Khalid came.	جَاءَ أَحْمَدُ ثُمَّ خَالِدٌ. ٣

Notice: Words consisting of only one letter are combined with the subsequent word. That is why you attach و and ف to the word which comes after them.

213. WHAT DOES لَمْ يَعُدْ MEAN?

The verb عَادَ (past tense) and يَعُودُ (present tense) is a wily verb. It generally means *to return* especially, if it is used with إِلَى

Therefore, لَمْ يَعُدْ could mean: *He did not return.*

1. However, if it is used in the past tense (usually negated and without a preposition), it normally means *to become* (*to grow into*) similar to the verb صَارَ. It is then treated as a sister of كَانَ which means the predicate has to be مَنْصُوب

2. If you use عَادَ in the past tense (<u>negated</u>) followed directly by a verb in the present tense, it will have a present tense meaning: *no longer (to) be; not any longer.*

3. If you use عَادَ in the past tense (<u>not negated</u>) followed directly by a verb in the present tense, it will usually mean *to do again.*

4. Sometimes, you can use عَادَ in the past tense together with the conjunction فَ followed by a verb in the past tense. This also expresses: *to do again*

Let us look at these examples:

I no longer remember....	...لَمْ أَعُدْ أَذْكُرُ
There is no alternative left.	لَمْ يَعُدْ هُناكَ بَدِيل.
I am now nothing more than; now I am only...	...لَمْ أَعُدْ سِوَى
I no longer think...	...لَمْ أَعُدْ أُفَكِّرُ
He hit me again.	عَادَ فَضَرَبَنِي.

331

214. إذا - WHAT DOES IT MEAN?

Don't confuse the word إذا ("idha") with إذًا (" 'idhan") which means *therefore; so; then*.

The word إذا is normally used to start a conditional sentence, meaning *if; when; whether*.

However, there is also a so called إذا الْفُجائِيّة which is used if something is unexpected (a kind of surprise).

→ Important: After إذا you have to use a جُمْلة اسْمِيّة.

Let us check some examples:

I entered the room and (surprisingly/all of a sudden) all the students were absent.	دَخَلْتُ الْحُجْرة فَإذا جَمِيعُ الطّلّاب غائِبونَ.
I opened my bag and (strangely/surprisingly) it was empty.	فَتَحْتُ حَقِيبَتِي فَإذا هِيَ خالِيةٌ.

215. WHAT IS THE PROBLEM WITH THE WORDS FOR "EXCEPT"?

It is mainly the grammar which can be complicated as we will see. There are several ways to express the meaning of *except, and* this doesn't make it easier. In Arabic, we call these forms أُسْلُوب الْاسْتِثْناء. There are several words you can use. All of them basically mean the same: *except; but; excluding; save*:

إلّا - غَيْر - سِوَى - عَدا - ما عَدا - خَلا - ما خَلا - حاشا

Notice: The expression ما حاشا doesn't exist.

Let us now check how to use them.

1. The construction with إِلَّا *(except)*

The word إِلَّا is a so called حَرْف

1	All students came except one.	جَاءَ الطُّلَّابُ إِلَّا طَالِبًا.
	الطُّلَّابُ is the الْمُسْتَثْنَى مِنْهُ (the majority where the exception is taken from). The word طَالِبًا here is مَنْصُوب. Grammatically speaking, it is called the الْمُسْتَثْنَى (the thing excepted).	

2	Only one student came.	مَا جَاءَ الطُّلَّابُ إِلَّا طَالِبًا.
		مَا جَاءَ الطُّلَّابُ إِلَّا طَالِبٌ.
	Both are correct. You can choose: مَرْفُوع or مَنْصُوب	
	Watch out: طَالِبًا in the مَنْصُوب-case is the so called الْمُسْتَثْنَى In the second sentence, however, we use the مَرْفُوع-case! So the grammatical function is different: The word طَالِبٌ is a so called بَدَل. Therefore, regarding agreement, it has to follow the word it is referring to (الْمُسْتَثْنَى مِنْهُ) - which is in the above sentence الطُّلَّابُ	

3	Only one student is here.	مَا جَاءَ إِلَّا طَالِبٌ.
	This form is called أُسْلُوب الْقَصْر and describes exclusivity (see chapter 216). The word طَالِبٌ is the subject (فَاعِل) In order to find the right cases you'll have to delete the negation in your mind. So read it like: جَاءَ الطُّلَّابُ – and then put case markers.	

2. The construction with ما

All students came except one.	.جَاءَ الطُّلَّابُ ما عَدَا طَالِبًا .جَاءَ الطُّلَّابُ ما خَلا طَالِبًا

In both examples, the word for *except* is a verb and is connected to a so-called ما المصدرية, an interpreted مصدر. Since it is a verb, the information/word after it functions as an object (مَفْعُول بِه) – which has to be مَنْصُوب

3. The construction without ما

1	All students came except one.	.جَاءَ الطُّلَّابُ عَدَا طَالِبًا
	Same meaning as above (2.) with ما (and same cases too). The word طَالِباً is a regular object (مَفْعُول بِه).	
2	All students came except one. Same meaning as the prev. example	.جَاءَ الطُّلَّابُ خَلا طَالِبٍ .جَاءَ الطُّلَّابُ حاشا طَالِبٍ
	Notice: Here, the word خَلا has the function of a حَرْف جَرّ (preposition). Therefore, the word after it has to be مَجْرُور. The same applies to the word حاشا	

4. The construction with: غَيْر / سِوَى

All students came except one.	.جَاءَ الطُّلَّابُ غَيْرَ طَالِبٍ .جَاءَ الطُّلَّابُ سِوَى طَالِبٍ

The word طَالِبٍ is the 2nd part of a إِضَافة-construction, it has to be مَجْرُور. Since the sentence is not negated, the word غَيْرَ has a فَتْحة.

334

1	Only one student came.	مَا جَاءَ الطُّلَّابُ غَيْرَ طَالِبٍ. مَا جَاءَ الطُّلَّابُ غَيْرُ طَالِبٍ.

The word طَالِبٍ is the 2nd part of a إضافة-construction → it has to be مَجْرُور. You can either write غَيْرَ or غَيْرُ. Both are correct.

2	Only one student came.	مَا جَاءَ غَيْرُ طَالِبٍ. مَا جَاءَ سِوَى طَالِبٍ.

This type of construction is called أُسْلُوب الْقَصْر.

The word طَالِبٍ is the 2nd part of a إضافة, it has to be مَجْرُور.

The word غَيْرُ here is the subject (فَاعِل). It has to take a ضَمّة.

If you want to find out about the case markers, just image the sentence as there was no negation.

Notice: In the sentence with سِوَى, the case marker is hidden!

Here are some examples:

I only met one student.	مَا قَابَلْتُ إِلَّا طَالِبًا.
There is only one student in the room.	لَيْسَ فِي الْغُرْفةِ إِلَّا طَالِبٌ.

لَيْسَ is a verb – so it usually stands in the singular form at the beginning! (Note: This is only different if the subject is inherent in the verb, e.g. *they*: لَيْسُوا فِي الْبَيْتِ – *they are not at home*.)

- خَبَر لَيْسَ is the فِي الْغُرْفةِ
- The word طَالِب is the so called إِسْم لَيْسَ

I only met one student.	مَا قَابَلْتُ غَيْرَ طَالِبٍ.

335

Delete the negation in your mind: غَيْرَ. – قابَلْتُ طالِبًا – so it must be غَيْرَ. It would be the same if you used سِوَى, but notice that the case ending is hidden/a presumptive vowel (مُقَدَّرة)	
Every one wanted to go except for me	أرادَ كُلُ واحِدٍ أنْ يَذْهَبَ إلّا إيّاي.

216. أُسْلُوب الْقَصْر - How do you express exclusivity?

If you want to put the stress on a fact or a person, you use the words *except* or *only* in English. In Arabic, there are plenty of ways to express this. These forms are called أُسْلُوب الْقَصْر

1	Negation and exception	النَّفْيُ وَالْاِسْتِثْناء
	Only the serious workers are successful. (For the correct case endings, just imagine the sentence without the negation!)	لا يَنْجَحُ إلّا الْعامِلُونَ بِجِدٍّ.

2	Combination of إنَّ + ما	إنَّما
	Notice that after it, a جُمْلة فِعْلِيّة or a جُمْلة اسْمِيّة can follow, it is up to you. The ما here is a so called ما الكاقّة. This ما deletes all the grammatical implications of a sentence starting with إنّ	
	Success is for serious workers only.	إنَّما النَّجاحُ لِلّعامِلِينَ بِجِدٍّ. or إنَّما يَنْجَحُ الْعامِلِينَ بِجِدٍّ.

336

3	Meaning: *but*	بَلْ - عَطْف
	Note that you have to start with a negation.	
	Fairouz is not a writer, she is a singer.	ما فَيْرُوز كاتِبةٌ بَلْ مُغَنِّيةٌ.

4	Meaning: *but*	لكِنْ - عَطْف
	Fairouz is not a writer, she is a singer.	ما فَيْرُوز كاتِبةٌ لكِنْ مُغَنِّيةٌ.

5	Emphasis by word order	التَّقْديم والتَّأْخِير
	I address my words to you.	إلَيْكَ أُوَجِّهُ كَلَامي or أُوَجِّهُ كَلَامي إلَيْكَ.

Watch out for the correct cases and use of grammar!

The friendship with an idiot is a burden.	صَداقةُ الْأَحْمَقِ تَعَبٌ.
Here, you have to negate the اِسْم with لَيْسَ The خَبَر لَيْسَ (predicate) has to be مَنْصُوب	لَيْسَتْ صَداقةُ الْأَحْمَقِ إلّا تَعَبًا.

I am a student (feminine).	أنا طالِبةٌ.
I am (only) a student.	لَسْتُ إلّا طالِبةً.
(It is that; because; only) I am a student.	إنّما أنا طالِبةٌ.
I am student, not a teacher.	أنا طالِبةٌ لا مُدَرِّسةٌ.

217. HOW CAN YOU SAY "I CAN"?

In colloquial Arabic, you will hear مُمْكِن most of the time. But in standard Arabic, there are several ways to express *can* depending on the situation. Here are some examples:

literal meaning	syntax	root	
with my capacity, possibility	بِمَقْدُورِي أَنْ	ق - د - ر	1
with my ability, capability	بِاسْتِطاعَتِي أَنْ	ط - و - ع	2
verb mostly used for *can*	اِسْتَطاعَ, يَسْتَطِيعُ		
to be able to	قَدَرَ, يَقْدُرُ أَنْ / عَلَى	ق - د - ر	3
to enable; to be possible	أَمْكَنَ, يُمْكِنُ أَنْ / مِنْ	م - ك - ن	4
with capability; capacity	يُوسْعِ	و - س - ع	5
often translated as *could*	مِنْ شَأْنِ (ه / ها) + أَنْ	ش - ء - ن	6
to allow; to permit	سَمَحَ, يَسْمَحُ لِ + أَنْ	س - م -ح	7

218. DOES A SIMPLE SENTENCE ALSO MEAN SIMPLE GRAMMAR?

Not really.

Sometimes a single word can change the grammar and the meaning entirely. Especially if you want to give emphasis on a part of the sentence, the (pronunciation of the) ending can be different. Let us have a look at three sentences:

	meaning	explanation	example
1	Safety lies in slowness.		السَّلَامةُ فِي التَّأَنِّي.
		مُبْتَدَأ	السَّلَامةُ
		خَبَر الْمُبْتَدَأ	فِي التَّأَنِّي
	The 2nd part of the sentence is a so called شِبْه جُمْلة. Grammatically speaking, it is actually مَرْفُوع (nominative case) – but hidden. We say: فِي مَحَلّ مَرْفُوع		

2	It is safety that lies in slowness.		إِنَّ السَّلَامةَ فِي التَّأَنِّي.
	Watch out for the cases:	اِسْم إِنَّ	السَّلَامةَ
	The اِسْم إِنَّ ("subject") is مَنْصُوب. The predicate is مَرْفُوع	خَبَر إِنَّ	فِي التَّأَنِّي

3	Nothing but/much more safety lies in slowness.		إِنَّما السَّلَامةُ فِي التَّأَنِّي.
		مُبْتَدَأ مَرْفُوع	السَّلَامةُ
		خَبَر الْمُبْتَدَأ	فِي التَّأَنِّي

219. الْأَسْماء الْخَمْسة - Why are these five nouns special?

They are special because they change their form dramatically when they are combined with a possessive pronoun, or are part of a إِضافة, or - generally said - need cases. They are called الْأَسْماء الْخَمْسة ("the five nouns") because they are five in number. These words are often misspelled. Grammar mistakes are pretty common as colloquial and standard Arabic mix in daily speech. Let's have a look at them:

	word	مَرْفُوع	مَجْرُور	مَنْصُوب	translation
١	أَبٌ	أَبُوه	أَبيه	أَباه	his father
٢	أَخٌ	أَخُوه	أَخيه	أَخاه	his brother
٣	حَمٌ	حَمُوه	حَميه	حَماه	his mother in law
٤	ذو	ذُو	ذي	ذا	of; with
٥	فُو (فَم)	فُوه	فِيه	فاه	his mouth

220. إِذْ AND إِذا AND إِذًا - WHAT IS THE DIFFERENCE?

All three words look very similar. So watch out and don't mix them up. Here is a list what they mean and how they are used:

إذا	when; as suddenly
إذا is normally introducing a conditional sentence. The verbal sentence after it is usually in the past tense – but it has the meaning of the present tense or even future tense! إذا can only be used if the situation in the conditional sentence can theoretically be achieved (if it is possible, or if it has happened.) This is different to إِنْ because the word إِنْ can be used for introducing a <u>possible or impossible</u> condition – see examples below. إذا ما is only used to emphasize a sentence (تأكيد)	

340

If you work hard/strive in your work, you will be successful in your life. (This leaves open if you are successful or not; you could be both.)	إِنْ تَجْتَهِدْ فِي عَمَلِكَ تَنْجَحْ فِي حَيَاتِكَ.
When the sun rises (and the sun does rise every day without an exception), people will go to their work.	إِذَا طَلَعَتِ الشَّمْس ذَهَبَ النَّاسُ إِلَى عَمَلِهِم.

as; when; since; as; because	إِذْ
إِذْ can be used as a causal or temporal conjunction. Normally, a verbal sentence in the past follows, very rarely you see a nominal sentence. It has usually the meaning of عِنْدَ ما	
She cried because she was sick.	بَكَيَتْ إِذْ كَانَتْ مَرِيضَةً.

then; therefore; hence; that's why; consequently; in that case	إِذًا = إِذَنْ
Often used in a dialogue in response to what was said before.	
A: We will meet at the centre.	سَنَلْتَقِي فِي الْمَرْكَزِ.
B: Let's have a coffee together then.	إِذَنْ نَشْرَبُ قَهْوى مَعًا.

221. "BEFORE" AND "AFTER" – HOW ABOUT THEIR ENDING?

Normally, the words قَبْلَ and بَعْدَ end with a فَتْحة – but not if they are preceded by the word مِن. In this case, they take a ضَمّة

Why is that?

The ضَمّة replaces a sequence, e.g.: مِنْ قَبْلِ ذٰلِكَ الْوَقْتِ

That's why you will find the ضَمّة at the end of بَعْد or قَبْل only in connection with مِن. Let us have a look at some examples:

previously; before	مِنْ قَبْلُ
I have not visited Luxor before.	لَمْ أَزُرِ الأُقْصُر قَبْلَ الْيَوْمِ.

Note the differences in the endings:

before	قَبْلَ + إضافة
before the lesson	قَبْلَ الدَّرسِ
After مِنْ! Notice that the word قَبْلِ takes a كَسْرة at the end as it is the 2nd part of the إضافة	مِنْ قَبْلِ + إضافة
before that	مِن قَبْلِ ذٰلِكَ
before; previously. It doesn't require further specification. Here, the word قَبْلُ takes a ضَمّة as we don't have a إضافة	مِنْ قَبْلُ

222. "NEVER" - HOW DO YOU SAY THIS IN ARABIC?

This is not so easy.

There are several possibilities.

Let us have a look at some of them:

I	(1) negation (past tense) + (2) قَطُّ	never; ever; at all
	The word قَطُّ itself comes from the root: *to carve; to cut; to trim*.	
	The director has never gone to the office. (For the purpose of explaining, I didn't use a helping vowel for يَذْهَبْ)	لَمْ يَذْهَبْ الْمُدِيرُ قَطُّ إِلَى الْمَكْتَبِ.
2	(1) verb + (2) أَبَدًا	never
	I never study.	لا أَدْرُسُ أَبَدًا.
3	(1) verb + (2) مُطْلَقًا	never
	I never study.	لا أَدْرُسُ مُطْلَقًا.

223. كَانَ AND إِنَّ ARE SOMEHOW THE OPPOSITE, AREN'T THEY?

Grammatically speaking: yes.

If you spot the verb كَانَ (*to be*) or the particle إِنَّ (*indeed; that*) in a sentence, you have to be particularly careful.

The regular rules for the case endings of subject and object don't apply any longer. Unfortunately, both of them have "sisters", other words that share the same grammar rules. Let us have a closer look at both groups as they are crucial for the correct understanding of Arabic grammar:

All sisters of كَانَ are verbs	كَانَ وَأَخَواتها
All sisters of إِنَّ are حُرُوف	إِنَّ وَأَخَواتها

كانَ	إِنَّ
Past tense of the verb *to be*.	To emphasize a جُمْلة اِسْمِيّة (nominal sentence).
كانَ - أَصْبَحَ - أَضْحَى - أَمْسَى - بات - ظَلّ - to be or to become صارَ: to describe a transformation لَيْسَ - for negation ما دامَ - for proof of duration ما بَرِحَ - ما اِنْفَكَّ - ما فَتِئَ - ما زالَ - for continuation; *still, as long as* (all of them have the meaning of the present tense)	إِنَّ - كَأَنَّ - لكِن - لكِنَّ - لَعَلَّ (*perhaps*) - لَيْت (*if only*) - Notice: Since it is emphasizing a nominal sentence, the word after إِنَّ has to be a noun or a pronoun (ها ,ه, ...) which turns it, in fact, into a nominal sentence. The "sisters" are conjunctions expressing doubt or objection.
subject: مَرْفُوع object: مَنْصُوب	subject: مَنْصُوب object: مَرْفُوع
an example	
صارَ الرَّجُلُ مُدِيرًا.	كَأَنَّ الْحَياةَ حُلْمٌ.
The man became director.	It seems that life is a dream.

224. سَنةٌ - How do you build the plural of it?

The word means *year*. There are two correct plural forms:

type	explanation	plural
A	regular feminine plural	سَنَوات
B	sound masculine plural pattern; for the nominative case (مَرْفُوع)	سِنُونَ
	sound masculine plural pattern; for مَجْرُور and مَنْصُوب and also used in dialects	سِنِينَ

Form (B) of this plural is subsumed under the masculine sound plural. So the same rules as for sound masculine plural forms have to be applied, i.e. you have to omit the ن in masculine sound plural endings if it is the first part of a إضافة

There are several other words that have a sound masculine plural form besides its other (and more often used) plural form. For example the word *son*: اِبْن – see chapter 225.

225. What does أُولُو mean?

The word أُولُو is a plural form of the demonstrative pronoun ذُو which basically means *master of; in possession of.* أُولُو is a very strange plural form, but they do exist in Arabic for other words too. When dealing with the word اِبْن (*son*), for example, you could encounter atypical plurals too following similar rules.

Let's take an example. Notice that the ن disappears!

sons of Israel	بَنُو إِسْرائِيل

Let us check these plural forms in detail:

A: regular feminine plural

B: sound masculine plural pattern

meaning; explanation	plural	type	word
Meaning: *sons.* This is the broken plural	أَبْناء	A	اِبْن
This is the sound masculine plural مَرْفُوع	بَنُون	B	
This is the sound masculine plural مَنْصُوب	بَنِين	B	
Type B is more often used in religious scripts. Notice that the ن disappears in a إِضافة because it is a masculine sound plural!			بَنُو إِسْرائيل
owner; people. It is the masculine plural مَرْفُوع of ذُو. You can't use it alone; it must be used as a إِضافة like ذُو – that's why there is no ن	أُولُو	B	ذُو
This is the sound masculine plural مَنْصُوب	أُولِي	B	
Meaning: *men of understanding* It comes from the word لُبّ (*mind* or *hear*).			أُولُوا الْألْبابِ
وَلَكُمْ فِي الْقِصاصِ حَياةٌ يَا أُولِي الْألْبابِ لَعَلَّكُمْ تَتَّقُونَ .			
"And there is for you in legal retribution [saving of] life, O you [people] of understanding, that you may become righteous." (Qur'an, سُورة الْبَقَرة (*The cow*), 2:179)			

Watch out: The word ذُو is sometimes mistaken with اذ and therefore mistranslated as *that*.

226. قَضَيْتُ أَوْقاتًا OR قَضَيْتُ أَوْقاتٍ - WHAT IS CORRECT?

The sentence means: *I spent time.*

The word *time* is the direct object (مَفْعُول بِهِ).

First of all, don't forget that Arabic feminine plurals don't take the ending "-an" (ـً) in the مَنْصُوب-case. For example:

I saw (female) teachers.	رَأَيْتُ مُعَلِّماتٍ.

Let us check the word أَوْقات now. It looks like it has the feminine ة-ending. But this is wrong - because the word أَوْقات is not a feminine plural. The ت is part of the root.

Therefore, it has to be: قَضَيْتُ أَوْقاتًا

meaning	plural	word	root
time	أَوْقات	وَقْت	و - ق - ت
I had a great time.		قَضَيْتُ أَوْقاتًا سَعِيدَةً	
sound	أَصْوات	صَوْت	ص - و - ت
I heard sounds.		سَمِعْتُ أَصْواتًا	

227. دَلَّ - WHAT IS THE إِسْم الْفاعِل OF THIS VERB?

The verb means *to point; to indicate.*

Verbs consisting of two root letters having the latter one doubled can be a bit nasty.

This brings us to the question: How do you build the active participle (إِسْم الْفَاعِل) of these verbs?

Let's see:

meaning	إِسْم الْفاعِل	الْمُضارِع	الْماضِي	root
to point; indicate	دالٌّ	يَدُلُّ	دَلَّ	د - ل - ل
to split; cut through	شاقٌّ	يَشُقُّ	شَقَّ	ش - ق - ق

→ You take the regular pattern فاعِل and the only thing to keep in mind is that the ل is not written twice, but gets a شَدّة

228. "AT THE SAME TIME" - HOW DO YOU SAY THAT?

There are many ways to express that something happened at the same time. We will focus on a possibility that uses a إِضافة-construction with إِذْ - a word denoting past time meaning: *at the time of; then.*

Here is how this works:

1st	Take a word indicating time or place.	ساعة
2nd	Add a فَتْحة at the end of the word. Note that the ة will become a ت in the next step.	ساعَت
3rd	Add the word إِذْ and add two كَسْرة as تَنْوين	ساعَتَئِذٍ
	This expression means: *at the same time; in this/that hour.*	

348

Here are some other examples. They all mean more or less the same: *then* or *at that time*:

وَقْتَئِذٍ	عِنْدَئِذٍ	فِي ذَاكَ الْوَقْتِ
ساعَتَئِذٍ	حِينَئِذٍ	آنَئِذٍ

You can use it with other words too, like *day* or *year*:

at the same moment/second	لَحْظَتَئِذٍ
on the same day	يَوْمَئِذٍ
in the same year	سَنَتَئِذٍ

229. إِنَّ AND أَنَّ - WHAT IS THE DIFFERENCE?

You might have noticed that especially after the verb *to say*, إِنَّ is used and not أَنَّ. But why is that?

First of all, أَنَّ can never stand at the beginning of a sentence.

إِنَّ on the other hand can only be used:

1. To start a complete sentence (e.g. to start a جُمْلة اِسْمِيّة) – used as an emphatic particle

2. After verbs that don't necessarily take an object (to say)

3. Reported speech (especially with the verb قَالَ (*to say*) and sometimes also with the verb عَلِمَ (*to get to know*)

349

إِنَّ is never followed by a verb. For this reason a dummy pronoun (ضَمِير الشَّأن) is occasionally used after إِنَّ – for example a ه. Instead of starting the sentence with a اسْم, the verb follows إِنَّهُ. Watch out for the case endings as with the dummy pronoun, the sentence follows the regular rules of a جُمْلة فِعْلِية

Let us have a look at an example. Both sentences mean the same: *He said that the teacher came.*

Here we use a dummy pronoun. Notice that *teacher* takes a ضَمّة as it is the subject (فاعِل).	قَالَ إِنَّهُ جَاءَ المُدَرِّسُ.
This is the usual construction. The word for *teacher* is the اِسْم إِنَّ and has a فَتْحة at the end.	قَالَ إِنَّ المُدَرِّسَ جَاءَ.

Let us dig deeper into the sentence-structure:

I said that the lesson is easy.	قُلْتُ إِنَّ الدَّرْسَ سَهْلٌ.

There has to be a complete sentence after إِنَّ. The reason for this has to do with the verb *to say* – as *to say* doesn't need an object!

The best way to understand why there is إِنَّ after قَالَ is the following rule: قَالَ is <u>always followed by a sentence</u> or clause – and never by a single word.

This, on the other hand, is not true with أَنَّ (with فَتْحة on the ن) as it <u>can be followed by a single word</u>.

To make it clearer, we will have a closer look at أَنَّ now. Try to imagine the following examples (although not 100 % grammatically correct) with a مَصْدَر (instead of أَنَّ). Notice also the cases!

I am pleased that you arrived.	أَسْعَدَنِي أَنَّكَ وَصَلْتَ
	= أَسْعَدَنِي وُصُولُكَ.
I mentioned to Karim that you arrived.	ذَكَرْتُ لِكَرِيمٍ أَنَّكَ وَصَلْتَ
	= ذَكَرْتُ لِكَرِيمٍ وُصُولَكَ.
I was happy that you arrived.	فَرِحْتُ بِأَنَّكَ وَصَلْتَ
(or: with the fact that you arrived.)	= فَرِحْتُ بِوُصُولِكَ .

What we learn from the examples: The expression أَنَّكَ وَصَلْتَ (*that you arrived*) could be replaced with وُصُولُكَ (*your arriving/your arrival*) which is the مَصْدَر.

إِنَّ - however - can't be paraphrased like that!

You can't replace قَالَ إِنَّكَ وَصَلْتَ (*He said: Truly, indeed, you arrived*) with the sentence: قَالَ وُصُولُكَ (*He said: your arriving/arrival*) because the latter doesn't make sense. Thus, إِنَّكَ وَصَلْتَ has the status of a full clause and not that of a مَصْدَر (infinitive). In English, we occasionally leave the word *that* out.

Some important remarks:

1. You have to use إِنَّ after قَالَ if you trust the information that comes after it. If you <u>doubt</u> it, you can use a construction with بـ and أَنَّ – to show that you do not believe what comes after it. Notice: This construction is also used for the reported speech! (see chapter 202)

Let us check an example (taken from a Syrian textbook):

Some scientists say that the universe is expanding.	يَقُولُ بَعْضُ الْعُلَمَاءِ بِأَنَّ الْكَوْنَ يَتَمَدَّدُ.

351

2. أَنَّ can start a sentence – but watch out for the meaning!

The child groaned.	أَنَّ الطِّفْلُ.
The child groans.	يَئِنُّ الطِّفْلُ.

In this sentence أَنَّ is not a particle – it is a verb! The particle أَنَّ can never stand at the beginning of a sentence – unless it is a verb (*to groan; moan*) which looks like this:

past tense	أَنَّ

present tense	يَئِنُّ

3. Sometimes, there is a لـ after a sentence with إِنَّ

It is you whom I know.	إِنِّي بِكَ لَعارِفٌ.
(German: *Dich kenne ich doch!*)	

After إِنَّ (which is here combined with the first person أنا – notice the ending ي) the information, which comes after it (predicate), is often introduced by لـ – which is NOT a negation. It is used to emphasize. This لـ has <u>no</u> influence on the case!

A remark: If you use the verb عَلِمَ in the meaning of *to hear about; to be told; to get to know* (German: *erfahren*), you can choose between إِنَّ or أَنَّ

Both sentences mean the same:	عَلِمْتُ أَنَّ الدَّرْسَ سَهْلٌ.
I was told/got to know that the lesson is easy	عَلِمْتُ إِنَّ الدَّرْسَ سَهْلٌ.

230. THE PARTICLE أَنَّ - WHAT WORD HAS TO COME AFTER IT?

The particle أَنَّ comes usually after a verb and means *that*. For example: *I think that...*

Arabic, however, works differently, so if you have an English sentence in mind that starts with *I think that..,.* you could get lost in translation as you might build an Arabic sentence that sounds "English". Here is an example:

I think that it isn't clear if...	...أَظُنُّ أَنَّ لَيْسَ مِن الْواضِحِ إذا	1
There is a mistake in this sentence! After أَنَّ you can never put a verb – and لَيْسَ is a verb!		
Here is the solution: You can correct the sentence by using a pronoun! Notice the pronunciation: "annahu"	...أَظُنُّ أَنَّهُ لَيْسَ مِن الْواضِحِ إذا	2
The pronoun converts the sentence to a جُمْلة اِسْمِيّة; so the word after أَنَّ is not a verb any more!		

231. إِنَّ - WHEN DO YOU HAVE TO USE IT?

The particle إِنَّ causes students a lot of problems. You shouldn't forget that إِنَّ changes the case endings:

- The subject (اِسْم إِنَّ) after it has to be مَنْصُوب
- The predicate (خَبَر إِنَّ) has to be مَرْفُوع

Let us check when you have to use إِنَّ

1	At the beginning of a sentence	
	Truly (indeed), work is important for people.	إِنَّ الْعَمَلَ ضَرُورِيٌّ لِلإِنْسانِ.

2	After a quotation	
	My professor said: "Indeed, the prices in this shop are high."	قالَ أُسْتاذِي:"إِنَّ الأَسْعارَ فِي هٰذا الْمَحَلِّ مُرْتَفِعةٌ."

3	After أَلا – so called أَلا الاسْتِفْتاحِيّة or *letter of inauguration; inceptive; initial particle*	
	Certainly men of knowledge are beneficial to the society.	أَلا إِنَّ أُولِي الْعِلْمِ نافِعُونَ لِلْمُجْتَمَعِ.

4	After the word كَلّا which can mean: *not at all; on the contrary; by no means! Certainly not! Never! No!*	
	No! Health is more important than money!	كَلّا إِنَّ الصَّحّةَ أَهَمُّ مِنَ الْمالِ!

5	After the particle إِذْ	
	I arrived when the students were leaving.	حَضَرْتُ إِذْ إِنَّ الطُّلابَ مُنْصَرِفُونَ.

6	After the word حَيْثُ	

354

I sat where the colleagues were sitting.	جَلَسْتُ حَيْثُ إِنَّ الزُّمَلاءَ جَالِسُونَ.

7	At the beginning of a sentence that is used as a حال
I said goodbye to my colleague while he was leaving.	وَدَّعْتُ زَمِيلِي وَ إِنَّهُ مُنْصَرِفٌ.

8	At the beginning of a sentence that has the meaning of a relative clause (جُمْلة الصِّلة)
I met those who master five languages.	قَابَلْتُ مَنْ إِنَّهُمْ يُجِيدُونَ خَمْسَ لُغاتٍ.

9	Used to start the sentence after an oath (قَسَم – جَوَاب الْقَسَم)
I swear that the temperature has reached fifty below zero.	وَاللهِ إِنَّ دَرَجَةَ الْحَرارةِ وَصَلَتْ إِلَى خَمْسِينَ تَحْتَ الصِّفْرِ.

232. قال AND AFTERWARDS أَنَّ - DOES IT WORK?

Yes, it does. Normally, the indirect speech after قَالَ is connected with إِنَّ. But what do you do if you have more than one information? For example: *It is said that.... and that...*

If you have 2 noun clauses in an indirect speech with قَالَ, there is a common way to deal with it: The first part is introduced with إِنَّ and the second part with أَنَّ.

Let us have a look at an example:

It is said that they are still alive and that they need water.	يُقالُ إنَّهُمْ ما زالُوا أَحْياءً، وَأَنَّهُمْ يَحْتاجُونَ إلَى مِياهٍ.
Notice the two occurrences of *that* and pay attention to the first letter and its pronunciation: first we have إنَّهُمْ and the second *that* is أَنَّهُمْ	

233. مَرْفُوع – WHEN DOES A WORD TAKE THIS CASE?

There are six situations. Let us have a look at them:

Subject of a جُمْلة اِسْمِيّة (nominal sentence). Literally meaning: *where it begins*. It is usually – as its literal meaning says - the <u>first word</u> of a sentence.	الْمُبْتَدَأ	1
Predicate of a جُمْلة اِسْمِيّة (nominal sentence). It completes the meaning of the الْمُبْتَدَأ. Without the الْخَبَر, a nominal sentence wouldn't make sense.	الْخَبَر	2
This is the subject (usually the first noun) in a sentence with كان. Notice that "sisters" here also mean: أَفْعال الْمُقارَبة والرَّجاء (verbs of approximation), (verbs of hope) and الشُّرُوع (verbs of beginning).	اِسْم كانَ and its sisters	3
Predicate of a sentence that starts with إنَّ. "Sisters" are: أَنَّ, كَأَنَّ, لَكِنَّ, لَعَلَّ, لَيْتَ; sometimes also the predicate of لا if used for an absolute denial, for instance: لا سُرُورَ دائمٌ (*there is no lasting pleasure*)	خَبَر إنَّ and its sisters	4

356

Subject of a verbal sentence.	الْفَاعِل	5
Subject of a verbal sentence in the passive voice.	نَائِب الْفَاعِل	6

234. تَمَّ قَتْل AND قُتِلَ - WHAT IS THE DIFFERENCE?

Both expressions mean: *was killed.* There is only a minor difference as both forms express the passive voice.

- قُتِلَ is the regular passive form of the verb

- تَمَّ قَتْل is another possibility to express roughly the same meaning. It follows the pattern: تَمَّ plus مَصْدَر

Let us have a look at some examples:

The man was killed.	قُتِلَ الرَّجُلُ.	1
We use the verb *to kill* in the passive tense. We don't know who the killer was. We use a so called نَائِب فَاعِل		
The man was killed.	تَمَّ قَتْلُ الرَّجُلِ.	2
The meaning here is slightly different. It means more like: *the killing was completed.* It is used like an intransitive verb.		
If you use this sentence without further information, it will express that there was an *order/assignment that has been fully completed.* It has the meaning of: *Okay, I did it; it is done.* Notice that the مَصْدَر here functions as the subject (فَاعِل) – and not, like in the sentence above (verb in the passive tense) as the نَائِب فَاعِل		

357

The مَصْدَر is normally definite: by the article ال, as a first part of a إِضافة (our example!) or by a pronoun-suffix.		
The lesson was completed.	تَمَّ الدَّرْسُ.	3
If you use this sentence without further information, it will mean: *I have finished the lesson; I did it.* (Rather than just: *The lesson is over*).		
The work will be finished.	سَيَتِمُّ الْعَمَلُ.	4
In this sentence, we express a future action by conjugating the verb تَمَّ. Notice: الْعَمَل here is the subject of the sentence (فاعِل)		

235. أَيّ - WHAT CAN THIS WORD MEAN?

It can mean various things: *which, each* or *that is.*

More interesting, however, is the application of أَيّ.

There are different ways of using the words أَيّ / أَيّةٌ (feminine form) – and each way leads to different meanings of the word. Grammatically speaking, the word أَيّ is the first part of a إِضافة – so don't forget that the word after it has to be مَجْرُور.

Let us examine how we can use أَيّ in a sentence:

1. Meaning: *which?* - الْإِسْتِفْهام

Which book is this?	أَيُّ كِتابٍ هٰذا؟	1
Here, the word أَيّ is the <u>predicate</u> (خَبَر) of a nominal sentence;		

هٰذا is the subject (مُبْتَدَأ)		
Which book did you read?	أَيَّ كِتابٍ قَرَأْتَ؟	2
Here, أَيَّ كِتابٍ is the <u>direct object</u> (الْمَفْعُول بِهِ) of the sentence. Therefore, it has to be مَنْصُوب which might confuse a bit as it starts the sentence. It can also function as a part of other types of objects. For example: أَيَّ جِهَةٍ اتَّجَهْتَ؟ - مَفْعُول فِيهِ or أَيَّ تَصَرُّفٍ تَصَرَّفْتَ؟ - مَفْعُول مُطْلَق		
Which book did you read? (same meaning as above)	أَيُّ كِتابٍ قَرَأْتَهُ؟	3
There is a grammatical difference: أَيُّ (example 3) is the subject (مُبْتَدَأ) of a (nominal) sentence as we have in this construction a جُمْلة اسْمِيّة. Notice the case on أَيُّ - it is مَرْفُوع! This is why you have to refer to the word *book* again by adding a pronoun - ه - to the verb. If you use a transitive verb, it must be connected with a pronoun. If you have an intransitive verb, you don't need a pronoun.		
Which student came?	أَيُّ تِلْمِيذٍ حَضَرَ؟	4
The word أَيُّ here is the مُبْتَدَأ مَرْفُوع. The verb in this sentence is intransitive and could stand alone. So we don't use a pronoun.		
Which man did you meet?	أَيُّ رَجُلٍ قابَلْتَهُ؟	5
The word أَيُّ is the مُبْتَدَأ مَرْفُوع. The predicate is the sentence comes after it (=verb connected with a pronoun): قابَلْتَهُ *To meet* is a transitive verb meaning that it has to be completed by		

an object (مَفْعُول بِهِ) – which is the pronoun o here.	

Which nationality?	مِنْ أيِّ جِنْسِيةٍ؟	6

Here, the word أيّ takes a كَسْرة as it follows a preposition.

Which student?	أيَّةُ طالِبَةٍ؟	7

Notice that we use the feminine form here as *student* is feminine.
But this is not always the case. Sometimes, the masculine form is
used although the word after it is feminine.

2. Meaning: *each/anything*

I like anything you like.	أيُّ شَيْءٍ تُحِبُّهُ فَأَنا أُحِبُّهُ.

In this construction, we have two sentences which are combined.
Watch out: The verb تُحِبُّ is not مَجْزُوم as this is not a conditional
sentence.

3. Meaning of a conditional – اِسْم الشَّرْط

A (each/every) student who works hard will succeed.	أيُّ طالِبٍ يَجْتَهِدْ يَنْجَحْ.	1

Both verbs are مَجْزُوم (the sentence has a conditional meaning!)

Whomever you honour shall praise you.	أيًّا تُكْرِمْ يَحْمَدْكَ.	2

If you skip the مُضاف after أيّ, you have to write أيًّا in the
مَنْصُوب-case with تَنْوِين ("an"). Notice: Both verbs are مَجْزُوم.

4. Relative pronoun (اِسْم الْمَوْصُول) meaning: *which, that*

I like the one who carries out his work.	يُعْجِبُنِي أَيَّ أَدَّى عَمَلَهُ.
(In order to understand the sentence better, we could rewrite it like this.)	أَيَّ يُعْجِبُنِي مَنْ أَدَّى عَمَلَهُ.

5. Meaning: *that is (to say); namely*

Here, أَيْ is used to explain what comes before. It can be translated as: *this means; that is to say; namely*. It is also used to address somebody (حَرْف نِداء). Notice: There is a سُكُون above the ي	أَيْ = يَعْنِي
You are accusing me of a crime, namely, that I am a thief.	تَّهِمُنِي بِالجُرْمِ ، أَيْ أَنا مُجْرِمٌ.
Oh Lord!	أَيْ رَبِّ!

236. "WHEN I WAS ELEVEN…" - HOW DO YOU SAY IT IN ARABIC?

There are several possibilities.

Let us examine one example that is a bit more complicated:

When I was eleven…	كُنْتُ فِي الْحادِيَةَ عَشْرَةَ مِنْ عُمْرِي…
1. Why is the word الْحادِيَةَ here مَنْصُوب؟	
Well, the number is مَجْرُور and not مَنْصُوب ! However, all numbers between 11 and 19, cardinal and ordinal, always end in فَتْحة, whatever	

the case. Other ordinal numbers follow the usual rules.

2. Why do you use the feminine form of the numbers?

Originally, the sentence was written with the word سَنة after the preposition – but although it is not written any more, the numbers are still declined according to the feminine word سَنة

When I was twelve...	...كُنْتُ فِي الثّانِيةَ عَشَرَ
I am 22 (variation one).	عُمْري اثْنانِ وعِشْرُونَ عامًا.
I am 22 (variation two).	أنا فِي الثّانِيةِ والْعِشْرِينَ مِنْ عُمْري.

Watch out: In the last sentence, the number after the preposition فِي has a كَسْرة at the end! It is مَجْرُور and follows the usual rules (unlike all numbers between 11 and 19 – see our first example!)

237. مَفْعُول لِأَجْلِهِ - WHAT IS A CAUSATIVE OBJECT?

A causative object (مَفْعُول لِأَجْلِهِ) is used to describe the purpose of an action.

It clarifies the reason for the occurrence of an action which originates from the doer. In order to identify it, you simply ask: *why?* or: *what for (reason)?*

- What is important to know: The مَفْعُول لِأَجْلِهِ is always مِنْصُوب

- The مَفْعُول لِأَجْلِهِ is not always just a word; it can also be an adverbial clause (شِبْه جُمْلة)

362

Notice the difference to the so called الْحَال! If you want to identify the الْحَال, you ask: _how?_

Here is an example:

مَفْعُول لِأَجْلِهِ		I.I
I went to Egypt to study Arabic. (Question: Why did I go to Egypt?)	جِئْتُ إِلَى مِصْرَ رُغْبَةً فِي تَعَلُّمِ العربِيةِ.	
The word رَغْبَةً describes the cause, the reason why I went to Egypt.	رَغْبَةً فِي = السَّبَب	
He cried of fear. (Question: Why did he cry?)	بَكَى خَوْفًا.	I.2

الْحَال		2
He came laughing. (Question: How did he come? It describes the subject while it/he was doing the action)	جاءَ ضاحِكًا.	

238.   Brother or Stepbrother?

In Arabic, the word أَخ means *brother*. But there is also another word for *brother*: شَقِيق

The root of the word ش - ق - ق means basically *to split*. شَقِيق describes that you have the same mother and father as your brother - whereas أَخ can also be used if either your mother or father is different.

شَقِيق is also frequently used by politicians when they talk about other Arab nations:

The sister states (with reference to Arab nations)	الدُّوَل الشَّقِيقة
Two sister nations	شَعْبانِ شَقِيقانِ

239.   "At the beginning of the century"- In Arabic?

You can't translate it word-for-word from English, but it is also not that different. The important thing in Arabic is that we use the plural form of the word that determines the time.

Let's have a look:

At the beginning of the 20ᵗʰ century	الْقَرنِ الْعِشْرِينَ	+	أوائِلِ	خِلال +
In the middle of the month	الشَّهْرِ		أواسِطِ	
At the end of the year	السَّنةِ		أواخِرِ	

364

The word after خِلال (*during; through*) has to be مَجْرُور. In our examples, the broken plurals are مَمْنُوع مِن الصَّرْف – but since they are definite (first part of a إضافة), they take the regular ending: a كَسْرة

Watch out: Don't mix خِلال with the expression مِنْ خِلالِ which means: *on the basis of*

240. مَمْنُوع مِن الصَّرْف - WHAT DOES IT MEAN?

First of all, what we are saying in this chapter is only important if you have to deal with <u>indefinite</u> words!

Words which are definite by ال or are functioning as the first part of a إضافة follow the regular rules.

مَمْنُوع مِن الصَّرْف (*diptotes*) means that you don't write the endings "un", "in" or "an" which we call تَنْوِين. Instead, it is just a simple vowel without the "n"-sound. *Diptote* means two case endings only. A regular اِسْم is a *triptote*!

Several types of words are مَمْنُوع مِن الصَّرْف. Let us check them in detail:

<u>I. I. Proper names: عَلَم</u>

Proper nouns are called عَلَم in Arabic. What is important here: All names of cities are feminine and don't take تَنْوِين

Feminine proper nouns - عَلَم مُؤَنَّث			A
Suad, Zainab, Damascus	سُعادُ, زَيْنَبُ, دِمَشْقُ	They look masculine – but have a feminine meaning	A.1
Osama, Hamza	أُسامةُ, حَمْزةُ	They look feminine – but have a masculine meaning	A.2
Fatima, Mecca, Khadija	فاطِمةُ, مَكَّةُ, خَديجةُ	They look feminine – and have a feminine gender	A.3
Egypt, India, sun	مِصْرُ, هِنْدُ, شَمْسُ	They consist of three letters; There is a سُكُون on the 2nd letter! You can choose if you want to add تَنْوِين	A.4
	مِصْرُ or مِصْرٌ both are correct		

Non-Arab names – عَلَم أَعْجَمِيّ			B
Ibrahim, Iran, Ramses	إِبْراهِيمُ, إِيرانُ, رَمْسِيسُ	These words are borrowed from foreign languages	B.1
Noah, Hud, Lot (prophets in the Qur'an)	نُوحُ, لُوطُ, هُودُ	Foreign names consisting of 3 letters. There is no vowel in the middle. You can choose if you want to add تَنْوِين	B.2
	نُوحُ or نُوحٌ both are correct		

Proper names which have Alif ا and ن at the end: ان			C
Ramadan, Ad-nan, Marwan	رَمَضانُ, عَدْنانُ, مَرْوانُ	These words are mostly names for persons	C.1

Proper names which follow the pattern of a verb عَلَى وَزْن الْفِعْل			D
Ahmed, Yazed, Yathreb (Medina)	أَحْمَدُ, يَزِيدُ, يَثْرِبُ	These words look like verbs (in present or past tense)	D.1

Proper names that follow the pattern "fuʒal": فُعَل			E
Omar, Zahal (name for the planet Saturn)	عُمَرُ, زُحَلُ	These words are formed of three letters and follow the special vowel pattern: "u-a"	E.1

Proper names that consist of two (blended) names			F
Hadramaut, Port Said	حَضَر مَوْتُ, بُور سعيدُ	These words consist of two words	F.1

II. Adjectives: صِفة

Now, let us check the adjectives. Please note that in Arabic, there are only three types of words: اِسْم, فِعْل, حَرْف

This means that an adjective in Arabic, a so called صِفة, is a اِسْم

Adjectives following the pattern fAʒlaan: فَعْلان			A
Watch out: The form " fuʒalan" - فُعْلان - gets تَنْوين!			
thirsty (2x), hungry	عَطْشانُ, ظَمآنُ, جَوْعان	These adjectives have the feminine form فَعْلَى and the plural form فَعالى	A.1

367

Adjectives following the pattern "af3al": أَفْعَل			B
bigger, smaller, nicer, most important	أَكْبَرُ، أَصْغَرُ، أَجْمَلُ، أَهَمُّ	These adj. have the feminine form فُعْلَى	B.1
Watch out for the difference in the feminine form between the comparative form and the patterns for colours. Comparative: أَفْعَل - فُعْلَى versus colours: أَفْعَل - فَعْلاء			
deaf	أَصَمُّ - صَمَّاءُ	Adjectives that describe if a person is blind, deaf, etc. So called: عُيُّون بِالإِنْسان	B.2
blind	أَعْمَى - عَمْياءُ		
dumb; not talking	أَبْكَمُ - بَكْماءُ		

Adjectives describing numbers and following the pattern "fU3aal" or "maf3Al": فُعال / مَفْعَل			C
one by one (in one row)	أُحادُ / مَوْحَدُ	These patterns describe how things are arranged. You can choose which form you prefer, they both mean the same. They are only used with numbers from 1 to 10. Used mainly in literature.	C.1
in pairs	ثُناءُ / مَثْنَى		
in pairs of ten	عُشارُ / مَعْشَرُ		

III. Broken plurals: جَمْع التَّكْسِير

We will now check <u>broken plural forms which don't take</u> تَنْوِين.

They are diptotes:

Irregular plural		A
If the broken plural consists of <u>more than three letters</u> and has an Alif ا after the first two letters, it doesn't take تَنْوِين. That's why the plural of رِجال (*men*) gets تَنْوِين because it consists of only three letters. On the contrary, a doubled letter (شَدّة) counts, so the plural of the following words don't get تَنْوِين: مَوادّ (*materials; topics*), مَضارّ (*adversities; harm*), مَشاقّ (*hardship; toil*)		A.1
house	مَنازِلُ	مَنْزِلٌ
school	مَدارِسُ	مَدْرَسةٌ
factory	مَصانِعُ	مَصْنَعٌ
If the broken plural consists of three letters at the beginning and has a ي before the end, then it doesn't take تَنْوِين		A.2
key	مَفاتِيحُ	مِفْتاحٌ
lamp	مَصابِيحُ	مِصباحٌ
bird	عَصافِيرُ	عُصْفُورٌ

IV. Special case:

A اِسْم which is coined by an Alif ا indicating a feminine form!

	مَقْصورة - The Alif ى is additional	A

Laila, fem. name	لَيْلَى
Salma, fem. name	سَلْمَى
great, major; larger	كُبْرَى

Strictly speaking, these words aren't diptotes. They are indeclinable, that is, they have only a single form, unlike diptotes which have two.

	المَمْدُودة - The Alif ا and the ء are additional	B

desert	صَحْراءُ
red	حَمْراءُ
friends	أَصْدِقاءُ

beauty	حَسْناءُ
scientists	عُلَماءُ

Watch out!

In the following examples, the ء is either part of the root or the root has a و or ي that turns into a هَمْزة. These words <u>are not feminine</u> – they take تَنْوِين!

news	نَبَأ - أَنْباءُ

building	بِناءُ - أَبْنِيةٌ

sky	سَماءٌ		enemy	عَدُوٌّ - أَعْداءٌ
name	اسْمٌ - أَسْماءٌ		member	عُضْوٌ - أَعْضاءٌ

One last but important remark: Feminine regular plurals have only two case endings („un" and „in") – but they can take تَنْوِين. They are not مَمْنُوع مِنْ الصَّرْف!

In مَنْصُوب and مَجْرُور, they share the same ending: ِ

241. مَمْنُوع مِن الصَّرْف - WHAT ARE THE CORRECT ENDINGS?

In chapter 240, we had a look at all kinds and forms of words that don't get تَنْوِين – in case they are indefinite.

But instead of تَنْوِين what ending do they take?

Let us check all three possible cases:

1. Nominal case (مَرْفُوع)

These are clean streets.	هٰذِهِ شَوارِعُ نَظِيفةٌ. 1
The word *streets* takes only one ضَمّة. The word *clean* takes two.	
These are new buildings.	هٰذِهِ مَنازِلُ جَدِيدةٌ. 2
The word *buildings* takes only one ضَمّة. The word for *new* takes two.	

2. Accusative case (مَنْصُوب)

I saw clean streets.	١ شاهَدْتُ شَوارِعَ نَظيفةً
The word *streets* takes only one فَتْحة. The word *clean* takes two.	
The engineers build new houses.	٢ يَبْني الْمُهَنْدِسُونَ مَنازِلَ جَديدةً
The word *buildings* takes only one فَتْحة. The word *new* takes two.	

3. Genitive case (مَقْصُور)

It is marked by a فَتْحة! Only the examples, marked in grey, are مَمْنُوع مِن الصَّرْف

I walked in clean streets.	١.١ مَشَيْتُ فِي شَوارِعَ نَظيفةٍ.
The word *streets* takes only one فَتْحة. The word *clean* takes two كَسْرة.	
I walked in <u>the</u> streets of the city.	١ مَشَيْتُ فِي شَوارِعِ الْمَدينةِ.
إِضافة – so it is treated as definite (→ use the regular rules). The word *streets* takes only one كَسْرة. The word *clean* takes one كَسْرة as *streets* is the 1st part of a إِضافة	٢
I walked in <u>the</u> clean streets.	١.٣ مَشَيْتُ فِي الشَّوارِعِ النَّظيفةِ.
Definite article! So, the word *streets* takes as usual one كَسْرة	

Also the word *clean* takes as usual one كَسْرة	
The people live in new buildings.	يَسْكُنُ النَّاسُ فِي مَنازِلَ جَدِيدةٍ. ٢
The word *buildings* takes only one فَتْحة. The word *new* takes two كَسْرة.	

242. HOW DO THE CASE ENDINGS OF آخر LOOK LIKE?

First of all, we have to notice that the meaning changes whether the vowel is above or under the second root letter.

آخر can mean *other* (آخَر) or *last* (آخِر) and has the form أَفْعَلُ

This form is also used for colours or for people who have a certain handicap.

This brings us to our initial question: Indefinite words following the pattern أَفْعَلُ don't take تَنْوِين. So, the word آخر belongs to مَمْنُوع مِن الصَّرْف

This means:

مَرْفُوع	آخَرُ
مَجْرُور	آخَرَ
مَنْصُوب	

243. حسناء - أَحْسَن IS THIS THE FEM. FORM OF أَحْسَن ("BETTER")?

No, it isn't.

The word أَحْسَن is the masculine form of the word *better/best* and is a so called *elative* (comparative/superlative). The feminine comparative (which is rarely used) is built by the pattern فُعْلَى resulting in حُسْنَى for the feminine word for *better/best*.

So what does the word حسناء mean? First of all, we have to know the correct vowel at the beginning. It is حَسْناء

The pattern فَعْلاءُ is the feminine form of colours and deficiencies which have the same pattern as the اِسْم التَّفْضِيل which is: أَفْعَلُ. For example: the word for *red* أَحْمَر / حَمْراءُ

So is the masculine counterpart of حَسْناءُ the word أَحْسَنُ?

Yes it is, but the meaning is not *best* - it is *beautiful*.

There are some adjectives of beauty that have the same pattern as colours and deficiencies: أَفْعَلُ for masculine forms and فَعْلاءُ for feminine forms. Interestingly, the word أَحْسَنُ is only very rarely applied to a man whereas حَسْناءُ is pretty common to describe a woman as *beautiful*. Instead, for a man, the word حَسَن is used which means practically the same. Both words أَحْسَنُ and حَسْناءُ are a صِفة مُشَبَّهة. So let us summarize:

meaning	grammatical type	feminine	masculine	
better; best	اِسْم التَّفْضِيل	حُسْنَى	أَحْسَنُ	١
beautiful; nice	الصِّفة المُشَبَّهة	حَسْناءُ	أَحْسَنُ (not used)	٢

374

Here are some other words to describe beauty and follow the same pattern as colours:

meaning	feminine form	masculine form
smooth	مَلْساءُ	أَمْلَسُ
nice; bright	بَلْحاءُ	أَبْلَجُ
brave; courageous	شَجْعاءُ	أَشْجَعُ

All words are مَمْنُوع مِن الصَّرْف – because of the pattern.

244. الْمَفْعُول مَعَهُ - HOW DO YOU USE IT?

This type of object is also called the concomitant object (which means: *to accompany; to be somehow connected*) or the object in connection. A مَفْعُولٌ مَعَهُ can be difficult to translate if you don't know its function. It is, basically said, a اِسْم مَنْصُوب that comes after the word و but has the meaning of *with*. You can also substitute the و with مَعَ which doesn't change the meaning of the sentence – but the case-ending as the اِسْم becomes مَجْرُور

Let us look at some examples:

I walked along the sea.	مَشَيْتُ وَالْبَحْرَ.
I walked along the sea.	مَشَيْتُ مَعَ الْبَحْرِ.
I work during the night.	أَعْمَلُ وَاللَّيْلَ.
I woke up by the chirping of the birds.	اِسْتَيْقَظْتُ وَتَغْرِيدَ الطُّيُورِ.

375

245. مِيناء - What is the root for this word?

مِيناء means *port*. The root is و - ن - ي.

The word for *port* was originally مِوْناي following the pattern مِفْعال. But this word would be difficult to pronounce, so it changed to a more convenient way: مِيناء

The plural of the word مِيناء is: مَوانِئ

It is, grammatically speaking, a اِسْم آلة like the Arabic word for *minaret* which was originally meant to be a tool and not a place. See chapter 176.

However, it is originally not an Arabic word, but a loanword, probably from ancient Egyptian (where port is *"mni"*), from where it entered Greek (*"limen"*) and Hebrew (*"namal"*).

246. Whereas; while - How do you express it in Arabic?

There are special constructions in Arabic if you want to express *whereas* – a contrast between two statements. Let's check it:

1	...أمّا... + فَـ...
I liked the mountains <u>whereas</u> my friends hated them.	الْجِبالُ أَعْجَبَتْنِي أَمّا أَصْدِقائِي فَقَدْ كَرِهُوها.
2	بَيْنَما
I asked her to come to the party, <u>whereas</u> she wants to stay at home.	طَلَبْتُها بِحُضُورِ الْحَفْلة، بَيْنَما هِيَ تُرِيدُ الْبَقاءَ فِي الْبَيْتِ.

But watch out:

بَيْنَما is more often used for something else: to join two actions or situations which are parallel (simultaneously) going on. It means in English *while*; in German: *während*. It has the same meaning as عِنْدَما or حِينَما

بَيْنَما is followed by a جُمْلة اِسْمِيّة or a جُمْلة فِعْلِيّة with the verb in the past or present tense – but don't forget that the tense (for translations) is marked by the main clause.

I read a book while you watched a soap opera.	قَرَأْتُ كِتابًا، بَيْنَما أَنْتَ كُنْتَ تُشاهِدُ مُسَلْسَلًا.

247. IS IT: "TO DRINK COFFEE COLD" OR "COLD COFFEE"?

It depends what you want to say.

Regarding *cold coffee*, the word *cold* is describing *coffee* and not the verb *to drink* – so the word *cold* is a نَعْت/صِفة which is describing a اِسْم. Whereas in the case of *to drink coffee cold*, the word *cold* is referring to the verb – this is a حال

The الْحال is a grammatical construction which describes how somebody did something. It describes an action.

In order to identify the الْحال, you ask the question: كَيْفَ؟

In our example: *How do you <u>drink</u> the coffee?*

The الْحال is a so called denotative of state. It is describing the <u>action (verb)</u> which is connected to a subject or object (صاحِب

الْحال) and is used to describe the condition or circumstance ob-taining at the time when the action of the main verb takes place.

If you ask *how are you?* in Arabic, you can ask: كَيْفَ الْحال؟

Some people are joking and answer: الْحالُ مَنْصُوبٌ

This is a link to the الْحال which grammatically speaking has to be مَنْصُوب. The الْحال can consist of a word (e.g. an active participle) or a full sentence. In German, these kinds of sentences are sometimes translated (connected) with the word *indem*.

A remark: Don't get confused as we are now analysing the word and its function in the sentence. We don't examine if a word is a ظَرْف or a إِسْم.

There are several possibilities to use a حال:

A. Single word in the مَنْصُوب-case: مُفْرَد

The man drank the coffee and smiled/smiling.	شَرِبَ الرَّجُلُ الْقَهْوةَ مُبْتَسِمًا.	١
Question: How was he drinking?		
فاعِل؛ صاحِب الْحال	الرَّجُلُ	
مَفْعُول بِهِ	الْقَهْوةَ	
حال	مُبْتَسِمًا	
The man drank his coffee cold. (Not: The man drank the cold coffee.)	شَرِبَ الرَّجُلُ الْقَهْوةَ بارِدةً.	٢

378

Question: How was he drinking the coffee?
And not: How was the coffee?

صاحِب الْحال	الْقَهْوة
حال	بارِدةً

If the حال is not مُفْرَد (only one word), it will need a connector
– a so called رابِط. Notice that you don't translate the connector.
So never say e.g. *and* or *and he*, etc. There are three possibilities
to connect the حال with the preceding sentence:

The particle وَ	وَ	1
A pronoun at the end of a verb, for example the ضَمّة (meaning *he*) in the verb: يَتَحَّدَثُ	ضَمير فَقَط	2
(1) plus (2) وَ ضَمير	وَهُوَ	3

B. Full sentence: جُمْلة

The الْحال can also be a full sentence:

- If you use a nominal sentence (جُمْلة اِسْمِيّة), you need a
  رابِط to connect it with the preceding sentence, e.g.: a وَ

- The verbal sentence (جُمْلة فِعْلِيّة) doesn't need a رابِط

I repeated my lessons and the people were sleeping.	راجَعْتُ دُرُوسِي وَالنّاسُ نائِمونَ.	1

راجَعْتُ - تُ	تُ = صاحِب الْحال
وَالنّاسُ نائِمونَ	حال, جُمْلة اِسْمِيّة

The whole second sentence, which is the الْحال, is مَنْصوب but you actually don't write/see it. The whole جُمْلة اِسْمِيّة is marked as مَرْفوع but grammatically speaking, it is considered to be جُمْلة اِسْمِيّة في مَحَلّ نَصْب - so called: مَنْصوب

	2 تَرَكْتُ الْبَيْتَ وَالْبابُ مَفْتوحٌ.
I left the house with open doors/and left the door open, etc.	
صاحِب الْحال	الْبَيْتَ
حال, جُمْلة اِسْمِيّة	وَالْبابُ مَفْتوحٌ

	3 شَرِبَ الرَّجُلُ الْقَهْوةَ وَهُوَ يَبْتَسِمُ.
The man drank the coffee and smiled/smiling.	
رابِط, جُمْلة اِسْمِيّة	وَهُوَ

Notice: Without the وَ it wouldn't be a حال!

	4 شَرِبَ الرَّجُلُ الْقَهْوةَ وَهِيَ بارِدةٌ.
The man drank his coffee cold.	
رابِط, جُمْلة اِسْمِيّة	وَهِيَ

	5 جَلَسَ الْمُديرُ يَتَحَدَّثُ.
The man sat down talking.	
صاحِب الْحال	الْمُديرُ
ضَمير مُسْتَتِر- حال	يَتَحَدَّثُ- تُ

The director came driving his car.	أَتَى الْمُدِيرُ يَقُودُ سَيارَتَهُ.	6
صاحِب الْحال	الْمُدِيرُ	
رابِط = ضَمِير فَقَط	يَقُودُ سَيارَتَهُ	

I started sleeping when the sun rose.	بَدَأْتُ النَّوْمَ وَ قَدْ طَلَعَتِ الشَّمْسُ.	7
These particles indicate a جُمْلة فِعْلِيّة	وَ قَدْ	

The شِبْه الْجُمْلة can be an adverb of time or place or a prepositional phrase.

I received the prize with joy/joyful.	إِسْتَلَمْتُ الْجائِزة فِي فَرَحٍ.	1
إِسْتَلَمْتُ - تُ	صاحِب الْحال	
فِي فَرَحٍ	حال - جارّ وَمَجْرُور	
I left the car in the parking lot.	تَرَكْتُ السَّيّارة عِنْدَ الْمَوْقِفِ.	2
عِنْدَ الْمَوْقِفِ	حال, ظَرْف مَكان	
وَجَدْتُ الْكِتابَ بَعْدَ تَعَبٍ		3
بَعْدَ تَعَبٍ	حال	

381

Let us summarize the conditions for the الْحال:

1. The الْحال has to be <u>indefinite</u> (نَكِرة) and مَنْصُوب

2. The الْحال صاحِب has to be <u>definite</u>. It can be either the subject (فاعِل) or the object (مَفْعُول بِهِ)

<u>An important remark:</u>

All three possibilities (A, B, C) which we examined above mean the same. Like in the following example: *He greeted me saying...*

participle	verbal sentence	nominal sentence
...سَلَّمَ عَلَيَّ قائِلاً	..سَلَّمَ عَلَيَّ وَ هُوَ يَقُولُ	سَلَّمَ عَلَيَّ وَ هُوَ قائِلٌ..

248. تَعْت حال AND - WHY ARE THEY SOMETIMES MIXED UP?

The word نَعْت means *description* in Arabic and is sometimes translated into English as *attribute* or *attributive adjunct*.

What we call an adjective in English (صِفة) can also be called نَعْت. It is important to understand that we don't look at the type of word (صَرْف) here – but at its function.

The نَعْت is a مُشْتَقّ which literally means *derivative*. It is a اِسْم that is derived from the root. It can have several forms, for example:

اِسْم الْفاعِل - اِسْم الْمَفْعُول

الصِّفة الْمُشَبَّهة - اِسْم التَّفْضِيل - النِّسْبة - صِيغة الْمُبالَغة

Let us check all this in detail:

I bought a new car.	اِشْتَرَيْتُ سَيَّارَةً جَدِيدَةً.
مَنْعُوت – the thing, that is being described	سَيَّارَةً
نَعْت – the description It needs agreement (مُطابَقَة) with the thing that is being described.	جَدِيدَةً

Al-Azhar is an Islamic university.	الأَزْهَرُ جامِعَةٌ إِسْلامِيَّةٌ.
خَبَر (predicate); the word *Islamic* is the النَّعْت for *university*.	جامِعَةٌ إِسْلامِيَّةٌ

The النَّعْت has to agree with the الْمَنْعُوت in four things:

1	same article; definite or indefinite	نَكِرَة / مَعْرِفة
2	same case marker	مَرْفُوع, مَجْرُور, مَنْصُوب
3	same gender (نَوْع)	مُذَكَّر, مُؤَنَّث
4	same number (عَدَد)	مُفْرَد - مُثَنَّى - جَمْع

The النَّعْت is different from الْحال and can be mixed up.

Here you see both - الْحال and النَّعْت - in one sentence:

I wrote the lesson in Arabic.	كَتَبْتُ الدَّرْسَ بِاللُّغةِ الْعَرَبِيَّةِ.
صاحِب الْحال	كَتَبْتُ - تُ

الْحال	بِاللُّغةِ
النَّعْت for the word *language*	الْعَرَبيّة

Rule:

- The sentence following a <u>definite</u> word is a حال. It is describing the action (verb) that is connected to the subject or object.

- The sentence following an <u>indefinite</u> word is a نَعْت (صِفة) – a description that is not connected to the action which the subject/object is doing.

Watch out for the difference:

I don't want to see a crying child.	لا أُحِبُّ أَنْ أُشاهِدَ طِفْلاً باكِيًا.
It is a نَعْت – and not a حال	باكِيًا
This is because the الْحال has to be <u>definite</u>!	
In our example, if it was definite, the sentence would describe the child: صاحِب الْحال. It would describe its condition right now as I am watching the child. So what is the difference? Here, as a نَعْت, it is more like a general statement. If the expression was definite - a حال -, it would describe a certain child that I see crying (at the moment).	

Another example:

I live in a house close to the beach.	أَسْكُنُ فِي بَيْتٍ بِحَيِّ الشَّاطِئ.

384

Indefinite. So it can't be a حال – it is the الْمَنْعُوت	بَيْتٍ
نَعْت الْجُمْلة	بِحَيِّ الشَّاطِئ

The following two sentences are also not a حال because the word which is being described is <u>indefinite</u>:

I live in a house with big rooms.	أَسْكُنُ فِي بَيْتٍ غُرَفُهُ واسِعةٌ.
I live in a house opposite the beach.	أَسْكُنُ فِي بَيْتٍ أَمامَ الْبَحْرِ.

249. WHAT DOES مَهْما MEAN?

It means: *despite; although; whatever*. If it has a conditional meaning, you should translate it as: *whatever the case...* or *no matter what/how*. Don't forget that if the sentence has a conditional meaning, the verb after مَهْما has to be مَجْزُوم.

If مَهْما doesn't start a conditional sentence, you frequently use a verb in the past tense that has the <u>meaning of the present or future tense</u>!

Let us have a look at an example:

I will be the same person whatever people say.	سَأَظَلُّ بِهذا الشَّكْلِ مَهْما قالَ النَّاسُ.
Notice in this example that we use the past tense of *to say* to express a present tense meaning.	

Let us look at some more examples:

Although (despite) that it (she) is difficult... (Notice that we use the past tense!)	مَهْما كانَتْ صَعْبَةً...
Whatever the case... (Notice here the مَجْزُوم-mood)	مَهْما يَكُنْ مِنْ الأَمْرِ...
No matter how I try, I can't. (Notice that we use the past tense to express a situation in the present or even future.)	مَهْما حاوَلْتُ لا أَسْتَطِيعُ.

There are, of course, also other words meaning the same as مَهْما:

مَهْما = حَتَّى لَوْ = إذا حَدَثَ

All three introduce a so called <u>indefinite conditional clause</u>. On the contrary, إذا, لَوْ and إِنْ are limiting the number of possible conditions in the if-part whereas words like *whatever, whoever, wherever* leave it open to almost any situation.

- Indefinite conditional clause: *Whatever the weather will be, we will go.* In indefinite conditional sentences, the verbs are almost always مَجْزُوم.

- *If the weather is nice, we will go.* In conditional constructions with إذا, لَوْ and إِنْ the verbs are only sometimes مَجْزُوم depending on the context.

250. اللّٰهُ إِلَّا إِلٰهَ لَا - WHY HAS GOD A فَتْحة AT THE END?

The sentence اللّٰهُ إِلَّا إِلٰهَ لَا is also called the *Islamic Shahada*. It means: *There is no God but God.*

A remark before with start our discussion: The long "*aa*" above the ل in the words *God* and *Allah* is usually written as a vertical dash (dagger Alif or أَلِف خَنْجَرِيَّة – see chapter 22).

Grammatically speaking, we are dealing with a so called *generic* or *absolute negation* (لَا النَّافِية لِلْجِنْس). The first word for *God* in the sentence has the singular form إِلٰه. But why is there a فَتْحة at the end of the word ("la ilah**a**...")?

First of all, let us check the different forms of the particle لا:

	type	translation	example
1	نافِية مَرفُوع	The boy doesn't play football in the street.	الْوَلَدُ لا يَلْعَبُ الْكُرةَ فِي الشَّارِعِ.
	Notice: The verb *to play* has a ضَمّة at the end.		
2	نافِية مَجْزُوم	Don't play soccer in the street!	لا تَلْعَبْ بِالْكُرةِ فِي الشَّارِعِ.
	Notice: There is a سُكُون at the end of the imperative *play!* It has to be مَجْزُوم		
3	الْعَطْف	Nagib Mahfouz is a writer, not a poet.	نَجِيب مَحْفُوظ كاتِبٌ لا شاعِرٌ.
	Notice: Both words (*writer; poet*) take the same case.		

4	لا النَّافِية لِلْجِنْس generic negation; جِنْس here means *gender*	There is no student in the room.	لا طالِبَ في الْغُرْفةِ.

This negation is called *generic* or *absolute negation* because it denies the existence of the preceding noun. Therefore, it has the meaning of *there is no... (at all).* Or: *there is not a...* Or: *none at all*

- There is no verb involved!
- The noun after لا is مَنْصُوب
- Basically you have to apply the same rules as after إِنَّ. It is even regarded as a sister of إِنَّ – provided that the اِسْم (noun) is indefinite and directly connected with لا
- The noun after لا never gets تنْوِين (only a single فَتْحة)
- The predicate is مَرْفُوع (and takes تنْوِين)

Watch out: If you are referring to a specific person or thing, you normally negate the nominal sentence with لَيْسَ. However, you could theoretically also use لا, but this is rarely used.

We will concentrate on type 4, the so called لا النَّافِية لِلْجِنْس

These are the three conditions for a *generic negation*:

1	The noun has to be indefinite! But watch out – never add تنْوِين!
2	The noun has to follow لا immediately
3	There is no preposition involved

388

What cases can the اِسْم have after لا?

A	مُفْرَد (single noun) The noun after لا is مَنْصُوب

There is no popular liar. (Lit. meaning: No liar is popular.) Notice the فَتْحة upon liar.	لا كاذِبَ مَحْبُوبٌ.	١
There are no popular liars. (Lit. meaning: No liars are popular.) Notice that the و turns into a ي as it is مَنْصُوب	لا كاذِبِيْنَ مَحْبُوبُونَ.	٢
There are no (female) popular liars. (Lit. meaning: No (female) liars are popular.)	لا كاذِباتِ مَحْبُوباتٌ.	٣

Watch out: Although the word *liars* is مَنْصُوب, you have to mark it with a كَسْرة. Why is that? Feminine sound plurals and duals have two cases only - nominative and oblique - but do not belong to diptotes (مَمْنُوع مِن الصَّرْف). Sound feminine plurals have nunation (تَنْوِين) whenever they are indefinite.

B	(إِضافة) مُفْرَد / مُضاف (single noun or إِضافة) The first part of the إِضافة noun is مَنْصُوب The second part of the إِضافة has to be تَكِرة (singular)

There is no professional who loses his wage. (Lit. meaning: No professional loses his wage.) Notice the فَتْحة as it is مَنْصُوب	لا مُتْقِنَ عَمَلٍ يَضيعُ أَجْرُهُ.	١

لا مُتْقِنِي عَمَلٍ يَضِيعُ أُجْرُهُم.	There are no professionals who lose their wages. (Lit. meaning: No professionals lose their wages.) 2

Notice that the ون turns into a ي as the ن disappears in a إِضافة and the و turns into a ي in the مَنْصُوب-case

لا مُتْقِناتِ عَمَلٍ يَضِيعُ أُجْرُهُنَّ.	There are no (female) professionals who lose their wages. (Lit. meaning: No (fe-male) professionals lose their wages.) 3

Notice the كَسْرة – although it is مَنْصُوب (feminine plural)

<table>
<tr><td>C</td><td>إِضافة not a – شَبيه بِالْمُضاف but similar
The 1st part takes تَنْوِين, the 2nd part is a direct object (مَفْعُول بِه)</td></tr>
</table>

لا مُتْقِنًا عَمَلاً يَضِيعُ أُجْرُهُ.	There is no professional who loses his wage. (Lit. meaning: No professional loses his wage.) 1

Notice: عَمَلاً is a مَفْعُول بِه. The part after the object is the pre-dicate (خَبَر) – in the form of a جُمْلة فِعْلِيّة

لا مُتْقِنِين عَمَلاً يَضِيعُ أُجْرُهُم.	There are no professionals who lose their wages. (Lit. meaning: No profes-sionals lose their wages.) 2

لا مُتْقِناتٍ عَمَلاً يَضِيعُ أُجْرُهُنَّ.	There are no (female) professionals who lose their wages. (Lit. meaning: No (fe-male) professionals lose their wages.) 3

But watch out:

١	لا الطُّلَّابُ حاضِرُونَ وَلا الْأُسْتاذُ.	Neither the students nor the professor are present.

The مُبْتَدَأ (subject) is مَرْفُوع (pronounced: "a-TTullaabU") because the first word is <u>definite</u>! This sentence is <u>not a general statement</u>. It is addressing a specific situation/certain people. Grammatically speaking, it is a normal لا النّافِية - so after the particle لا, there must be a مُبْتَدَأ مَرْفُوع

٢	لا فِي الْعالَمِ سَلامٌ وَلا عَدْلٌ.	There is no peace nor justice in the world.

It is تَكِرَة (indefinite) - so it should follow the rules for a لا النّافِية لِلْجِنْس. However, between the words لا and سَلام there is something written in between - so it turns into a normal لا نافِية

٣	أنْتَ ذَكِيٌّ بِلا شَكٍّ.	You are clever without doubt.

The preposition بـ changes the sentence into a regular لا نافِية - and a regular نافِية never changes the case. Just treat it as it would be written without the لا

٤	بِلا رَيْبٍ = لا رَيْبَ فِي ذٰلِك.	No doubt.

٥	لا شَكَّ فِي ذٰلِك.	No doubt in that.

This sentence which fulfils all conditions for the لا النّافِية لِلْجِنْس - singular, nothing in between, no preposition!

251. WHY ARE IF-CLAUSES SO DIFFICULT TO TRANSLATE?

In most languages, if-clauses give non-native speakers a headache, so in Arabic. I was teaching German in Egypt. In one lesson, I talked about New York and said a sentence which in English means: *If I had money, I would fly to New York.* After the lesson a student came to me and said: *Congratulations! When are you going to New York? We will miss you!*

In English or German we love to speak in *would-*, *could-* and *should-*sentences. But in Arabic, there is no easy way to express all this. The Arabic verb lacks tenses and moods and specific rules for if-clauses. Instead, it all depends on the context!

Some general rules:

- The verbs in conditional sentences have no real temporal significance. The actual tense is determined by the context.

- The verb in the first part of the if-sentence is typically in the past tense – regardless of whether a reference to a past, present or future situation is intended.

- The verb in the second or main clause is usually in the past tense too – but other tenses are also possible.

- The actual meaning of the verbs corresponds to a number of English tenses depending on the meaning of the condition and the context.

252. مَجْزُوم - WHAT DOES IT ACTUALLY MEAN AND IMPLY?

In Arabic, the word مَجْزُوم literally means: *cut short; clipped*. It describes a certain mood of a verb which is marked by a سُكُون at the end of the conjugated verb.

When you see a مَجْزُوم-verb,

a) probably there is a connection to the meaning of *should*

b) maybe there is a command involved (*imperative*)

c) maybe it can have the meaning of a conditional clause – no wonder why we call this verb mood *jussive*

A <u>verb in the present tense</u> (مُضارِع) needs the مَجْزُوم-mood when it is preceded by a letter of elision (حَرْف الْجَزْم) or a conditional particle (أَداة الشَّرْط):

since	لَمَّا
whenever	إِذْما
to	لِ

negation	لَمْ
no	لا
(even) if	إِنْ

253. IF-CLAUSES - WHEN DO YOU NEED THE مَجْزُوم - MOOD?

Several words can start a conditional sentence and it depends on the initial word if the verb after it needs to be مَجْزُوم.

In this chapter we will have a look at words which put a verb into the مَجْزُوم-mood. They are called: أَدَوات جازِمة

word	explanation	example
إِنْ	*if*; used for time or place	
	If you put an effort in your work, you'll succeed in your live.	إِنْ تَجْتَهِدْ فِي عَمَلِكَ تَنْجَحْ فِي حَيَاتِكَ.
مَتى	*when*	
	If/when you come to Egypt, you will find beautiful weather.	مَتى تَأتِ إِلَى مِصْرَ تَجِدْ جَوَّها جَمِيلاً.
	Notice that the weak letter in أتى / يَأتي is elided.	
مَنْ	*who*; for persons	
ما	*who; whoever; which* – for animals, trees; non-human things	
	Whoever travels a lot will see different people.	مَنْ يُسافِرْ كَثِيرًا يَرَ شُعُوبًا مُخْتَلِفةً.
	The weak letter in رَأى / يَرَى is elided. A remark: رَأى is one of the very few pretty irregular verbs. You cannot conjugate it by using the common rules. The same is true for its IV-form أفْعَل, which looks like أرَى in its basic form (past tense).	
مَهْما	*what; which; whatever*	
	What you do for the good of the people will make you happy.	مَهْما تُقَدِّمُوا مِن خَيْرٍ لِلنَّاسِ تُصْبِحُوا سُعْداءَ.
أيْنَما	*where*; for places	
	Wherever you travel you will find friends.	أيْنَما تُسافِرْ تَجِدْ أصْدِقاءَ.

كَيْفَما	how?	
	The way you treat friends the way they will treat you.	كَيْفَما تُعامِلْ زُمَلاءَكَ يُعامِلُوكَ.
أَيُّ	every; whoever. For people; places; time; Notice that there has to be a noun (اِسْم) after أَيُّ and never a verb; you have to treat it like a إِضافة	
	Every worker who works diligently will find the fruits of his work.	أَيُّ عامِلٍ يَعْمَلْ بِجِدٍّ يَلْقَ ثَمَرَةَ عَمَلِهِ.
	Notice that the weak letter in لَقِيَ/ يَلْقَى is elided.	

254.   DO YOU ALWAYS NEED THE مَجْزُوم - MOOD IN IF-CLAUSES?

No, you don't. It is true that we should be careful to choose the correct verb mood in if-clauses. There are particles that turn the (present tense) verb into the مَجْزُوم-mood. But there are several other words too that start a conditional clause and don't affect the verb. In this chapter, we will have a look at particles that don't change the verb to مَجْزُوم

if; when	إِذا
The condition expressed by إِذا is generally a <u>situation which is likely or expected</u> – that is why it is usually translated as *when*. The only doubt is the time of the event. Notice: The verb which comes after إِذا has to be in the past tense although it has a future meaning.	

If morning comes, people will go to their work.	إِذا طَلَعَ الصَّباحُ ذَهَبَ النَّاسُ إِلَى أَعْمالِهِم.

if; whether	لَوْ

Some important general remarks:

- لو is used for <u>hypothetical questions</u>, for things that are <u>improbable</u> or <u>contrary to fact</u>. We are either talking about something that has already occurred. Or we know that the scenario we are introducing doesn't match reality.
- Similar to إذا, the temporal meaning of the verb is determined by the meaning of the condition.
- Regarding the use of ف in the main clause - see chapter 255.

<u>What is important about</u> لَوْ:

- If the first part of the if-clause doesn't happen, the second part of the if-clause is also not going to happen.
- That's why you need the <u>(emphatic) particle</u> لَ ("la") <u>to connect the second sentence</u> - so called اِمْتِناع الشَّرْط. The word اِمْتِناع means *refusal*.

Had you put effort into your work you would have won the prize.	لَوْ اِجْتَهَدْتَ فِي عَمَلِكَ لَحَصَلْتَ عَلَى الْجائِزَةِ.

Watch out: The normal interpretation of this sentence would be as a <u>counterfactual</u>. So don't get confused: The sentence does not mean: If you put an effort in your work, you will earn the prize.

If I had known (it), I would have walked.	لَوْ عَرَفْتُ لَمَشَيْتُ.

if not; if it were not for; if it had not been for; if there was no	لَوْلا

لَوْلا precedes a single noun or phrase and <u>hypothetically denies it</u>.

- After لَوْلا there has to be a nominative noun (اِسْم مَرْفُوع) – always!

- You have to use the particle لَ as this is crucial for the second part of the sentence. The لَ is a form of التّأْكِيد – emphasis. See chapter 125; 5.2.3.

If there was no Nile, Egypt would be a desert	لَوْلا النّيلُ لَأَصْبَحَتْ مِصْرُ صَحَراءَ.

Notice: The word مَوْجُودٌ (*found*; *existing*) is implicitly understood after the word *Nile*, however, it is not written.

every time	كُلَّما

Every time I walked in the streets of Cairo, I found a crowd.	كُلَّما سِرْتُ فِي شَوارِع الْقاهِرة وَجَدْتُ اِزْدِحامًا.

Notice: In the 2nd part of the sentence, you have to use the past tense!

255. WHEN DO YOU USE فَ AND لَوْ IN CONDITIONAL SENTENCES?

In most conditional clauses which start with لَوْ or مَنْ or إِذا you will find the particle فَ to connect the first sentence with the main clause. The letter فَ is used as a conjunction meaning: *then*; *thus*; *hence*; *therefore*. So when do you have to use it?

As a rule we could say: If the <u>second sentence</u> (main clause) <u>doesn't start with the verb directly</u>, you should add the فَ!

Generally speaking, ف usually comes after:

هُوَ	إِنَّ	قَدْ	سَ سَوْفَ	لِ	لَمْ	لَنْ	ما	لا
or any other pronoun to emphasize and start a جُمْلة اِسْمِيّة	to stress the main clause	to emphasize the meaning of the past tense	future indicator		negation			

Whoever enters the room is safe.	مَنْ دَخَلَ الْغُرْفة فَهُوَ آمِنٌ.
If you get married, you won't marry me.	إِذا تَزَوَّجْتَ فَلَنْ تَتَزَوَّجِيني.

If you start the second part (main clause) directly with a verb, you don't need the particle فَ – but instead, maybe the particle لَ, which underlines one thing: <u>The situation, which is described in the second part, will only be true if the first part happens.</u>

Or in other words: If the first part doesn't happen, the second part won't either. The لَ is normally used for if-clauses type II (*if I was...*) and III *(if I had been...)*. Notice the difference to the particle لِ with a كَسْرة - which means *in order to*.

Let us have a look at another example for لَ:

If I had known (it), I would have walked.	لَوْ عَرَفْتُ لَمَشَيْتُ.

Notice that in the following examples, the Arabic sentence means basically always the same despite the different tenses: *Whoever works hard, will succeed.*

1	We use only the verb – we don't need a فَ	مَنْ يَعْمَلْ بِجِدٍّ يَنْجَحْ.
2	Nominal sentence (جُمْلة اِسْمِيّة) Here, we need a فَ! The subject - فَنَجاحُهُ - and the predicate - مُؤَكَّدٌ - are مَرْفُوع	مَنْ يَعْمَلْ بِجِدٍّ فَنَجاحُهُ مُؤَكَّدٌ.
3	The future tense needs فَ. Notice that the second verb has a ضَمّة at the end ("yanjah**u**"). Don't get confused: Grammatically speaking, the verb is regarded فِي مَحَلّ مَجْزُوم – so called: مَجْزُوم	مَنْ يَعْمَلْ بِجِدٍّ فَسَيَنْجَحُ.
		مَنْ يَعْمَلْ بِجِدٍّ فَسَوْفَ يَنْجَحُ.

256. إِذا AND إِنْ - WHAT IS THE DIFFERENCE?

Theoretically, you can use both words to express *if* or *when*. Practically, however, there is a difference:

This word implies a positive or negative meaning; something can happen – or not!	إِنْ
This particle indicates that <u>something is going to happen</u>.	إِذا

Here is an example:

When morning comes (and it will definitely come)	إِذا طَلَعَ الصَّباحُ

What is important: It doesn't matter which time you use!

All three sentences in the following table have the same meaning: *If you strive in your work, you will be successful in your life.*

1	إِنْ اِجْتَهَدْتَ فِي عَمَلِكَ نَجَحْتَ فِي حَيَاتِكَ.
	<u>Past tense:</u> There is no مَجْزُوم-mood in the past tense. Although the verb is in the past tense, it has the meaning of the future.
2	إِنْ تَجْتَهِدْ فِي عَمَلِكَ تَنْجَحْ.
	<u>Present tense:</u> You have to use the مَجْزُوم-mood of the verb.
3	اِجْتَهِدْ فِي عَمَلِكَ تَنْجَحْ.
	<u>Imperative:</u> Don't forget the سُكُون – the verbs are مَجْزُوم

257. WHAT ARE THE ESSENTIAL RULES FOR WRITING NUMBERS?

Numbers are among the most difficult things in Arabic grammar. There are various rules which do not always follow logic. Let us examine them step by step:

<u>The number 1</u>

The Arabs did not distinguish between one or two. They used the dual for two. Otherwise, it was just one. So you never use a إِضافة for *one* or *two*. For emphasis – use an adjective.

A man came.	جَاءَ وَاحِدُ رَجُلٍ.	wrong
	جَاءَ رَجُلٌ.	correct

Two men came.	جاءَ اِثْنا رَجُلٍ.	wrong
	جاءَ رَجُلانِ.	correct

	feminine	masculine
I	واحِدة	واحِد
1st	الْأُولَى	الْأَوَّل
II	إِحْدَى عَشْرةَ	أَحَدَ عَشَرَ
11th	الْحادِيةَ عَشْرةَ	الْحادِيَ عَشَرَ
21	إِحْدَى وعِشْرُون or: واحِدة وعِشْرُون	واحِد وعِشْرُون

When should you use واحِد and when أَحَد؟

واحِد	In English, this would be the <u>adjective</u> one. In Arabic too, it is used as a صِفة/نَعْت which means it <u>always comes after the word it describes</u> and never before! E.g.: one word (a single word; German: ein Wort): كَلِمة واحِدة
أَحَد	In English, this would be the <u>noun</u> one. (German: einer). <ul><li>Normally, this word is used as the <u>first part of a</u> إِضافة. Meaning: one of.</li><li>It is often used independently and functions as an indefinite pronoun (anyone, someone). It is normally part of a negated sentence! See chapter 114.</li></ul>

2	اِثْنَتانِ - اِثْنَتْيْنِ	اِثْنانِ - اِثْنَيْنِ
2nd	ثانِية	ثانٍ
12	اِثْنَتا عَشْرةَ - اِثْنَتَيْ عَشْرةَ	اِثْنا عَشَرَ - اِثْنَيْ عَشَرَ

- The numbers from 3 to 10 are regular. The feminine form is built by adding a ة

- The numbers 30, 40, 50, ... have only one form, so there is no feminine form, e.g. 40: أَرْبَعُونَ

- Regarding *ten* and the correct vowels – see chapter 259

The numbers 100, 100 and 1 million

These are nouns that have either only a masculine or feminine form:

	feminine	masculine
100	مِئة	---
1000	---	أَلْف
1 million	---	مِلْيُون
1 billion	---	مِلْيار

Now let us check how to connect the numbers with nouns (e.g. apples, pens, trees, etc.). These words are called مَعْدُود – the word/noun which is connected with the number. The مَعْدُود is the word that gives <u>the number</u> the right gender.

<u>First step: Check the singular form of the مَعْدُود</u>

Let us see some examples:

meaning	masc. singular	fem. singular	plural
pen	قَلَم	---	أَقْلَام
tree	---	شَجَرَة	أَشْجَار
* Gini; Egyptian currency unit	جُنَيْه	---	جُنَيْهات
* A remark: In English, the currency is called *Egyptian pound*. The Arabic word comes from English *Guinea*, a one-pound-sterling gold coin, named after the Guinea gold mines in Africa.			

<u>Second step: Find the correct form + agreement for the number</u>

Rule A	The number has to <u>agree</u> with the مَعْدُود and the مَعْدُود has to be <u>singular</u>.

This rule is applied to:

- the numbers 1 and 2

- 11 and 12

- 21, 31, 41,...

I bought (only) one pen.	.اِشْتَرَيْتُ قَلَمًا واحِدًا
I bought (only) two pens.	.اِشْتَرَيْتُ قَلَمَيْنِ اِثْنَيْنِ
I read (only) one page.	.قَرَأْتُ صَفْحَةً واحِدَةً
I read (only) two pages.	.قَرَأْتُ صَفْحَتَيْنِ اثْنَتَيْنِ
11 days have passed.	.مَرَّ أَحَدَ عَشَرَ يَوْمًا
12 days have passed.	.مَرَّ اثْنا عَشَرَ يَوْمًا
I read 11 pages.	.قَرَأْتُ إِحْدَى عَشْرَةَ صَفْحةً
I read 12 pages.	.قَرَأْتُ اثْنَتَيْ عَشْرةَ صَفْحةً
21 days have passed.	.مَرَّ واحِدٌ وعِشْرُونَ يَوْمًا
22 days have passed.	.مَرَّ اِثْنانِ وعِشْرُونَ يَوْمًا
I read 21 pages.	.قَرَأْتُ إِحْدَى وعِشْرِينَ صَفْحةً
I read 22 pages.	.قَرَأْتُ اثْنَتَيْنِ وعِشْرِينَ صَفْحةً

Rule B	The number has to <u>disagree</u> with the مَعْدُود and the مَعْدُود has to be in <u>plural</u>.

This rule is applied to:

- the numbers from 3 to 10

I bought 10 books.	اِشْتَرَيْتُ عَشَرَةَ كُتُبٍ.
I read 10 pages.	قَرَأْتُ عَشْرَ صَفَحَاتٍ.

Notice here that the word for *ten* in our examples have different vowels that the word for *ten* in combinations, like in 15, 17,... See chapter 259.

Rule C	The number has to <u>disagree</u> with the مَعْدُود and the مَعْدُود has to be <u>singular</u>.

This rule is applied to:

- 13, 14, ... 19 and so on

Let us have a look at some example for Rule B and C:

I bought 3 books.	اِشْتَرَيْتُ ثَلَاثَةَ كُتُبٍ.
I read 3 pages.	قَرَأْتُ ثَلَاثَ صَفَحَاتٍ.
14 days have passed.	مَرَّ أَرْبَعَةَ عَشَرَ يَوْمًا.
14 years have passed.	مَرَّتْ أَرْبَعَ عَشْرَةَ سَنَةً.
I have 26 books.	عِنْدِي سِتَّةٌ وَعِشْرُونَ كِتَابًا.
I read 26 pages.	قَرَأْتُ سِتًّا وَعِشْرِينَ صَفْحَةً.

A remark: Theoretically (although very rarely used) you could also place the number after the noun. If you do so, you can either use the masculine or feminine form.

For example:

| Three men came. | جاءَ رِجالٌ ثَلاثةٌ or ثَلاثٌ. |

| Rule D | Numbers which never change their form |
| | → no agreement |

This rule is applied to:

- 20, 30, 40,...
- 100 (for the writing of *hundred* – see chapter 196)
- 1000
- 1 million

| Rule E | How to combine *hundred* and *thousand* |

There is a difference whether you are talking about 300, 400, 500... or 3000, 4000, 5000...

- In most cases you use the word for <u>*hundred*</u> in the <u>singular</u> form and the word for <u>*thousand*</u> in the <u>plural</u>.

- The number (e.g. three) and the word for *hundred* or *thousand* are combined as a إضافة-construction!

- This means: ثَلاث is the first part and مِئة or آلاف is the second part of the إضافة

Let us have a look at some examples for rule D and E:

In the room are 20 (masc) students.	فِي الْغُرْفةِ عِشْرُونَ طالِبًا.
In the room are 20 (fem) students.	فِي الْغُرْفةِ عِشْرُونَ طالِبةً
A century has 100 years.	الْقَرْنُ مِئةُ عامٍ
I read 100 pages.	قَرَأْتُ مِئةَ صَفْحةٍ
In the faculty are 100 (masc) students.	فِي الْكُلِّيّةِ مِئةُ طالِبٍ
In the faculty are 100 (fem) students.	فِي الْكُلِّيّةِ مِئةُ طالِبةٍ
In the faculty are 300 (masc) students.	فِي الْكُلِّيّةِ ثَلاثُمِئةِ طالِبٍ
In the faculty are 300 (fem) students.	فِي الْكُلِّيّةِ ثَلاثُمِئةِ طالِبةٍ
In the faculty are 3000 (masc) students.	فِي الْكُلِّيّةِ ثَلاثةُ آلافِ طالِبٍ
In the faculty are 3000 (fem) students.	فِي الْكُلِّيّةِ ثَلاثةُ آلافِ طالِبةٍ

258. ARE NUMBERS TREATED AS A اِسْم REGARDING CASES?

Generally said, yes, numbers are treated like any other اِسْم – which also means that a number can be a subject or an object.

It is already difficult to build the numbers correctly, but there is still something left to think about: the right case marker.

Let us have a look at some examples:

Three days of the months passed.	مَضَتْ ثَلاثَةُ أَيَّامٍ مِن الشَّهْرِ.	١
فاعِل مَرْفُوع	ثَلاثَةُ	
I read three chapters of the book.	قَرَأْتُ ثَلاثَةَ فُصُولٍ مِن الْكِتابِ.	٢
مَفْعُول بِهِ مَنْصُوب	ثَلاثَةَ	
The book consists of three chapters.	يَشْتَمِلُ الْكِتابُ عَلَى ثَلاثَةِ فُصُولٍ.	٣
اِسْم مَجْرُور	ثَلاثَةِ	

Let us now focus on the rules:

Rule A	Regarding the numbers 20, 30, 40, ... → watch out for the correct ending: ونَ or ينَ

20 (fem) students study in the centre.	تَدْرُسُ بِالْمَرْكَزِ عِشْرُونَ طالِبَةً.	١
فاعِل مَرْفُوع	عِشْرُونَ	
The centre receives 20 (fem) students.	اِسْتَقْبَلَ الْمَرْكَزُ عِشْرِينَ طالِبَةً.	٢

408

مَفْعُول بِهِ مَنْصُوب	عِشْرِينَ	
The centre welcomes 20 (fem) students.	رَحَّبَ الْمَرْكَزُ بِعِشْرِينَ طالِبَةً.	3
إِسْم مَجْرُور	بِعِشْرِينَ	
In the centre are 25 (masc) students.	فِي الْمَرْكَزِ خَمْسَةٌ وَعِشْرُونَ طالِبًا.	4
إِسْم مَعْطُوفٌ عَلَى خَمْسة - مَرْفُوع	وَعِشْرُونَ	

Rule B	Numbers between 11 and 19 always have a فَتْحة

11 (male) students came.	حَضَرَ أَحَدَ عَشَرَ طالِبًا.
I met 11 (male) students.	قابَلْتُ أَحَدَ عَشَرَ طالِبًا.
I met 11 (male) students.	اِلْتَقَيْتُ بِأَحَدَ عَشَرَ طالِبًا.

Rule C	A special case – the dual: Numbers which are combinations of the number *two* are treated like a dual.

Two (masc.) students came,	حَضَرَ طالِبانِ اثنانِ,	1

two (fem.) students came.	حَضَرَتْ طالِبَتانِ اثْنَتانِ.	
نَعْت مَرْفوع	إِثْنانِ , اِثْنَتانِ	
I met two (masc.) students, two (fem.) students.	قابَلْتُ طالِبَيْنِ اثْنَيْنِ, قابَلْتُ طالِبَتَيْنِ اثْنَتَيْنِ.	2
نَعْت مَنْصُوب	اِثْنَيْنِ , اِثْنَتَيْنِ	
I met two (masc.) students, two (fem.) students.	اِلْتَقَيْتُ بِطالِبَيْنِ اثْنَيْنِ, اِلْتَقَيْتُ بِطالِبَتَيْنِ اثْنَتَيْنِ.	3
نَعْت مَجْرُور	اِثْنَيْنِ , اِثْنَتَيْنِ	
In the department are two hundred (fem.) students, in the faculty there are two thousand (fem.) students.	فِي الْقِسْمِ مِئَتا طالِبةٍ, فِي الْكُلِّيّةِ أَلْفا طالِبةٍ.	4
مُبْتَدَأ مُؤَخَّر مَرْفوع	مِئَتا , أَلْفا	

259. WHY CAN IT BE DIFFICULT TO PRONOUNCE "TEN"?

You may have noticed that the number *ten* - عشر - doesn't always get the same vowels. Therefore, it is pronounced differently.

There is a reason for this. In order to find the correct vowel, you have to check the gender of the noun to which it is referring to.

Rule 1	If عشر points to a <u>masculine</u> word, there is a فَتْحة on the letter ش

I bought 10 pens.	اِشْتَرَيْتُ عشرة أَقْلَامٍ.
I bought 13 pens.	اِشْتَرَيْتُ ثلاثة عَشَرَ قَلَمًا.

Rule 2	If عشر points to a <u>feminine</u> word, there is a سُكُون above the letter ش

I read 10 pages.	قرأتُ عشْرَ صَفْحاتٍ.
I read 13 pages.	قرأتُ ثَلاتَ عشْرةَ صَفْحَةً.

260. DOES "SOME" SOMETIMES CHANGE ITS FORM?

Yes, it does! The word بضع changes its gender, at least in some expressions.

If you want to express that you are talking about *few* or *some*, you can use the word بِضْع – but only if you are dealing with numbers from 1 to 9, e.g.: *for a few days; a few hundred.*

The rules for بِضْع are similar to the rules for writing numbers. This means, you have to use the opposite gender of the word that comes after it. For example:

for a few days	Here, you have to use the feminine form of *some* as the word for days is masculine.	لِبِضْعةِ أَيّام
some years	Here, you use the masculine form	بِضْعُ سَنَوات

411

	of *some* as the word for years is feminine.	
There were a few hundreds.	Here as well, use the masculine form of *some* as the word for *hundred* is feminine.	كانَ بِضْعُ مِئاتٍ

261. WHAT IS AS "LOGICAL SUBJECT"?

Let's start the discussion with a sentence: *Many (a lot of) devices support the operating system.*

What is the subject of this sentence? Is it *many* or *devices*? This is crucial for the correct form of the verb. Let's have a look:

	verb refers to	
1	الْعَدِيدُ	يُدَعِّمُ الْعَدِيدُ مِنَ الْأجْهِزةِ نِظامَ التَّشْغِيلِ.
2	الْأجْهِزة	تُدَعِّمُ الْعَدِيدُ مِنَ الْأجْهِزةِ نِظامَ التَّشْغِيلِ.

Does the verb refer to الْعَدِيدُ – which means the verb should be يُدَعِّمُ؟

Or does it refer الْأجْهِزة – which means it should be تُدَعِّمُ؟

This is indeed an interesting topic. It has to do with the so called "logical subject". First of all, I guess there is no right or wrong on this issue. The problem with quantifiers is whether they should be treated like real (masculine singular) nouns or ignored in verbal agreement. In English you ignore quantifiers: You say *some/a lot of people <u>are</u>* here – and not: *<u>is</u> here*.

But in Arabic they are true nouns (اِسْم), and form compound constructions (إِضافة) with the following اِسْم, so they should be treated as the main اِسْم. But since semantically they are not the salient part, people often make the verb agree with the following word.

In short: Classically you should write يُدَعَّم, since the word عَدِيد is technically a masculine noun (اِسْم) and serves as the الْفاعِل (subject). It is مَرْفُوع and marked by a ضَمّة!

However, you can use the logical "subject" as well for agreement. The verb is تُدَعَّم then. Although it is grammatically semi-correct, you will hear and see it occasionally.

This is similar to كُلّ. The word كُلّ is a masculine singular noun, verbs and adjectives may (should) agree in the masculine singular.

But it is also common for the verb or adjective (صِفة, نَعْت) to agree with the gender and number of the word governed by كُلّ (i.e. the so called "logical subject").

Let us have a look at both possibilities:

1. Verbs and adjectives agree in the masculine singular as كُلّ is a masculine singular اِسْم:

They are all silent.	كُلُّهُم صامِت.

413

2. The adjective or verb agrees with the gender and number of the logical subject (=second part of the إِضافة)

We will all go.	كُلُّنا سَنَذْهَبُ.

The same is true for the word جَميع. When it is the first part of a إِضافة, the agreement is usually with the number and gender of the logical subject (=second part of the إِضافة).

262. HOW DO YOU EXPRESS: AMPLIFICATION OR LIKENESS?

If you write an article, these expressions might be useful to express amplification or likeness – التَّوْسِعة / التَّشابُه

Moreover; furthermore	وَفَضْلاً عَلَى ذلِكَ
In addition to that	وَبِالإِضافةِ إِلَى ذلِك
Moreover	ثُمَّ إِنَّ
As; just as; quite as; on the other hand	كَما أَنَّ
As to, as for, as far as... is concerned; but; yet, however; on the other hand	فَأَمّا / أَمّا...فَ...
Regarding; concerning	فِيما يَتَعَلَّقُ بِ... فَ...
Perhaps it would be useful to say that	وَلَعَلَّ مِن الْمُفيدِ الْقَوْل إِنَّ
Perhaps it is clear	وَلَعَلَّ مِن الْواضِح

It is known	وَمِن الْمَعْلُومِ
It is noticeable	وَمِن الْمُلاحَظِ
And also	وَأَيْضًا
As well as	وَكَذَلِك
A question arises here, which is	وَيَبْرُزُ هُنا سُؤَالٌ هُوَ
It should be noted here	وَتَجْدُرُ الإِشارَةُ هُنا إِلَى
It is worth mentioning that	وَجَدِيرٌ بِالذِّكْرِ أَنَّ
It is worth mentioning that	وَالْجَدِيرُ بِالذِّكْرِ أَنَّ
Likewise	وَعَلَى نَحْوٍ مُماثِلٍ
Similarly	وَعَلَى نَحْوٍ مُشابِهٍ
It seems that	وَيَبْدُو أَنَّ
It also seems that	وَكَذَلِكَ يَبْدُو أَنَّ
It is strange that	وَمِن الْغَرِيبِ أَنَّ
The strange thing is that	وَالْغَرِيبُ مِن الأَمْرِ أَنَّ
Not only this, but	لَيْسَ هذا فَحَسْبُ وَلِكِنْ

263. HOW DO YOU EXPRESS: EMPHASIS?

If you write an article, these expressions might be useful to express emphasis or accentuation – التَّأْكِيد

There is no doubt that	وَلا شَكَّ فِي أَنَّ
	وَمِمَّا لا شَكَّ فِيهِ أَنَّ
Surely	بِلا شَكٍّ = رَيْبٍ
In fact	وَفِي وَاقِعِ الْأَمْرِ
	وَفِي حَقِيقَةِ الْأَمْرِ
	وَوَاقِعُ الْأَمْرِ
	وَحَقِيقَةُ الْأَمْرِ
I totally reject this opinion.	وَإِنِّي أَرْفُضُ هٰذا الرَّأْيَ بِرُمَّتِهِ
I am supporting/accepting this opinion.	وَإِنِّي أَرْتَضِي هٰذا الرَّأْيَ
This opinion is not acceptable from my point of view.	وَلَيْسَ هٰذا الرَّأْيُ بِمَقْبُولٍ مِن وِجْهَةِ نَظَرِي
Of course	وَبِالطَّبْعِ
In the same book	وَفِي هٰذا الْكِتابِ نَفْسِهِ
He himself preferred this opinion.	وَقَدْ ذَهَبَ هُوَ نَفْسُهُ إِلَى هٰذا الرَّأْي
The scientists/academics all agree	وَالْعُلَماءُ كُلُّهُم مُتَّفِقُونَ عَلَى
This matter is only but	وَلَيْسَ هٰذا الْأَمْرُ إِلَّا
Without limitation we could say	وَما مِنْ حَدٍّ يَسْتَطِيعُ الْقَوْلَ إِنَّ
I (indeed) think that	وَأَظُنُّ ظَنًّا أَنَّ
And particularly	وَبِخاصَّةٍ

416

In particular	وَعَلَى وَجْهِ الْخُصُوصِ
Generally	وَعامّةً
In general	وَبِعامّةٍ
And the Arabs in general and the Egyptians in particular	وَالْعَرَبُ بِعامّةٍ وَالْمِصْرِيونَ بِخاصّةٍ
Though it clearly seems that	وَإِنَّ الْأَمْرَ لَيَبْدُو وَاضِحًا إذا...
And one should never think that	وَلايَحْسَبَنَّ أَحَدٌ أَنَّ
It is an opinion that is really worth mentioning.	وَهُوَ رَأيْ جَدِيرٌ بِالْقَوْلِ حَقًّا

264. HOW DO YOU EXPRESS: CONTRAST OR CONCESSION?

If you write an article, these expressions might be useful in order to express contrast or concession – الْمُقابَلة / التَّسِليم

But	وَلكِنَّ	وَلكِنْ
However	بَيْدَ أَنَّ	إِلّا أَنَّ
However; nevertheless		غَيْرَ أَنَّ
although		وَعَلَى الرَّغْمِ مِن... فَ...
If it was not for		وَلَوْلا أَنَّ
In contrast to		وَعَلَى النَّقِيضِ مِن ذلِك

In contrast to this view	وَفِي مُقَابِلِ هٰذا الرَّأْي
The other opinion is that...	وَيَذْهَبُ رَأْيٌ آخَرُ إِلَى
Nevertheless	وَمَعَ أَنَّ وَمَعَ ذٰلِك
On the other hand	وَمِنْ نَاحِيةٍ أُخْرَى
Whilst	فِي حِينٍ يَرَى
One could say that	وَقَدْ يُقَالُ إِنَّ
If we compare this view to	وَإِذَا قَارَنَّا هٰذا الرَّأْيَ بِ
After examining this view/opinion it looks to me that	وَعِنْدَ تَمْحِيصِ هٰذا الرَّأْي يَبْدُو لِي أَنَّ
And if we challenged this	وَإِذَا وَضَعْنا هٰذا بِإِزَاءِ
It is acknowledged	وَمِن الْمُسَلَّمِ بِهِ
It can't be denied	وَمِمَّا لا يُمْكِنُ إِنْكَارُهُ
Whatever the case is	وَمَهْما يَكُنْ مِن أَمْرٍ
Most likely	وَفِي أَغْلَبِ الظَّنِّ
It is likely	وَمِن الْمُرَجَّحِ
Probably	وَالأَرْجَحُ
I agree with this opinion.	وَإِنِّي أَتَّفِقُ مَعَ هٰذا الرَّأْي
I accept this opinion.	وَإِنِّي أَرْتَضِي هٰذا الرَّأْيَ
I tend to agree with this opinion.	وَإِنِّي أَمِيلُ إِلَى الأَخْذِ بِهٰذا الرَّأْي

265. HOW DO YOU EXPRESS: TO GIVE AN EXAMPLE?

If you write an article, these expressions might be useful if you want to give an example for something or if you want to explain something – المِثال

For example	فَمَثَلاً
	فَعَلَى سَبِيلِ الْمِثالِ
As a way of example	وَمِن الأَمْثِلةِ عَلَى هٰذا
The clearest example for this	وَأَوْضَحُ مِثالٍ عَلَى هٰذا
The closest example	وَأَقْرَبُ مِثالٍ عَلَى هٰذا
It illustrates	وَمِمَّا يُوَضِّحُ هٰذا
What makes this idea clearer	وَمِمَّا يَزِيدُ هٰذِهِ الْفِكْرَةَ وُضُوحًا
An example that illustrates my opinion	وَمِن الأَمْثِلةِ الَّتِي تُوَضِّحُ رَأْيِي
This is similar to	وَيُشْبِهُ هٰذا بِ
	وَهٰذا شَبِيهٌ بِ
Like this; similar to this	وَشَبِيهٌ بِهٰذا
Likewise	وَنَظِيرُ هٰذا
This is like	وَهٰذا مِثْلُ
One example cited/given by the author	وَمِن الأَمْثِلةِ الَّتِي ذَكَرَها الْمُؤَلِّفُ

266. HOW DO YOU EXPRESS: PROOF?

If you write an article, these expressions might be useful to give your reader evidence or proof of something – الدَّليل

The proof	الدَّليلُ = الحُجّة = البُرْهان = البَيِّنة
The evidence for this	وَالدَّليلُ عَلَى هذا
The evidence that supports this view	وَالدَّليلُ الَّذِي يَدْعَمُ هذا الرَّأْيَ
I quote this from	وَأَسْتَدِلُّ عَلَى ما أَذْهَبُ إِلَيْهِ بِ
What supports my opinion	وَمِمَّا يَدْعَمُ رَأْيِي
I support my opinion with several evidences	وَأَدْعَمُ رَأْيِي بِعِدَّةِ أَدِلَّةٍ
This is conclusive evidence	وَهذا دَليلٌ قاطِعٌ عَلَى
This is a clear proof for	وَهذا بُرْهانٌ ساطِعٌ عَلَى
A proof for this from real life	وَالدَّليلُ عَلَى هذا مِنْ واقِعِ الْحَياةِ
What confirms this opinion and supports it are the words of... (insert a name of a person)	وَمِمَّا يُؤَكِّدُ هذا الرَّأْيَ وَيَدْعَمُهُ قَوْلُ (فُلان)
Perhaps the best evidence for what (name of a person) said	وَلَعَلَّ خَيْرَ دَليلٍ عَلَى هذا ما قالَ (فُلان)
And (name of a person) agrees with	وَيَتَّفِقُ مَعِي فِي هذا الرَّأْي

420

me in this opinion	(فُلان)
I don't agree with this opinion because it seems to me that	وَلَسْتُ أَتَّفِقُ مع هٰذا الرَّأْي إِذْ يَبْدُو لِي أَنَّ
The clearest evidence of my opinion are the words of (name of a person) in his book "xxx" in which he says: "xxx"	وَأَوْضَحُ دَلِيلٍ عَلَى ما أَذْهَبُ إِلَيْهِ قَوْلُ (فُلان) فِي كِتابِهِ " xxx" حَيْثُ يَقُولُ: " xxx"

267. HOW DO YOU EXPRESS: CAUSE AND EFFECT?

If you write an article, these expressions might be useful to express cause and effect or a consequence – السَّبَب و النَّتِيجة

From here it becomes clear	وَمِنْ هُنا يَتَّضِحُ أَنَّ
Thus, we conclude that	وَمِنْ ثَمَّ نَسْتَنْتِجُ أَنَّ
And so it is evident that	وَهٰكَذا يَتَّضِحُ أَنَّ
It is true to say that	وَعَلَى هٰذا يَصِحُّ أَنْ يُقال إِنَّ
This is a result of	وَيَنْتُجُ مِنْ هٰذا بِالضَّرُورةِ
This necessarily requires	وَ يَقْتَضِي هٰذا بِالضَّرُورةِ
As a result of this	وَنَتِيجة لِهٰذا
Though	وَإِنْ
Accordingly, we can say that	وَعَلَى هٰذا يَصِحُّ الْقَوْلُ إِنَّ

We can conclude from this	وَيُمْكِنُ أَنْ يُسْتَنْتَجَ مِن هذا
So	لِذَلِكَ | لِهذا | لِذا
For this reason we can say that	وَلِهذا السَّبَبِ يُمْكِنُ الْقَوْلُ إِنَّ
And the explanation of that	وَتَعْلِيلُ ذَلِكَ
This goes back to	وَهذا راجِعٌ/عائِدٌ إِلَى
Perhaps the reason for this is that	وَلَعَلَّ السَّبَبَ فِي هذا أَنَّ

268. HOW DO YOU EXPRESS: TIME OR PLACE?

If you write an article, these expressions might be useful if you want to focus on time – الزَّمان

And then	وَحِينَئِذٍ
	وَعِنْدَئِذٍ
	وفِي ذَلِكَ الْحِينِ
At that time	وَوَقْتَئِذٍ
And then	وَبَعْدَئِذٍ
Previously	وَمِنْ قَبْلُ
And beyond	وَما بَعْدُ
Following that	وَعَقِبَ ذَلِكَ

Immediately	وَعَلَى الْفَوْرِ
Since then	وَمُنْذُ ذَلِكَ الْحِينِ
And in a later stage	وَفِي مَرْحَلَةٍ مُتَأَخِّرَةٍ
At the turn of the century	فِي مَطْلَعِ الْقَرْنِ
Until	إِلَى أَنْ
Until; even	وَحَتَّى
Before	وَقَبْلَ
When	وَعِنْدَما
As	وَلَمَّا
As soon as this book appeared, the general concept began to change.	وَما إِنْ ظَهَرَ هَذا الْكِتابُ حَتَّى بَدَأَ الْمَفْهُوم العام يَتَغَيَّر
They promised to help him *as soon as* they could.	وَعَدُوهُ بِالْمُساعَدةِ حالَما يُصْبِحُونَ قادِرِينَ عَلَى ذَلِك

If you write an article, these expressions might be useful if you want to focus on a place or the position of the narrator – الْمَكان

It appears from far	وَيَظْهَرُ عَلَى الْبُعْدِ
At a short/long distance	وَعَلَى مَسافةٍ قَرِيبةٍ/بَعيدةٍ
At a closest distance it seems	وَعَلَى مَسافةٍ أَقْرَبَ يَبْدُو
If we take a good look	وَإِذا دَقَّقْنا النَّظَرَ

At first glance, the place seems	وَيَبْدُو مِنْ خِلالِ النَّظْرةِ الأُولَى إلَى الْمَكان
And after a closer look, it appears	وَيَبْدُو مِنْ خِلالِ النَّظْرةِ الفاحِصةِ
In the heart of the place	وَفي صَدْرِ الْمَكانِ
The front view appears	وَيَبْدُو فِي الْمَنْظَرِ الأمامِيِّ
The back appears	وَيَبْدُو إلَى الْخَلْفِ
At further distance the place appears	وَعَلَى مَسافةٍ أَبْعَدَ يَظْهُرُ الْمَكانُ
The general overview of the place shows that	والنَّظْرةُ الْعامَّةُ لِلْمَكانِ تُظْهِرُ أنَّ

269. HOW DO YOU EXPRESS: RESTATEMENT?

If you write an article, these expressions might be useful if you want to summarize or restate a thought – إعادة تَقْريرالْفِكْرة

In a summarized form	وَبِعِبارةٍ مُوجَزةٍ
In short	وَبِعِبارةٍ مُخْتَصَرةٍ
Briefly	وَبِإيجازٍ
It can be summarized as	وَ يُمْكِنُ إجْمالُ هذا فِي
To summarize this we can say that	وَإيجازًا لِهذا يُمْكِنُ الْقَوْلُ إنَّ

In other words	وَبِعِبارةٍ أُخْرَى
Briefly, this means	وَيَعْنِي هٰذا فِي إِيجازٍ
This means	وَمَعْنَى هٰذا
To explain this idea I say that	وَإِيضاحًا لِهٰذِهِ الْفِكْرةِ أَقُولُ إِنَّ

270. HOW DO YOU EXPRESS: CONCLUSION?

If you have to write an article, these expressions might be useful to express a conclusion – الْخاتِمة

Finally	وَخِتامًا	وأَخِيرًا
In short		وَجُمْلةُ الْقَوْلِ
		وَخُلاصةُ الْأَمْرِ
In all of the above		وَإِجْمالاً لِما سَبَقَ
To sum it up, I say that		وَعَلَى سَبِيلِ الْإِجْمالِ أَقُولُ إِنَّ
In conclusion, I say that		وَفِي الْخاتِمةِ أَقُولُ إِنَّ
I conclude by saying that this topic		وَأُخْتِمُ هٰذا الْمَوْضُوعَ بِقَوْلِي إِنَّ
So		وَإِذَنْ
And so we can say in conclusion		وَهٰكَذا يُمْكِنُ الْقَوْلُ فِي الْخِتامِ

To conclude this article I say that	وَخِتامًا لِهذا الْمَقالِ أَقُولُ إِنَّ
At the end, and to summarize what's above I say that	وَأُوثِرُ فِي الْخِتامِ أَنْ أُوجِزَ ماسَبَقَ فَأَقُولُ إِنَّ

INDEX

431

432

436

438

439

440

442

43592529R00257

Made in the USA
Middletown, DE
13 May 2017